NORMAN:
Through My Eyes

A social and personal history of Leicester

DEDICATION

To Norman's great grandchildren:

Izzy Bradley

Ayla Julia Mason

Ella Dotty Mason

Jared Anthony Hastings

Percy John French

Grace Hastings

Thomas Hastings

Aurelia Joyce Irene Hastings

Alanah-Faye Rita Hastings

CONTENTS

'

Foreword

For many years, in fact, right up to her going deeply unconscious into that final sleep which comes so often just before death gives final ease from suffering, Our Mam used to tell anyone prepared to listen within the family, of how she was the cleverest girl in her class at school. Our Mam would then go on to say,

'And my Headmaster always used to tell me, one day Mary Wileman, you will write a book and I hope I will be alive to read it.'

One of her deepest regrets in later life was that the prizes she won at school were taken from her by her father, my Grandfather, and pawned to buy basic food for her family. I think one of these was 'Pilgrims Progress,' for that was the title she remembered.

I think her Headmaster was a very observant man and when he spoke about her writing a book, he was referring to the appalling poverty in which she, her parents and her brothers and sisters lived.

Our Mam never did get to write that book and, as you read the pages to follow, then you will understand why.

In a way, I suppose I am writing some of what I know her book would have contained; those parts which she recounted to us as children, and other parts of her life which my siblings and I shared, nitty gritty and all.

I have tried to set down our story truthfully, for even one untruth can, if proven, destroy credibility. Perhaps those close to me may say,

'Ah, you have been a little unfair here' or 'I don't remember that'.

If so, remember that one incident observed by five different people will bring conflicting reports as to what actually happened.

Here then, is our story and, if as you read the following pages, you feel pity, then I will have failed in what I have set out to do. Our Mam was a very happy person basically. Unfortunately for me, I reminded her too much of her husband. However, towards the end, it all came right. The Sunshine followed the Rain and, in any case, as Our Mam used to say,

"There's plenty worse off than us."

To Mary Sarah Jane HASTINGS, ALLEN Nee Wileman 1894 -1983 R.I.P

Beeson: Line of Descent 1811 – 1929

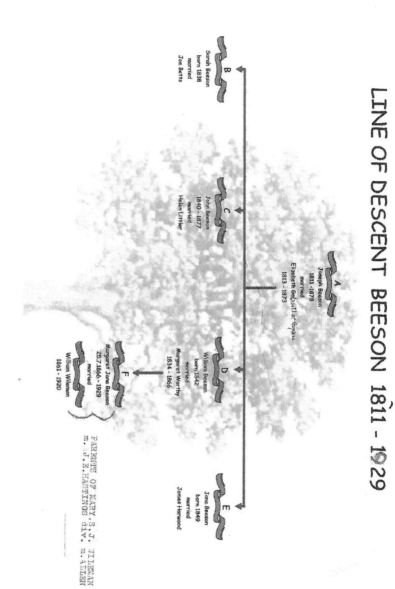

LINE OF DESCENT BEESON 1811 - 1929

A — Joseph Beeson 1811 -1878 married Elizabeth Gabriel le Grand 1813 - 1873

B — Sarah Beeson born 1838 married Joe Betts

C — John Beeson 1840 - 1877 married Helen Littler

D — William Beeson born 1842 married Margaret Worthy 1834 - 1866

E — Jane Beeson born 1849 married James Harwood

F — Margaret Jane Beeson 25.7.1866 - 1929 married William Wileman 1861 - 1920

PARENTS OF MARY.S.J. WILEMAN
m. J.E.HASTINGS div. m. ALLEN

Wileman: Line of Descent 1798 – 1983

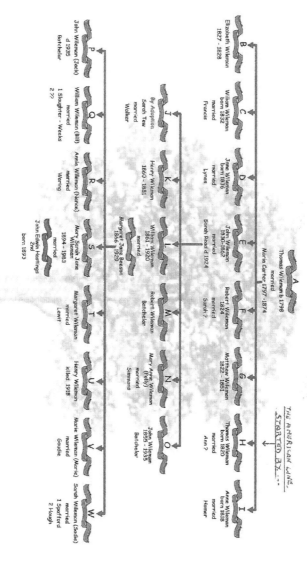

LINE OF DESCENT WILEMAN 1798 - 1983

THE ANGLICAN LINE
STARTED BY ...

A Thomas Wileman b 1798
married
Maria Carter 1797 - 1874

B Elizabeth Wileman 1827 - 1828

C Wileam Wileman born 1832
married
Frances

D Jane Wileman born 1836
married
Lynes

E John Wileman 1830 - 1862
married
Sarah Read d 1924

F Robert Wileman 1824
married
Sarah ?

G Matthew Wileman 1822 - 1861
married
Ann ?

H Thomas Wileman born 1820
married
Homer

I Anne Wileman born 1818
married
Homer

J By Adoption Sarah Tew married Walker

K Henry Wileman 1860 - 1881

L Willem Wileman 1863 - 1881
married
Margaret Jane Beezon 1866 1929

M Robert Wileman Betchelor

N Mary Anne Wileman (Polly) married Simmons

O John Wileman 1855 - 1935 married Betchelor

P John Wileman (Jack) d 1935 Betchelor

Q William Wileman (Bill) married Annie Wileman (Nance) married Waring
1 Slaughter - Weeks
2 ??

R married John Edwin Hastings 2nd born 1893

S Mary Sarah Jane Wileman 1894 - 1983

T Margaret Wileman married Lewit

U Henry Wileman killed 1918

V Marie Wileman (Marie) married Goudie

W Sarah Wileman (Sadie) married
1 Spafford
2 Hough

Hastings: Line of Descent 1819 – 1999

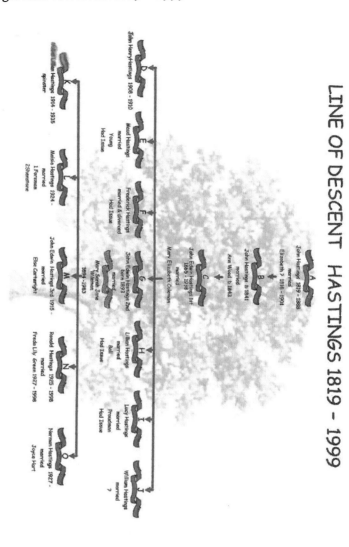

1: A Brief Family background

My Mother, hereinafter, always referred to as Our Mam in the same way we always referred to our father as the Old Man, was born 27 March 1894, at Stoughton Cottages, Stoughton Street, Leicester, the third of what would eventually be the eight children of William WILEMAN and Margaret WILEMAN nee BEESON.

The Wilemans were a very prominent family around the Earl Shilton area of Leicester, a Coat of Arms being registered in the 1600's. Early registers show their prominence and connections with the Hosiery Industry. Others of the clan were land owners.

Sadly, by the time my Grandfather appeared on the scene most, if not all of the family possessions, had gone.

William Wileman (1861 – 1920) and Margaret (Nee Beeson) (1866 – 1929)

Sometime around 1880, at which time my Grandfather WILEMAN would have been in his early 20's, the family moved from Earl Shilton to Leicester City. This was minus Grandfather's own father, John WILEMAN, who had died in 1862 of typhoid fever, when Grandfather was just a few months old. The family at that time consisted of the Mother, Sarah WILEMAN, and her children Mary Ann, John, Robert, Henry, William and an adopted girl child, Sarah TEW. Sadly, Henry was to die aged 21 months of Pthisis (consumption), soon after the move to 21 Melrose Street, Leicester - now demolished. It was from this address that in 1891 my Grandfather, William WILEMAN, married Margaret BEESON, at St Matthews Church, Leicester. His brothers, John and Robert did not marry although their sister, Mary Ann and adopted Sarah TEW, did.

Can we now move on to William's bride, Margaret BEESON, born ? Right from the start, Grandmother WILEMAN kept throwing up more questions than answers and it would be true to say that her own children, Our Mam included, knew nothing very much about her.

I was only 2 years old when Grandma Wileman died, and all her own children could tell me was her maiden name and that she was born in Leamington Spa. She said many times she was born a twin and that the other twin had died, as did her Mother, soon after giving birth.

My search began because I knew that without some background on my Granny, I could not do justice to my own Mam's story.

When I began, the only one of my Grandmother's children still alive was an elderly Aunt, who would not or could not tell me anything very much about my Granny Wileman, born Beeson who, on her wedding certificate, had, instead of signing her name, had written 'Mr Beeson's daughter' and yet she could neither read nor write! Also, why did she call herself Margaret Elizabeth when, in fact, her birth name was Margaret Jane? To compound the mystery, my Aunt and her husband hinted that Granny Wileman was a bastard, although they never actually used that word.

I worked out rough dates and surnames after much research and applied to St. Catherine's House, London.

Question: Do you have a marriage entry of a BEESON m WORTHY around 1860?

Answer: No.

So, my Granny had been born out of wedlock, BUT HAD SHE?

Some two months later, I was in the Mormon Church Records Office in Leicester when I mentioned to a helper of my failed search. He asked for details; names, approximate dates etc and came back with the proof.

In 1865, in Leamington Priors, William BEESON married Margaret WORTHY. A child was born a year later and five days after the birth, the new mother, my Great Granny, died of Puerperal Fever. Was there a twin to the child? We will never know for unless it was a live birth, it was not recorded.

Question: Was the name my Granny used, Margaret Elizabeth, to have been the dead twin's name?

Answer: Oh yes.

St. Catherine's House were most apologetic.

Just a few questions remained. Who brought the motherless mite up? When did the father and child come to Leicester? And why did the bitterness well up so that she was to say, 'My father treated me like a dog.' We will never know for we know nothing about him.

But if I may pick up the story with Our Mam's family, headed by William and Margaret Wileman, whose children were, Margaret, Henry, Mary (Our Mam), Maria (Marie), Sarah (Sal/ Sadie), Annie, William and lastly John (Jack), the last being born in 1909.

It was not until most of these named were dead, that a daughter of the first born, Margaret (always called 'Our Mag') confided to me that at her grandfather's funeral, his sister, Great Aunt Polly, pulled Aunt Mag from the front of the funeral line up where she was standing with her mother and said,

'Our William's eldest goes first with his widow.'

Standing: Mary (Polly) Simmons (Nee Wileman) 1855 – 1946 daughter of Sarah Wileman (Nee Reed) 1833 – 1924 (seated)

She then put Our Mam in Margaret's place. Had Mam's brother Henry not been killed in the Great War, then he would have led with his mother. So,

Mam, the third born of my Granny, was the second born to Grandad! To be fair, if Great Aunt Polly had kept quiet at the funeral this would never have emerged. None of Aunt Mag's brothers or sisters ever repeated this piece of scandal. It was Mag's daughter who let the cat out of the bag when I was in my 60's. More research........... Leicester! Workhouse admission register, 1889, to Margaret BEESON of Leamington, a child Margaret.

Our Mag – born in the workhouse and not recognised by Aunt Polly as the eldest child of William Wileman and Margaret Beeson

No name was given for a father. By trade, my Grandfather Wileman was a Currier or worker in leather. He was a tall man, around 6 foot, with grey eyes, a full head of hair and he walked with a pronounced limp due to the poor setting of a bone in his ankle. Like so many others before and after, he had the curse of gambling in his blood. Due to his constant frittering away of his money on the horses, the family were constantly on the move, dodging the Rent Man and sundry debt collectors. Often, his family were to know real poverty and hunger as the money that should have put clothes on their backs, shoes on their feet and food in their bellies, went into the 'Bookies' pockets. Years later, Our Mam saw and recognised the main 'Bookie' that her dad bet with and made herself known by mentioning her dad's name. The Bookie's comment,

'Your dad was a bloody fool but if I hadn't taken his money someone else would have.'

So, that was his conscience satisfied.

Working for a local tannery, Grandad Wileman was no better or worse off than thousands of other workers in his class but a piece of good fortune brought him ill fortune and reduced the family to the direst poverty. You see, an uncle of his, brother of his long deceased own father, died, and left a piece of land that was to be sold and the proceeds of the sale divided between two nephews and a niece. (The uncle was a former butcher, also a Wileman, of Hill Top, Earl Shilton.) With the few pounds burning a hole in his pocket, Grandad set off to the Leicester Races, hoping to skin the 'Bookies'. He did not, of course, but far worse, he was seen, recognised and reported to his boss, Briggs the Tanners. He was sacked on the spot and as far as I can see he was blacklisted, for he never could get regular work again and was reduced to selling newspapers outside the Leicester Railway Station. Poor Granny Wileman, his long suffering wife, was reduced to even greater poverty and began to take in other people's washing and ironing, charging just a few coppers a bag, not knowing if those she was skivvying for would pay her. God alone knows how she managed to cope with her workload, pregnancies and the inevitable miscarriages. Our Mam told me how, finding that her mother was once again pregnant, she said to her,

'You can't be pregnant 'Our Mam,' we can't afford the babies we have now, let alone you to have another one!'

Looking back, all these years on, I realise my Granny Wileman must have had the heart of a lion. She had a weakling husband who, as fast as she gained a few coppers, took it and gambled it away and yet her daughters spoke and acted as ladies, looked and dressed in later life like ladies, had beautiful homes, and, most important to me as a small child, they could always dip into their purses to find me a copper or half penny for a few sweets. Of her three sons: Henry or 'Our Harry' as he was always to be known was killed in the Big War; John or 'Our Jack' died aged 26. Both were single men although both had sweethearts. Only William 'Our Bill', their brother who came in the middle birth wise, married, was divorced and then remarried. Bill had a son, Reg Wileman, by his first wife. Reg would be about my age, born around 1927, but I have not seen him for over 60 years. Reg is the last in the direct Great Grandad line of Wilemans. I don't think he married.

L-R: Sarah (Sadie), Annie, Maria (Marie)

Henry Wileman died 1918

Jack Wileman died 1935

With family fortunes fluctuating due to no set income, the rent was often unpaid and worse still often there was not enough money for food. Again, Our Mam,

'At school, our Headmaster would come into the classroom and say hands up those children who haven't had any breakfast before they came to school. Our hands were the first to go up because Mam couldn't afford to feed us some days if my Dad had gambled the Housekeeping on the horses.'

The Headmaster would then send those who were hungry across the road to the 'ragged mission' where they would be given a round of dripping and a cup of watered milk.

The girls of the family were often sent on errands to the local shops where they would ask for a ha'pennys worth of tea or sugar or a pennorth of stale bread bits etc. etc.,

'We were always hungry but still my Dad gambled, even at times pawning our shoes if he thought he had a winner.'

Minor ailments were treated at home e.g. The treatment for a toothache was to get the tip if a darning needle red hot in the fire and poke this into the offending molar. Annie had a bad heart, as did John (Jack) the youngest, and suffered from fainting spells. Their father's remedy for these was to pour cold water over the unconscious child.

The family now lived in the very poorest part of town. Mean poky little streets, bug and flea infested houses, with only their lion hearted Mother between them and the Union (Workhouse), for Grandfather's luck was still bad even selling newspapers. One day at his stand he forgot and shouted,

'Chronicle, Leicester Chronicle!'

A policeman passing by heard him. In those days it was permitted to sell newspapers in the street but you couldn't call out your wares. He was summoned to Court and fined Half a Crown (12 and a half pence). His family were the ones that paid that debt off though, by going short of food that week.

'Moonlighting' was part of life for the poor in those days, although it was more often described as 'flitting'. It went like this: Unable to pay the rent, poor tenants would seek out an empty slum house not too far away and persuade the landlord to rent it to them by giving the man a week's rent in advance. More often than not this was all he would get for that was how the previous, now unpaid landlord, was persuaded to part with the key. That day, Grandad would hire a push cart from a local firm who were making a good living by hiring carts out for just this purpose. (Moonlight Flitting) Everybody was doing it. Then, late in the evening, the family's few meagre possessions were loaded aboard the said cart and, with the big kids carrying or dragging the infants and babies along by the hand, and with the mother struggling along in the rear, more often than not heavily pregnant, the family would sneak away. The landlord, I assume, was not too bothered, for he hadn't a cat in hells chance of getting a penny of the arrears and the next ones in would at least pay a week in advance, just to get the key. That is if there was a key!

One house the family moved into had a ghost in residence. It came about in this way. It was a mean little place, no better and no worse than the rest of the 'drums' in that street. (Slum houses were often referred to as drums.) Upstairs was half passaged and my Grandparents slept with their bedroom door open in case one of their brood should awaken in the night. On this particular night Grandad woke up. The room was full of moonlight and the view down the passage was uninterrupted. To his horror he saw, hanging from a rope dangling from the attic trap door, the spectre of a man who was obviously a previous tenant who had chosen to end his life. Again, 'Our Mam,'

'It frightened my dad to death and we moved out the next morning. Fortunately, we hadn't returned the hand cart, so he didn't have to pay for that twice.'

This then, was my Grandparents miserable, mean existence. Hunger, poverty and very little charity. Fleas, bedbugs and the pawnshop on Monday morning; down the little concealed entry at the side, arguing over what was offered for rotten, worn out bedding and meagre items of family possessions. Mean little slum houses with outside earth toilets, kitchens and living rooms full of steam from laundry belonging to those better off people being taken in and the smell of the smoothing iron, heated on the coal fire hob.

Once a year there was a treat. This was at the Barwell/ Shilton 'Wakes' (a street fair) for this was the one day in the year my Grandad could be 'with his own.' The night before, Grandma would have her hair washed and tied in pieces of rag to try to impart a curl. Grandad would hurry off to hire a horse and cart big enough for all the family (no buses in those days) and with the family aboard they would set off. The most memorable year for all of them was the time the poor horse, pulling the overloaded cart up Earl Shilton Hill, fell and badly cut its knee. Grandad Wileman knew that if the local constable saw the state of the poor horse's knees, he would order it off the road. Before arriving at 'Hill Top', Grandad went in front and purchased a knob of 'blacking.' He then smeared it over the nag's knees to hide the blood and gore. I know it sounds hard but I don't think he had any other choice for if he'd been ordered off the road there was no way he could get a pregnant wife and a host of children back to Leicester.

In Barwell the family were greeted by the rest of the family. There would be brother John, bearded and a very good living man. Robert (Bob), a poacher type who knew where all the best game could be found and then, of course, the mother of the family, known to all as Granny Wileman. Sarah, my Great Grandma - I never knew her.

Sarah Wileman was a most remarkable woman. She was born in Bagworth, a coal mining area in Leicestershire, the daughter of Mary Read, a single woman. I suspect that as the stigma of 'bastard' was a cross hard to bear, little Sarah would have had a hard time of it during her childhood in such a small and tightly knit community as Bagworth. (Her mother, Mary, did eventually marry.)

Eventually, Sarah met John Wileman. Sarah was working as a servant at the time and John Wileman was a blacksmith, probably in the colliery. They were married at Bagworth Church, Sarah's home parish. Born to the couple were Mary, John, Robert, Henry and William. Henry, I am sure, died as a boy for my Grandfather is quoted as saying,

'I woke up one morning and the boy lay dead in bed at the side of me.'

Great Grandad John was to die young, at 32 years to be exact, so Sarah was now widowed. One would have thought that with her own fatherless family to bring up she would have had enough to cope with, but not at all, for she adopted legally a child, also a Sarah. Sarah Tew. What the story was behind the adoption I can only guess, but certainly, at the time, there was an outbreak of Diphtheria, so probably Sarah Tew had lost her parents.

It was during this outbreak that my Great Granny Wileman became so loved in the Earl Shilton/ Barwell area for, without hesitation, she went into infected homes and brought help and comfort to the sick and dying. One man said that if he recovered, he would leave a bequest that when 'Granny' died, as she surely would exposing herself as she did to infection, then he would pay for her grave to be tended in perpetuity. He died, she did not. Years later, I met a man who knew 'Granny Wileman.' (she died in 1924) He too had a story to relate:

When his father-in-law died, Granny stopped the widow, (who was penniless) in the street and, taking a sixpence from her purse, gave it to her saying,

'Here you are my dear; you need this more than I do.'

It was her last sixpence, all she had in the world but she gave it willingly. That same night, Granny went to the house wherein the dead man lay and, kneeling at the side of his bed, prayed for his departed soul. The man who recounted this ended by saying,

'Everyone around here loved her.'

My own Aunt told me how, as a sickly child during the Great War, she was sent via the Carrier's cart to stay with her Granny:

'Every night we went to bed as dusk fell and before getting into bed, my Granny would put a little mop cap on and, kneeling at the side of the bed say a prayer for every member of her family. This then, was the Wileman family of Earl Shilton/ Barwell.

Mam told me that the first thing Granny did when her son's family arrived for the 'wake' was to go round various houses asking if there were any outgrown shoes waiting to be thrown out as 'Our William's' come with his little brood and their shoes are in tatters.

Next, she would force food on the new arrivals, she was so proud of them, and then it was time to go to the wake - a sort of fair, cum cattle market.

When the festivities were over and the children were falling asleep on their feet, Granny Wileman would press a piece of bloodstained paper into her son's (my grandad's) hand. In it would be a choice cut of pork, for Sarah kept a pig at the bottom of her garden in a brick sty, and all her family shared in it at killing time. And so, as all the best books say, 'Home to bed.'

With so many mouths to feed and with so little money coming in, it was all hands to the pumps. Even Grandma Margaret helped with sorting out the different Sunday papers in spite of the fact she couldn't read a word. Who brought her up after her mother and twin died so tragically must remain a mystery, as must when her father brought her to Leicester.

2: Mam's story begins

1911: Mam was 17 and it was about this time she met the Old Man.

John Edwin Hastings was an extremely good looking chap and a year or so older than her. He too came from a largish family; seven in all I believe. His father, also John Edwin, had married Mary Elizabeth Coleman, and the family lived in the West Bridge side of Leicester - Thorpe Street. It was from this address the family were to emigrate to Paris, Ontario, Canada in 1912. John Edwin, my father didn't go with them nor did his sister, Lucy, who had married a Proudman and lived in Dannet Street, the same area as her parents.

Lucy had been blamed for the tragic death of the youngest Hastings' child, John Henry (2 years), in 1910. It was reported he'd followed another sister sent on an errand by Lucy and was run down and killed by a horse drawn milk float in New Parks Street.

Lucy Hastings: blamed for her brother John's death

I had no idea this youngest brother of my dad and therefore my uncle, had even existed until around 1980. My Mam's mind had started to deteriorate by this time and, as so often is the case with an old mind, had begun to remember things from the past. She told me of a child whose head had been crushed by a horse and cart. That was all she said; no more. It was enough to set me off on a search that was to uncover my roots, solve many mysteries, bring about reunions and explain much.

After consulting old records and newspapers, I had the story: John Henry Hastings, aged 2 years, had followed an older sister into the street. The older child had been sent on an errand by their older sister, Lucy. Not 20 yards from his home John stepped off the kerb and a passing horse drawn milk float knocked him down; the cart wheel passing over his head. Death was instantaneous. The old newspaper recorded the inquest the following Monday. My grandmother said she never sent her younger children on errands and she blamed her daughter, Lucy, for doing so. The verdict was accidental death. The first mystery of why Aunt Lucy did not emigrate to Canada with the rest of the family was solved! How could she face the rebukes of her embittered parents every day?! Lucy carried this terrible feeling of guilt all her life and on her own death bed, dying of cancer, in her delirium, cautioned those keeping the death watch, to be aware of the needs of the long dead infant. It may be that the Old Man stayed with Lucy to keep an eye on his sister who may not have been married when the first moves were made to go to Canada. If so, and I truly believe that he did love his sister, then that was one of the few decent things he did in his life, as we shall see.

My parents' courtship did not follow the normal path of true love for my father was an extremely erratic man who wasn't averse to using his fists on his love. At times Grandma Hastings would send one of the Old Man's brothers to follow the happy and devoted couple, to report back lest the young swain (or should it be swine) punched 'his lovely' too hard.

From 1911 the Old Man was in the Territorial Army, the Leicester's, and he attended all their summer camps.

Back now to Our Mam:

'My Mam said to me one day (it would be about 1913) Isn't it about time you got married my girl?' and I said, Why should I want to get married just yet, Mam, there's plenty of time? And Our Mam said to me, Well, you know you're pregnant don't you?!'

In fact Mam was 5 months pregnant when she went up the aisle although the one remaining photo taken on her wedding day shows no sign of this. Every other photo of her and my dad was destroyed by her or my dad cut out of it.

1910s this scene at the corner of Freme Road North and Noble Street
NOBLE STREET FROM WHERE JOHN EDWIN AND MARY SARAH WERE MARRIED FROM

Mam and the Old Man were married at St Pauls Church, and their first born arrived not very long after: Mabel Lillian, my sister.

3: The Great War

Now came the Great War. My father, along with his contemporaries, belonged to the part-time or Territorial Army and, with the deepening crisis in Europe you did not have to be a genius to work out that before very long the nasty stuff 'would hit the fan!' So, after confiding to his wife (my mother) that he did not intend to become 'cannon fodder' for King and country or family, he set about making enquiries for emigrating with his family to Canada to join his parents.

In 1915, the Old Man was given his discharge from the Army before the Territorials had even been sent to France. This was on the grounds he was unfit for overseas war service. He suffered from Otitis Media, an ear complaint. Before long though, he hit a snag to his plan. Whilst there were plenty of single berths for single men, double cabins were at a premium. Running true to the form he was to display so many times in the years to come, the Old Man did not hesitate in taking a berth on the first available steamer leaving Mam to follow on as best she could with Mabel 2 years and another baby, also John Edwin (Our Ted).

'Mam's' elder brother, Henry (Harry) had, by now, joined the Leicester's and was fighting on the Western Front. He was the rock on which that poor family's fortunes were to be built after the war; the one that would uplift his Mam, Dad, brothers and sisters out of poverty. Alas, it wasn't to be as we shall see.

Mam now made arrangements to follow her husband to Canada. Mam's sister, Maria (Marie), wanted to go with her and so they travelled together to a Scottish port to get a ship. The only berth they could get was on an old tramp steamer with very limited passenger accommodation and so around the middle of the war, Mam, Marie and the two infants in arms, set off across the North Atlantic in some of the worst weather of that notorious ocean's history. I've been across that ocean in February and it's frightening what those mountainous seas can do even to a new modern steamer. Convoys had not been introduced at that time and German submarines were sinking Allied ships left, right and centre. Fortunately, the bad weather and huge seas provided some degree of protection, but even so, time after time, the crew would drag their passengers up on deck to stand by the life boats as submarine activity was suspected in the area.

There was no refrigeration on aboard and the babies were living on watered down tinned condensed milk, but water was short and rationed as the voyage went on and on against mountainous seas. It was just like the old song, "Two steps forward and three steps back."

The ship's rats were a nuisance and on a number of occasions Mam woke in the night to find huge rats licking dried milk from her babies' chins. Eventually they arrived and the tired and worn out little brood were given temporary sleeping accommodation for the night in the port of disembarkation in Canada. Mam was in a single bed. Mabel ditto, whilst baby Ted was in a cot. It was a place used to accommodate families emigrating to that part of Canada before the war, for the years up to 1914 saw the largest numbers arriving in the Canadian Ports. Worn out, the weary travellers quickly fell asleep. Let Mam now take up the story again,

'I woke up the next morning, and the first thing I did was to check that the little ones were still safe and fast asleep. I nearly went out of my mind, for whilst Teddy was still curled up snug and warm, little Mabel was missing from her bed. I checked the door. It was closed though not locked as no bolts were fitted. I ran into Marie's room as she was in a room of her own. No Mabel. Together, Marie and I ran through those long corridors crying and calling out Mabel's name. There wasn't sight nor sound of her. Hysterically I was crying out 'My baby, someone has taken my baby.' People joined in the search. We turned that place inside out and upside down. Mabel was gone. Weeping and out of my mind with grief, I returned to my room. Teddy, with all the commotion, was now wide awake and had joined in the wailing and weeping without knowing why. I sat on Mabel's empty bed to comfort him and as I did so my eyes fell onto a bundle underneath my own bed which I'd so recently vacated. I laid Teddy down, reached under the bed and gently slid that bundle out. It was Mabel. In the night she must have stirred, fallen out of bed still wrapped in her blankets just as I'd laid her down and still fast asleep, and rolled under my bed to lay just as I was to find her.

Poor Mam! Years after, when recounting the incident to me, she visibly cringed. With all the passport and entry formalities completed, the weary travellers took a long train ride across Canada, to eventually join her 'ever loving' in Paris, Ontario, at his parents' house, her in laws' home. Soon after, and running true to form, the Old Man joined the Canadian Army, 'The Princess Pats Own Light Infantry' and, would you believe it, he was sent overseas to England!

Back Left: Jack Ball married Ted Snr's sister, Lil Hastings

Back Right: Relative 'Coleman' on Maternal side

Front Right: John Edwin (Ted) Hastings (The Old Man)

Front Left: Bill Hastings (Ted's brother) Stripes on left cuff shows wounding in 1914-1918

At first Mam and Marie stayed on at my Grandparents' (Hastings) home with the children. Mam got a job at the Mill making men's/ soldiers socks. She earned good money, for she was always quick to learn, and was a first class worker. Then she fell out with her mother in law.

Grandma Hastings was a big strong woman. She suffered with migraine, which at times was so bad she would grind her teeth with the pain. Grandpa Hastings was a small nervous man and I think it was all too much for them minding two small children and worrying about their two sons in the Canadian Army. One, was my Uncle Bill, who was wounded three times in

France, and the other was the Old Man, although due to recurring ear trouble (remember the Otitis Media), he was never was sent to fight. Mam claimed years later, that her mother in law had hit Teddy and this was the reason she left, taking the children with her.

Sister Marie stayed on for a time and eventually married Big Jim Goudie, a Canadian Mounted Policeman who later transferred to the Government Secret Service. In World War II Jim Goudie was sent to spy on the Russians across the common border shared by Canada and the Soviet Union and after the war Jim was part instrumental in catching and breaking up the communist cells in Canada. After he retired, he and Aunt Marie retired to Leicester. I think it was to get away from the possibility of communist reprisals. Both died in Leicester.

Anyway, Mam found a bungalow to rent in Paris. She made friends and began a social life. Living near to her was a neighbour, a one armed painter and decorator named 'Wingy Robinson'. It was he who, when the heating stove outlet became blocked, found the family unconscious and dragged them into the fresh air to revive. How did 'Wingy' hang lengths of paper only having one arm? Well, I wondered myself and then, years later, I got in touch with another of the Old Man's brothers who was still alive, Fred Hastings. He lived in St Catherine's, Ontario and he answered the query for me. It seems that after pasting the paper, 'Wingy' would hold the length in his mouth and using just the one arm he had, smooth it on to the wall.

When the war ended in Europe, the Old Man returned to his family and the war started again in Paris, Ontario. Honestly, if the Old Man had put as much effort into fighting the Germans as he did in fighting Mam, the war wouldn't have lasted longer than six months!

Around 1919, Mam sailed home to England. I was told, she travelled alone, leaving the Old Man to follow with the children, but I don't know if this was so.

In 1920, Mam's father, my Grandpa Wileman, died. I never knew him as I wasn't due for another seven years. I was told he filled up with water and died in the Leicester City General Hospital. It was likely the death in France of his eldest son Henry (Harry) had knocked the guts out of him, for he never came to terms with his loss. Mam and Maggie (her sister, not her mother) went to identify him. Mam told me he lay in the mortuary on a slab, as naked as the day he was born,

'You'd have thought they would have covered him decent, wouldn't you?'

For a time, the family of four (Mam, Dad, Ted and Mabel) lodged with Aunt Lucy, the Old Man's sister, although how she coped heaven knows! Mam and Dad had the front room upstairs. I was also told the Old Man would go and have a lay down every Sunday afternoon after having his mid-day booze. When it was time for him to get up, Lucy would get the broom and hit the ceiling with the handle to wake him up. (If the house was still standing I would go and see if the dents in the ceiling were still visible)

Old Granny Wileman of Barwell died in 1924. On the day of her funeral the streets were packed with people wishing to say farewell and curtains were tightly drawn out of respect for this much loved and respected woman. In the same year, Grandma Hastings, who'd recently visited Leicester from Canada, also died.

By now, Maisie had also been born to my parents. Ronald was to follow in 1925, with me coming into the household of woes, blows and tears, in 1927. I was born on 5th August, 1927, the youngest, and what proved to be the last born of my parents.

Perhaps one of the best known paintings in the world is the one entitled "When did you last see your father?" If that question was ever put to me or my siblings we would reply that within our family Ted Snr was always referred to as the 'Old Man' for the very simple reason he was never a father to us.

Mabel & Ted Jnr

Mam with Mabel (left) and Ted Jnr in Canada

4: 9 Martival, Leicester

When I came into the world my family were living at 9 Martival, Leicester, which was one of those 'Homes for Heroes' built to accommodate families who the Government realised would not be satisfied with the drab terraced homes available up to then to the main populace. 9 Martival was a rented council house erected around 1925 that features so prominently in the Social History books of today. Prior to these homes being built the only type of housing stock available was the sort of home provided by speculators and the Victorian/ Edwardian factory owners, aided and abetted by 'Jerry Builders.' In the main these terraces had minuscule rooms, had shared entries to the back leading to shared yards and often shared toilets (one lavvy to two homes) and were gas lit etc. etc; all were bad. We then, were better off than most, judging by housing standards of the day. Do understand though, that the amenities provided in this new type of council home were still pretty basic compared to the private sector properties which were now beginning to get off the ground. What we did have was electric light when gas light was still the order of the day for most. Remember, this gas was not the odourless natural gas of today but rather a thick, heavy, coal gas which, after a very short time, laid a thick layer of grease over the ceilings which no amount of whitewashing could ever cover over for long, and that left a smell, even after the gas was disconnected, that permeated the whole house. We had a bathroom which contained a cast iron bath but no wash hand basin and no inside toilet. We didn't have any sort of hot water system either for the bath or sink, and central heating? You're joking of course!!!

The house had three bedrooms, a living room and a front room whilst at the back was a nice sized garden which the Old Man cultivated with a few vegetables, but mainly flowers. He also planted an apple tree. Garden cultivation was a condition of tenancy. At the front of the house we had a small garden with grass and a small privet hedge under the window.

Every room in our house was large by any standards of the time, but unfortunately, probably to save costs or to avoid the charge of doing too much for their tenants, the Council had left both the kitchen and bathroom walls un-plastered. Both were plain brick.

The Council insisted that all decorating be left in their hands and so many rules and regulations were imposed. Their 'threats of eviction' notices flew in all directions.

In one corner of our bare brick kitchen stood the Old Brick Copper in which water was heated for washday (invariably Monday) and for heating the bath water. The water for both was heated by burning coal slack; tiny pieces of coal or dust which was the residue left over in the coal house when the coal lumps had been used up. This coal house was situated just inside the back door and ran under the stairs. Just outside the back door was our lavvy. It doesn't need much imagination to realise how filthy the hall and staircase became after the coal-man had tipped a load of coal in. That coal dust got everywhere and the house designers were well cussed by housewives who were forced to wash the paintwork and the walls down after 5cwts of Gedling best had been tipped. One thing though, and I have often wondered if this was the thinking behind putting the coal house in such a seemingly daft position, there was little chance of the neighbours helping themselves whilst the occupier was out; it being locked in

27

with the family, as it were. This was a regular cause of rows between neighbours in the older housing stock where the coal house was outside and easily accessible to all. Being fair though, with the method of selection used by the Council Officers, our neighbours were first class.

O.K. so we had a bathroom, but no hot water supply to it, so how did we get the water up to the bathroom? Simple. Every tenant's kitchen was fitted with a hand pump bolted to the kitchen wall, just above the copper, which was just below the bathroom. First, the copper in the kitchen was lit, having first been filled with water from the sink tap via a length of hose pipe or by using a bucket. Next, the kitchen door was opened wide, even if blowing a force 9 gale, as a good 'updraft' was needed to get the slack roaring. With the water near or at boiling point, a length of hose was attached to the base of the pump pipe and the other end dropped into the water. Next, the small priming cup at the top of the pump was filled with water which drained into the pump innards. The tap on the priming cup was closed and, with no time lost lest the water drain away from the pump innards (thus causing the whole operation to be gone through again) the pump handle was grabbed and worked vigorously to and fro. If the sequence of steps had been followed properly (and if the child dispatched beforehand to the bathroom had not gone to sleep) the 'bite' as the first stream of water sent aloft, was followed almost at once by the shrill cry of 'it's coming' as the bath began to slowly fill. From then until the whole family was bathed, it truly was 'All hands to the pump.'

To gain the fullest benefit from heating the Copper, most Mams would first do the family wash then, using the lovely soapy water, bathe the kids. Remember, there were no fancy detergents in those days! If the thought of it doesn't sound very hygienic, then all I can say is that few suffered from the eczema or skin conditions of today. The old bar soaps and soft soaps were kind to the skin. By the time the laundry and family bathing were over, the kitchen floor would be awash, and the walls and ceiling dripping with condensation. In addition, Our Mam's temper was very uncertain and not to be tested!

Any meals partaken that day were of the 'make shift' variety. That we got a meal at all was miraculous because by mid-day Mam was about on her knees. What with wielding the 'dolly peg' in the zinc corrugated 'dolly tub' to knock the dirt out of our clothes before rinsing, and putting them through the great cast iron monstrosity of a mangle, with the wooden rollers creaking and groaning like a dying man as the water was squeezed out, only to have the ritual repeated as the pressure was increased by the top pressure screws, sending even more of the rinse in a steady stream into the bucket put underneath. This too took a lot of effort as the contents were lifted up into the sink for disposal. Sleeves rolled up, red of face, Mam was constantly warning us little ones to 'keep your fingers away from the rollers.' Many a mangle handle turned without due care and attention, had crushed and maimed little fingers between those brutal cogs and rollers. Finally, the wash was pegged out on the line for neighbours to inspect at leisure and to pass judgement as to condition and cleanliness etc.

With the red brick tile kitchen floor mopped dry or as dry as one could get it, for it really had been swimming in water, and what with the carrying back and forth (no lino on kitchen floors in those days) Mam put into operation phase 2 of wash day. One of us, usually the eldest, was sent into the bathroom to observe whilst the 'pumping up' began and we, in turn, were thoroughly scrubbed clean. Events were arranged so by the time 'our lord and master' came home, we had all been bathed, and all he had to do was go and get into the bath, which had been half emptied, then topped up with fresh water from the copper.

Over forty years later, there were still Council homes using this same system of coppers and pumps. I know of one old gentleman whose son paid for a complete bathroom suite to be fitted in the Council house he'd occupied for years as the Council refused to do any improvements. A modern bath, toilet and pedestal wash hand basin, plus all the plumbing in. The Council maintenance office only sanctioned the work if the old bath was kept in the old gent's garden shed. He soon found out why when a few years later his old dad had to go into more suitable accommodation, for, hardly had the removal van left the street, when the Council workmen appeared, ripped out the complete suite and put that by now rusty old iron bath, back in.

It sometimes happened that to save time and energy, for all that pumping really took it out of the poor mums in those days, that having completed the family wash, the mothers would check the temperature of the copper water and having satisfied themselves it wasn't too hot, they would sit their child on the rim of the copper with their feet dangling in the water (just like a bird on a perch), and bathe them that way. Tragically, there were many recorded instances of little ones who loved to be bathed in this manner, climbing up whilst mum's back was turned and being severely, if not fatally, scalded. I cannot ever remember being bathed in this way but certainly, I can remember how I envied little playmates that were.

In the late twenties and early thirties, many men and women were unemployed, due to the world recession but we, as a family, were far better off than most. We had, for example, probably the most comfortable and certainly, the cleanest home in the district. Financially, we were sound. We didn't go short of anything in essentials and we had a few luxuries. The Old Man was a skilled elastic web weaver who could keep more than one loom going at a time and weaving paid well. Even so, he had a reputation of being an agitator. One boss once told Mam,

'Your husband is a born troublemaker but he's a damn good weaver and I need the work he turns out, otherwise, I'd get rid of him'.

So, even if one firm were on short time, he could always go somewhere else.

The Old Man was ever on the look-out for ways of making even more money e.g. A popular form of gambling in those days, at a time when any form of gambling was frowned upon, was the Football Tickets. These tickets carried inside a sealed card (Goal scores), for two league teams which once the tickets were purchased, revealed the scores. They were opened by ripping along the machined edges. The Old Man would purchase the tickets direct from the printers and it was then Ted and Mabel's job (Ted would be about 14 and Mabel 16) to sit at a sewing machine in the front room and, while Ted turned the handle, Mabel would sew them up by stitching all around the edges. With the bundle of tickets in his pockets, the Old Man would tout them around the Clubs, Pubs and his place of work. I think he charged tuppence for the sealed tickets and the winner won about 5/-. The beauty of the ticket buying and selling was there was no guarantee the winning ticket had been sold, so, in that case it would still be in the Old Man's possession. Any disputes were quickly settled by a method the Old Man was a master at, 'the fist', and it was a very brave or foolish man who tangled with him in his prime, for when violence decided who was king, our Old Man wore the crown.

Early Memories:

As a small child, my earliest recollection was being nursed on my mother's knee. It was early evening, just as the light of day was fading and the gentle shadows of dusk, closed in. Mam was nursing me on a chair just outside the French windows in the back garden. I had earache and as she comforted me she was humming a tune. I was to treasure that moment, and the tune stayed with me over the years until I found out its title. It was the 'Barcarole' from the tales of Hoffman. In the twilight of that evening, cuddled in my mother's arms, I was happy. It is the one memory I was to retain and treasure for the years that lay ahead - me being close to my mother. As a child I never again remembered being cuddled or kissed spontaneously by her in any way.

All too soon the peace was to be shattered by the sound of blows and the screams of Mam and we children as the Old Man returned home raving drunk from the Pub or Club. He would threaten to maim or kill Mam and anyone who stood in his way, and in one of his drunken, mad, rages he was capable of doing just that. When his voice was heard in the street, raving and raging, Mam would barricade us all in one bedroom and trembling in fear we'd await his onslaught on the bedroom door. In his good times, he would bring home chocolate with nuts and raisins, but we never knew what to expect. So, what caused the short circuits bringing on the almost maniacal behaviour? Who knows! Just around the corner to us lived two brothers who were Policemen. At first we would appeal to whoever answered their door to our frantic knocks, to help us but they were

32

never at home – or so it seemed. Another Policeman, after looking at the Old Man's mad goings on, said to Mam,

'Missus, he's mad; stark raving bloody mad.' (As if we didn't know that!)

Years later, I sussed it out. Realisation hit me that my parents' marriage stood no chance at all. The Old Man was a very jealous natured, very violent man, who liked his drink, and he was married to a very attractive woman. At best this was a lethal combination of circumstances but compounded by the simple fact Mam loved to be in company and positively glowed if a member of the opposite sex showed her any attention. Through no fault of her own, and because her looks and willingness led her to flirt a little, men were drawn to her as though by a magnet. The Old Man tried, but the anger must have built up in him. He would draw all the wrong conclusions in his mind, and 'BANG.'

There was a terrible scene one evening but finally the Old Man had calmed down a little and peace and quiet was restored. In the early hours of the morning, I, a mere baby, awoke, and crying wouldn't be comforted. Mam was walking the floor with me, trying to get me back to sleep again but wasn't having very much luck. The Old Man, still with the drink in him, accused her of deliberately using me to keep him awake. Mam protested – fatal! Working himself up into one of his terrible rages, he aimed a blow at her. Naturally, and instinctively, she ducked, for, as she was to say to me years later,

'I could ride a punch better than Joe Louis,'

But, as she got out of the way, she inadvertently put me right into it. Bang......I stopped it! In fairness, I know it was never intended for me. He might have 'pasted' his children but never would he have done us serious harm -

physically. The damage was done though and I went out like a light, unconscious! Later on, much later on, Mam was to say,

'The swine was terrified; he thought he'd killed you.'

The next and subsequent days I was terribly ill. I was only a year old and couldn't keep any food down. The flesh fell away from my bones and I was crying and whimpering non-stop for days at a time. I couldn't even sleep. From a normal baby (I was 10lb born) I became little more than a skeleton. The hollows in my arm pits were such that a clenched fist could be inserted therein. I was dying as they watched me. Alma Cleaver, a long-time friend of Mam's, called round, took one look at the skeleton I'd become and, without a by your leave, wrapped me in a blanket saying,

'You can't cover up for your rotten Old Man any longer Mary or this baby will die.'

Alma then marched us down to the doctor's surgery, to see the doctor who'd been treating me in absentia, thinking I had mild stomach colic. (Mam hadn't dared tell the truth else the 'cruelty man' would've been sent for)

In the doctor's room, Alma Cleaver, stripped the blanket from me and said, (for she was a very forthright sort of a soul)

'Just you look here doctor; look what her rotten Old Man has done to this poor little bleeder.'

The doctor immediately re-wrapped me and ordered that I be taken to the Leicester Royal Infirmary,

'Before he dies on you!'

In those days of the 'Panel', ambulances were for the 'well to do' so I was taken to the local hospital by tramcar; no expense spared! At the Infirmary, the blanket was stripped from my wasted form. Various doctors and specialists 'tut tutted' over my emaciated, whimpering, cringing little skeleton and, after much head shaking, I was admitted with a diagnosis of Nervous Unrest, Nervous Dyspepsia and Wasting Disease. They didn't mention the displaced septum caused by the blow, probably because they'd run out of room on the diagnosis sheet. After seeing me tucked up in a cot on the babies' ward annexe, Alma Cleaver turned to Mam and said,

'Come on then Mary, we'll go for a glass of beer. You won't see that little bleeder again!'

Ah well! How wrong she was. It may have been the peace and quiet, it might have been one of the nurses who, whenever I started to cry would come to my cot and say, 'baby Norman SHUSH....... Whatever, after three days I was taking food and keeping it down, preparing myself for the next few decades.

Taking her mother's part as she always did meant Mabel was always at loggerheads with the Old Man. At this time, she would have been around 19 years old but being so young my memories aren't very clear. From what I can remember Mabel was very small and dainty, with very clear, grey eyes and the longest eye lashes. When first seen, the abiding memory anyone had of Mabel was her eyes. She adored Mam and was adored in return. The one feature she inherited from the Old Man though, was his temper, but while her heart was large, her frame and stamina could not match it. Already the pallor was in her face and she had no way of escaping what fate had ordained for her.

My memories of early childhood are few and disjointed: I can remember the woman from around the corner who minded me standing in front of the mirror combing her hair. It was waist length and every few moments, whilst combing, she would pull the loose strands from the comb and throw them onto the fire. Afterwards, the hair, now combed and shining would be swept into separate strands and plaited into a round bun which was pinned at the back. With her hair long and loose her face had been soft and round, but now plaited it was hard and angular.

Another memory was looking into a deep drain hole that had been dug and uncovered before being connected into drains and sewers and feeling a terrible irrational fear of falling into it and disappearing forever. Why should I be so afraid of a hole in the ground? Perhaps my older siblings had been laying it on too thickly about the 'Bury Hole' - where people were put when they died.

I don't remember (thank God) hurting my shoulder/ collar bone as a little boy and running around like a bird with a damaged wing. When Mam pointed out I may have broken something, the Old Man had apparently 'pooh poohed' this idea and commented, 'If his bloody shoulder was broken, I wouldn't be able to do this now would I?!' whereupon he took my arm and swung it around in a full circle. I was told I went deathly white, screamed and fainted, proving that, in fact it was, and he couldn't. I've often wondered whether the scar found at the top of my lung some three years later was in fact caused by the broken bone piercing it whilst Daddy was showing off his expertise in first aid.

On my first day at school I can remember Mam taking me to enrol at the local school (1932) before she went to work. I knew that somewhere in the building was my brother and sister but that was no consolation. I was taken to the classroom door and the teacher who came to greet us seemed to be a hundred years old. Her name was Miss Flinders and she wore one of the old fashioned hats that covered her hair back and front. It had huge artificial roses on it and she never seemed to take it off in all the time I knew her. She tried to be very kind to me and it was 'Dear' this and 'Dear' that, until Mam slipped away whilst I was momentarily distracted, then it was 'Into the classroom mate and no messing.' I set off weeping and wailing but with a room full of kids, all new to the school like me, it was a case of 'Get on with it.' I soon settled.

Maisie had charge of me one day and I was being taken for a walk. It was early evening and summer. We'd walked down our road, passing the new council houses that were being tacked onto the end of our estate. We reached what was eventually to be the major road (Portway) which skirted our estate, although at this time it was still a rough field dotted with small mounds and hollows. Coming towards us were two girls who obviously knew Maisie for they shouted a greeting, to which Maisie replied. As the two girls redirected their steps in our direction, Maisie whispered, 'They're twins.' Now, I knew what twins were and I looked at my sister in disbelief for the only thing these two seemed to have in common was age, about 12 years. One alleged twin was very fat and the other very thin and, on that summer evening the fat girl was perspiring gently. I gazed at them with interest and they gazed back until the fat one said,

'Is he your little brother?'

Maisie answered in the affirmative. At once, the fat twin grabbed me and planted a big smacking kiss on my lips, her twin followed suit. It was the first time a female other than a member of my own family had kissed me, but what made it so memorable was that both must have just finished a meal of fish and chips, very greasy fish and chips and, as I wiped my sleeve across my mouth, some, in fact a lot of grease, smeared on my face along with the smell and taste of their meal. To this day I can still smell and taste it.

Those parts of the estate where 'the brickies' (bricklayers) worked, rang with the sound of trowels, as bricks were tossed into the air and with two or three whacks, it was cut cleanly into shape and size. (Unlike today where chisels and lump hammers are employed and still a bodge job is made of it) One of the perks of having the builders working in the district was that at the end of the day when the workmen had gone, the neighbourhood kids would go foraging around, mainly for off-cuts of wood to be used as kindling. Careful sifting would often provide enough to fill a carrier bag full. Unfortunately, there was a snag, and this came in the form of 'Dummy.'

'Dummy' was a big lad for his age, about 12 or 13. Always neatly dressed and clean, he was a very dark, handsome child. Unfortunately for him, as his name implies, he was what we termed in those days as 'deaf and dumb.' His obviously caring parents used to send their darling boy collecting this 'gash wood' but what they probably didn't know was that 'Dummy', before setting off, used to hide a lethal weapon under his jacket, to wit, the coal house hatchet. Now this hatchet wasn't to chop the waste wood, Oh dear no. That hatchet was to chop any kid in the area who had more wood in his bag than 'Dummy' had. He didn't live in our street, so that made him some sort of foreigner. The sight of him coming down the road used to clear the building sites far quicker than the 'Coppers' ever could, and it wasn't funny running like hell down the road with 'Dummy' slinging his bloody axe at your head.

Things at home, unfortunately, were going downhill fast. When they did go out together, the Old Man would have too much to drink and then the accusations would fly thick and fast. Any man in the near vicinity, be he eight of eighty, would be accused of, 'standing in with my old woman.' Denial of such patently untrue accusations only made matters worse. Blood, had to flow and when a certain point was reached 'BANG', it flowed. The neighbours soon learned to keep out of it and the only sign of their involvement was the twitching of a front room curtain when the level of noise from our house had reached a certain pitch or the shadow of someone with a little more courage than the rest, flitting down the street to fetch the police.

Yet, we had more going for us than most in the area; if only that mad so and so of a father had been able to control his mad rages and jealous nature. Our home furnishings were the best in the district. Mam was spotlessly clean and set us the same standards. We were all toilet trained well before the average age and were polite and well trained in our dealings with others at all times. School was a must, no excuses accepted, and each in turn was warned that any punishment at school would bring more when we got home. We rarely squabbled among ourselves and that was understandable as our parents did enough of that for the lot of us. As an elastic weaver the Old Man was rarely on short time. Mam had a good job in a shoe factory and put all her earnings into the house. Mam had left school before she was 14 and told us how she went knocking at factory office windows asking,

'Please have you got a job for me? I've got my pinny (pinafore) with me. I'll be a good girl and work hard.'

The first place she went to eventually took pity on her (she came from a very poor, large family and it showed) and set her on. Soon after, the forewoman went to her and complimented her saying,

'You're a good girl Mary Wileman; you do work hard.'

The Old Man had a most glorious Tenor voice and at the drop of a hat he would sing. An evening out when he was behaving himself would cost nothing. The family would go into the country on a service bus (only professional people had cars and not even all of them), find a country pub that had a piano and he would start to sing. From then on all the food and beer he could eat and drink was his for the asking. Not only did he sing the song, he lived it, and should it be 'Mother' or a 'Sonny Boy' type ballad, he would bring the house down. His favourite was a gem called 'Little Pal'. For this, one of us young ones would be sat on his knee, and he would sob the words, some of which I remember as, 'And if someday you should be on a new daddy's knee, don't forget about me, Little Pal.' At this there wasn't a dry eye in the house. Encore after encore was demanded and the freebies flowed faster and faster whilst the Publicans begged him to, 'Come again next week, Ted.'

Asked to describe the Old Man, I would say he was about 5ft 10ins tall, round faced with a good skin but rather pale complexion, although this means nothing as, apart from his ear problems, I don't think he had any major illness. His eyes were brown and they could be very expressive. His hair began to recede at a very early age but only at the front and top - he kept the back and sides. His mouth was wide and his teeth not very good, but certainly not bad; he'd lost them all by the age of 49. He smoked cigarettes but very infrequently, mainly, I think, because of his voice, although we didn't have the cigarette 'witch hunts' in those days that we do now. Perhaps his most noticeable trait was his reluctance to wear a collar and/or tie. Winter or summer, he scorned cardigans or pullovers and, if seen, he would be striding down the street, raincoat unbuttoned and flapping in the breeze, no collar or tie, and usually around his neck, a white silk scarf. Definitely not a scruff but certainly not a man to tangle with. Ah yes, always on his head, a soft cap, as are still worn today. He hated trouser braces, so his trousers were always self-supporting or he wore a belt. His very presence in a street seemed like a challenge from this bull of a man and so he became the focus of female eyes, drawing them in like moths to a flame; perhaps this was the reason Mam put up with him for so long without complaint. He even smelled like I imagine a man should smell; a clean surprisingly good smell.

I was about 4 years old and had been playing in the street in the gathering dusk when I hurt my finger. At this time, things must have been getting to boiling point between my parents, and the Old Man was living in the front room. I told Mam my finger hurt and she said,

'I'm busy, go and tell your dad.'

Over 65 years later (1997) I can see it as it was then. I went into the front room. There was a good fire and the curtains were drawn, the light on. The room was spotlessly clean and he sat at the table in the centre of the room drinking tea out of an earthenware basin (he never used a cup if he could help it, claiming the tea tasted better that way) but what overrode all else was the smell of him, a masculine smell; a smell I noticed even after he'd vacated a room long before. I've described the Old Man as a 'Bull of a Man', perhaps that was part of the whole which so often made him such a brooding, menacing figure.

Ted Junior had already suffered his dad's uncertain, often homicidal, temper. On this occasion Ted Jnr. was about 15years old. He was watching the Old Man trying to kick start his pride and joy, a motorbike which, in spite of everything, just wouldn't fire. The Old Man, never noted as you may have guessed for his sweet temper, was turning the air blue as he twisted the throttle and stamped down on the kick start, all to no avail. Ted Jnr. suddenly realised what was wrong and laughed. At once, the Old Man's head spun round,

'What the bleeding hell are you laughing at?' he snapped.

Without a word, Ted Jnr. leaned forward and twisted the petrol feed to 'ON'.

'Oh, you are silly Our Dad,' he was unwise enough to say.

Years later Ted Jnr recounted,

'That Old Bugger hit me so hard I was laid out on the grass verge on the other side of the road; I don't remember my feet touching the floor as I went! And he didn't even say 'Thank You' for spotting what was wrong!'

But this was the 'Old Man,' and everything that could be, was said by 'the fist'. Another story stored in the family archives concerns the self-same motor bike. Mam was being taken for a spin on the pillion when they came at high speed to a sharp bend in the road. Quite sure that at their speed there was no way the bend could be negotiated, Mam tightly closed her eyes. On opening them a few moments later she realised that not only were they still alive but they'd made it around the bend.

'Ted,' Mam had said, 'I was sure we were coming off at that last corner so I shut my eyes!' to which the Old Man had answered back, 'Well, so did I!'

In those days of the early thirties, one of the most common and widely used expletives was the word 'Bleeding' but let me hasten to add that although 'bad' language was used so frequently around us, children hardly ever swore, especially in the home, for fear of the ultimate sanction; a swift clip round the ear. The punishment was rarely more severe than that, for parents were aware that to impose a stricter sanction would make the whole idea of swearing more attractive. In every street though, an exception to this rule could be found, and our street had such an exception. It was a family: Mum, Dad, 2 girls and 4 boys. Walter, the youngest at nearly 5, was already an accomplished swearer with 'Bleeding' being the favourite family word. Walter was due to start school and on the appointed morning his mum set off, dragging a very reluctant Walter with her. As they went along, Walter's mum was shouting to any neighbour who might be listening, that now the great day was here she would soon 'be shut of the little bleeder' and she 'would get some bleeding peace at last.' Having registered and deposited her little darling with the Headmistress, Walter's Mam went back home chortling and looking forward to putting her feet up and enjoying the peace that was now due to her after 20 years of childbearing and minding. How wrong she was. Within ten minutes, a loud and persistent banging at the front door brought her to her feet. Opening it she found a very red faced, irate Headmistress and a loudly bawling Walter gripped tightly by the hand. It emerged that after only ten minutes in the classroom, Walter had called his teacher 'a rotten bleeder!' This surely must have set an all time record for the suspension of an infant on his or her first day from school!

Perhaps the fondest memory of that family was some 7 years later. The War had started and one of the sons was home on leave from the Navy. His whole family were joining in on the chorus of one of those ditties so beloved by 'Matelots.' I remember it went,

'We'll make a farce, kiss my arse, make fast the dingy.'
The tune was catchy, the words easy to remember, so I joined in too.

Once again, the Old Man had another money making idea. With one of his pals, they decided to take on an allotment and grow vegetables, selling off any surplus. They thought this would make a profit, allowing them to take on further allotments etc. etc. Give him his due he would always look out for ways of making more money. So, the first rule of good husbandry..........manure the ground well! A big load of horse muck was required which in those days of the horse and cart was easy to obtain. The pair hired a horse and cart and set off for the local co-op stables just off Leicester High Street, right in the heart of the City Centre. With visions of monster cabbages, and onions as big as a person's head, the cart was loaded to capacity and then, remembering the road back was all down-hill, further horse muck was added. Off they set, cart piled high with steaming, smelly horse manure; heads down, trying not to be seen by anyone who might know them. All went well until they arrived at the Centre of our fair City - the Clock Tower! It was a hive of activity with Tramcars, the first Buses, a few cars and plenty of other horse drawn vehicles. It was at this place I like to think the Dear Merciful Lord, who'd been watching the agony of my family at the hands of this sod for so long murmured, 'Got you, you Bugger,' and reached down from heaven and caused the cart wheels to collapse on one side. Whatever, God or fate, for the time it took to unharness the poor overloaded horse, fetch another cart and reload it, all under the eyes of a not very sympathetic Policeman plus a crowd that had gathered to see the fun as crowds do, the proceedings were helped along with comments such as, 'Blimey, it don't half pong,' and 'that's a funny place to have a load of shit delivered.' The market gardening idea died that day.

Another time, the Old Man went to Skegness with one of his mates, or dare I say 'partners in crime'. Mam and the kids were left behind as there was a good chance he'd have to leave 'Skeggy' quickly, but mainly because there would probably be unescorted females around and having a wife and children in tow would cramp his style. Years later, my brother Ted told me the drill: Now remember, betting was illegal in those days so if you wanted to bet you needed to find the local 'Bookie' (usually in a pub); also, telephones were not usually available to the ordinary man in the street. Finding where the local 'Bookie' worked from, ie. 'The Red Lion' or 'Dog and Duck', the Old Man would go in alone and, turning on the charm, get into conversation with him. (the Old Man could certainly charm and chat if he wanted) For the first day or so, the Old Man would pick a horse and, waiting till it was time for the 'off', would ask the 'Bookie' if he could take his bet. Now, the 'Bookie' knew full well that this new friend 'Ted' hadn't left his side for the last half hour, so was most happy to oblige, naturally, the horses chosen by the Old Man lost, and he lost his bets. The third day was 'kill time'. The Old Man's pal kept right out of the way but in the meantime had located a telephone near where the 'Bookie' and his nibs were. Perhaps even the pubs own telephone was used, after all, the landlord wasn't to know the man who'd dashed in asking if he might ring the hospital urgently was up to skulduggery with the 'Bookie's' new customer who had, up to now, lost pretty much consistently. With a line through to the racecourse or to a friend in the know, the stage was set. Eg The races (sprints or short distances) were due to take place at say, 2.30pm. At 2.30pm exactly, the Old Man would say to the 'Bookie',

'I fancy a bet in this one, is it still OK? Will you take it?'

After consulting his watch the 'Bookie' would say,

'Of course it is Ted, which do you fancy?'

Precious seconds, would pass with the Old Man consulting his newspaper whilst one eye was cocked for his accomplice. With a direct line to the course and now with the name of the sprint winner, the accomplice would signal the number of the horse to the Old Man. He would write the horse down and pass his betting slip to the 'Bookie' before sitting back and waiting for the 'Bookie's' runner to dash in breathless. The Old Man was now home & dry and from now on only bet on the horse with better odds. By the end of the day he was quid's in. The holiday 'digs', the beer, the fags and the women were paid for by the 'Bookie' and usually there was a pound or two left over to come home with. You couldn't do it today now betting's legal and the Betting Shops have a direct line to the Racecourse, but older brother Ted swore that the Old Man worked this fiddle and was one of the first to do so.

When my sister Mabel was in her teens, she was found to have scar tissue on her lungs and when tested was found to be consumptive. Never a strong girl, so slight and petite (even frail) she must have known she had little chance of beating that scourge of a disease, so aptly called 'The White Death' or 'Spitting Disease.' It touched nearly every family in the land. Sometimes it took whole families but always the dearest, prettiest and best loved. Several spells in hospital were to follow. I have a very faint recollection of Mam taking me into a long room that had several beds down each side of the wall. The overwhelming impression was of black and white - the black of the old iron bed frames and the white of the sheets, coverlets and pillowcases. Of course, it must have been the Isolation Hospital or 'Sanny' as we learnt to call it. I was very young but there, sitting up in one of those beds, was 'Our Mabel', her eyes big and shining at seeing her little brother and her adored and adoring Mam. I wanted so desperately to give her a kiss, for there was little else I could give her, but I wasn't allowed. Consumption or T.B. as we call it today is very contagious. I clearly remember how she kept coughing great wrenching coughs that shook her frail frame; how Mam would support her as the filth off her chest would rattle as she brought it up into her throat, and how she would reach out for the hideous metal sputum mug with the hinged lid that stood on her bedside locker, tainting the air with the smell of Lysol which covered the bottom. As the lid closed, hiding the often blood stained contents, poor Mabel would sink back, whiter than the pillows on which she lay, exhausted. That terrible cough and the metallic clang of the sputum mug haunts me to this day. The Old Man, who I'm sure was only trying to help her when she came out of the 'Sanny', forbade her to go to dances, which she loved, and tried to force her to live the life of an invalid. Unfortunately, you can't put wise heads on young shoulders and the rows between them flared up again & again. Eventually, Mabel left home to live with friends and only came back when he abandoned us.

One of the local boys was around 9 or 10 years. In those days all boys wore short trousers and he was no exception. This lad had a habit that had us doubling up with laughter whenever we saw him do it. He would stand in deep thought, obviously miles away, at the same time putting his hand up the back of his trouser leg. After poking his finger round his backside for a while, he would withdraw his hand and for the next half hour walk around with obvious relish sniffing his finger. I wonder what the child psychologists of today would make of that one?!

In our household, we had two pets. One was Peggy, an old English rabbit, and the other was Rover, an Airedale dog. Pegs, a lovely black and white darling of a rabbit, had been obtained originally to be fattened up for the pot and now she was 'pot' size. Came the awful day and Peggy disappeared into the garden shed in the Old Man's arms. A dull thud of a blow sounded and that was it. Farewell Peg! Ten minutes passed then we children were taken into the shed. Hanging on a nail was our pet's skin ready for the rag and bone man. The next time we saw Pegs, she was on our dinner plates. Dinner was a dismal failure. Maisie especially refused to eat our pet, I don't know about Ron. Me? Well, I just got stuck in; I liked rabbit and I still do.

I can only just remember Rover the dog as a brown blur, but with three young children he must have been pretty good natured with kids. Unfortunately, he took a bite out of the postman and the Old Man got a summons to go to court. He sent Ted Jnr in his place with the excuse he couldn't afford to lose time off work. He did have to pay the fine though. As for Rover, he was 'put down'. Mam used to say 'it was a pity it wasn't the Old Man........'

You could say things couldn't get any worse between our parents but how wrong you'd be. Mad, was a word often used to describe his behaviour and if you think the word 'Mad' too strong, then read on.....

The Old Man developed an interest in spiritualism and began, accompanied by Mam and another couple, to attend séances. Picture the scene..... The participants, some 20 to 25 people, all strangers, are seated in a circle. What happens next is hard to believe but Mam swore to the truth of it, so let her now tell the story.

'The medium went into a trance, moaning and muttering and now and again making 'Go Away' motions to any spirits who were getting too pushy. Suddenly, your Old Man began to go off. He grunted and groaned, his eyes rolled and then so did he, all around the floor. Wise people in the circle hurriedly left the room because the Old Man started to punch hell out of the chap who'd been sitting opposite him and with no further ado, the bloke started to punch the Old Man back. It was then me and our friends left hurriedly, before the coppers arrived.' Two hours later, the Old Man arrived home looking very much under the weather and a 'post-mortem' was held. The conclusion reached was that the Old Man and the other fellow's spirit guides, were in conflict, or as Our Mam put it, 'we had two mad buggers instead of one'.

During the late twenties and early thirties there was much unrest in Leicester City due to high unemployment, the general strike and the world recession. This led to the hated 'Means Test'. Let one of the Old Man's pals tell this next story as he did years later to Mam who was hearing it for the first time:

'Your mad old bugger (daddy) and me were in town when we saw a large crowd of men outside the Assistance Offices. Well, you know Ted, trouble draws him like a magnet and in one minute flat he was in front of the crowd shouting abuse and insults at the police as hard as he could, keeping at all times a weather eye open to make sure he had a clear line of retreat, especially as some of the coppers were on horses and had their batons out. Suddenly, and without any prior warning, your Ted bent down and, pulling a drain grating up, slung it straight through the Assistance Board's plate glass window. That did it. The 'hosses' were spurred into a gallop, the coppers on foot charged, batons swinging, and dear old Ted, true to form, was off like a bloody greyhound, out of it, leaving those who couldn't move very fast, to take the hammering. Of course, I'm no hero and I ran like hell as well. We ran down the main street and turned into a side road with the law close on our heels. Just inside the side road, as it was a warm day, some poor soul had left their front door open to cool the house down and get a breeze. With no hesitation, your Old Man ran through the front door, through the middle door into the living room cum kitchen, and into the back yard. He jumped over the wall with me running a close second and the coppers, on foot, by now a poor third (I think the front door was too narrow for the 'hosses' to get through). We got clean away'.

Here, the narrator paused and began to shake with laughter.

'It was funnier than the keystone cops but the really hilarious bit was the family who lived at the house, for, as we ran through, they were all sitting round the table having a late breakfast. I can see them now, mouths gaping open, cups or bread and dip halfway to their mouths, frozen. It was better than a bloody Charlie Chaplin chase'.

Mam knew the Old Man had a fancy woman tucked away and she was supposed to accept that. Mind you, if another bloke so much as looked at her the Old Man would hammer him and her to the floor, be the chap eight or eighty, it didn't matter; down he would go. Mam's suspicions were confirmed when, answering a knock at the front door, she beheld a strange man who demanded to know,

'Where's my missus?'

Mam asked by way of reply, 'I don't know your wife do I?'

The man had replied,

'Perhaps you don't but your lousy Old Man does, he's cleared off with her to Skeggy. They've gone on his motorbike!'

And so it proved to be. When the pair of them returned, the Old Man dumped her back where she lived before returning to the bosom of his family. We found out later her husband forgave her but only after insisting that she went to the local clinic for a VD test - wise man. Another young woman broke down and told Mam that because she had no money, she had let him have his way with her on the understanding he would pay her for the service. He paid her all right - 6 old pence (or 2½ new pence). When she was in her eighties, Mam broke down one day and confided to me,

'Your Old Man gave me a disease. I had you little ones to raise and poor Mabel dying and the rotten sod gave me that.'

No, she didn't have much to laugh about, none of us did.

It must have been about this time I began to develop septic spots on my heels. Why this complaint came to plague me I don't know for, unlike many kids around me at that time I never had to wear shoes that were too small or hand me downs. Anyway, Mam would spot I was hobbling around and the small red blemish would, within a matter of hours, change into a large blister full of fluid, with a clear red line extending from it, up the leg and into the groin. My temperature would rise and, with no time wasted, I was whipped down to the local Infirmary 'Out Patients Dept.' What I knew was to happen next, filled me with dread. We would go into a large, waiting room with a high ceiling and sit on one of the long oak forms, highly polished by the numerous bottoms that had slid along it as the queue 'otched' along. The walls were tiled in aseptic thick green tiles and the room reeked of a particular orange coloured paste or unction universally used and liberally spread, or so it seemed, on everything from a dog bite to a boil on the bum. In the background was the hissing of the sterilisers and the steam that arose whenever the stainless steel lid was lifted by the seemingly, always on the run, nurses, supervised by Sister, with her lace cap buckled under her chin and silver belt buckle twinkling. Lady of all, she surveyed, always with a kind word for the children but seeming to me never to meet the gaze of the accompanying mums. The call went out, 'Next patient, please' and in we went, the green card listing the injury held out. The doctors were always so kind to frightened little boys. Doctor would hum and ha and, after writing on my card, smile, pat me on the cheek, then go to get ready. Again, we would sit waiting. Then Sister would come to us.

'Alright, we're ready for Norman now, I'll take him.'

At this, I would scream and fight and try to hold on to Mam. 'It's alright', everyone near would say, but it wasn't alright. In spite of my struggles, I was half carried, half dragged into the next brilliantly lit room where the doctor was waiting, standing at the side of a table covered by a white sheet. Several nurses would grab and hold me down whilst another man, in a white coat, would hold what looked like an old fashioned gramophone horn over my face and head. I would hear a hissing noise as the gas came in and I would really go mad trying to escape until, mercifully, oblivion came. When I came to, I would be tightly clasped in my Mam's arms. Everyone would be telling her 'what a good boy he's been,' (sodding liars) and my foot and ankle would be swathed in bandages where the blisters had, after being pierced and drained, been cut off. Because temperatures usually soar at night, it was usually after the trams and buses had stopped running that all this happened and so my Mam, my poor Mam, had to carry me all the way home again, a distance of three miles or more.

Like most of the kids of those days, I was caught up in the 'Every child needs to lose its tonsils' thinking. Today, of course, we know that our tonsils are nature's filters and the pendulum has swung the other way but I was getting sore throats and a cough, so the powers that be decided....Tonsillectomy! This was deduced from the equation of sore throat + cough = Tonsil Removal. On the day I was to go into the clinic for this operation, my brothers and sisters spoke to me and treated me as though this was to be my last day on earth, and their constant and repetitive assurances that I would be alright did nothing to reassure me. I'd like to think the Old Man broke down and hugged me to his breast, perhaps he did, most likely he didn't, for around this time he'd most probably decided on a certain course of action as you will see later. With Mam holding me tightly by the hand, we set off down the road to catch the tram which was to take us to near the clinic where the local kids with coughs and sore throats got the chop. It was a big old Georgian house near the centre of the city and the waiting area smelt like the hospital waiting area. I wasn't the only kid there looking wild eyed and apprehensive. In these more enlightened times, mums not only stay with their offspring up to the actual 'op', but help nurse them during those traumatic few moments just before and just after it all happens, but not so then. No, what we got was a momentary distraction and when we looked again, Mam was gone, or worse, a huge nurse interposed herself between mum and child so mum had a flying start before the wails went up. With parent gone, we scared and frightened kids were herded (that's the only word to described it) into a large dormitory type room. I think it was all boys one session and all girls the next. We were told to get undressed and get into bed. I believe there were six to a room. With much lower standards in the thirties, not many of the working class men, women or children wore purpose made pyjamas; these were counted a luxury item. What went for sleeping apparel were vests, and in the cold weather shirts were kept on in bed. So, if hospitalised, pyjamas were borrowed if possible. I was lucky, my Mam had bought me some. The thick red hospital blankets on the beds looked marvellously warm to kids who, in the main, were used to 'snuggling up' often six to a bed, for warmth in the winter, although the colour of them, red, seemed ominous. I lay in the bed allocated to me, wittering and whining to myself inside and trying not to show it outside. I wasn't a baby (want to bet) and could easily see others were as nervous as I was. Then the door opened and a jolly man came in, carrying in his arms a stack of rubber hats, which he promptly threw at us, one to each child. The one he threw to me was thrown too hard and it hit me, 'thwack', right in the face ......it hurt. The hat was to be worn during the operation, although I wasn't to know that at this time. What I did know was my face was stinging from the impact and the other kids were laughing. I remember wishing Our Teddy was here; that he would hit them for laughing at me, but that was really wishful thinking. Mostly, like all big brothers, he would sooner hit me himself. I fought back the tears and to his credit the man came over and said he was sorry. I suppose they wanted us as calm as possible for what they knew was to come. Then it was time and the conveyor belt started up. Now, I'd been reassured that having ones tonsils out was not unlike being wheeled into a room and seeing Santa Claus, although I hadn't altogether swallowed this because of the repetitive 'it's not going to hurt you'. I just couldn't marry this with the picture they were trying to create in my mind of the 'good fairy' waving her magic wand, giving me a bag of sweeties, everyone telling me what a good boy I was and then home. No, I decided, there had to be a catch and I found out what it was then, wearing that ridiculous ruddy red hat I was wheeled into quite a small room; there was a window, a sink, a white coated doctor, a table and then......... 'Oh God nooooo'......... there was also one of those bloody great gramophone horn things that they put over my head in the Infirmary. I think that until the gas mercifully put me right out, I went quite insane. Kids today, after a tonsillectomy, get ice cream; if memory serves me right, we got either Oxo or it may have been Bovril. I can taste it now. For my return home Mam insisted on a taxi. It was my first time in a motor car.

Some twenty years later, I needed to have a tooth extracted. Up to then I'd only known local anaesthetics for dental jobs, but this man (who was new to me) without giving me a choice, told me he was giving me gas. I wasn't afraid, but when I got the first whiff of the stuff and tasted that rubber gag dentists put in to keep your mouth open etc., I felt my heart begin to speed up, faster and faster, until it was thundering in my ears and I thought it would burst. That 'Old Mab' was rearing its ugly head in my mind, deep, deep, in my subconscious and then nothing...... A split second later, or so it seemed to my disorientated mind, the dental surgeon was leaning over me shouting, 'It's alright' whilst at the same time pushing me hard back into the chair. His nurse at the back of me was hanging on hard, also restraining me. Over my shoulder I saw she was pale and frightened. When order was restored and I was clearly back in the land of the living, the dentist said,

'For God's sake, don't ever let me attempt to give you gas again old lad, you're bloody useless under it; now don't forget!'

I was to stay with that dentist for over thirty years. I was never again given gas by him for, as I said before, that 'Old Mab' was still slumbering just beneath the surface and when it emerged that day it certainly frightened the living daylights out of the dentist. After that episode he would come towards me and, after pushing the gas and air machine to one side, would wave the hypodermic needle under my nose as he muttered,

'We don't give you 'gas' do we lad!'

Mam was in the kitchen washing up the breakfast pots having seen me into school. Ronnie, who thought himself no end of a big lad at the age of 6 or 7, always insisted he went to school with his chums, unescorted. Suddenly, there came a knocking on our front door and when Mam answered it she was greeted by a neighbour with,

'Your Ronnie's just been knocked down by a car on the main road.'

'No, you're wrong, Our Ronnie's at school,' but no, Our Ronnie wasn't, Our Ronnie had decided to play 'hooky' and for his sins got cleaned up by a lorry and had a broken leg to prove it. One thing though, it cured him of ever playing truant.

Ronnie and I were now standing in our front garden, every now and again getting out of the way of the men who were helping the Old Man carry furniture out of our house and put it into a van. Ronnie was about eight; I was about six. Maisie was in the house. I knew that as I could hear her raised voice. She was shouting something at the Old Man. Young as I was I knew something was wrong, very wrong. I remember thinking Mam would know what to do but she was at work; so was 'Our Teddy'. I didn't know where Mabel was but she certainly wasn't at home because the men had just put her bed in the van. Chairs, tables, linoleum and rugs - I wanted to ask but daren't. Looking at Ron's face I knew he was near to tears, so was I, but I didn't know why. The van was nearly loaded with our home. I started to cry and the Old Man gave me and Ronny a penny but it didn't placate us. He told us to be quiet and looked furtively up and down the street. Window curtains around the houses were beginning to twitch; we were being watched. We gripped the pennies tightly. We didn't know it then but it really was 'hush money', our pay-off, all that our lives and future was to become, a penny whilst he took away our home and the roof over our heads, leaving us defenceless. Judas sold a man for 30 pieces of silver; my family, less the Old Man, went for tuppence. The house was now empty. All that remained was the piano, standing in solitary splendour in the front room in its position of honour. Both Teddy and Mabel could play it, and in the good old days we'd gather round as one or the other played and sing our hearts out. We hadn't got much to sing about now. One of the men advanced towards the piano with a muttered,

'Come on, this is the last and then we're finished.'

Immediately, Maisie (12) flew at him.

'You leave that piano alone' she screamed, standing arms outstretched in front of it, daring him to touch it.

'You're not taking it,' she yelled, 'My Mam paid for it.'

The men stopped dead in their tracks, halted by the vehemence in her voice. In full flood it took a lot to shut 'Our Mais' up as we young ones knew only too well, and screaming and crying, all without seeming to take a breath, she was a pretty daunting sight.

'It's me Mam's' she shouted again, 'Our Dad never paid for it, Our Mam did out of her wages.' (Which was true).

9 Martival, Leicester

Of course the neighbours, who by now were gathering at the front gate, drawn by the shouting, had begun to chime in with cries of 'shame' and 'leave that girl alone you rotten sods,' at the same time making sure they were part of the crowd and not to be identified as the Old Man wasn't fussy as to who he punched in the face, as has been said before. One of the removal men settled the issue, for with a long look at the near hysterical Mais, then at Ronnie and me, both bawling our eyes out and being comforted by the now, fast swelling crowd of neighbours, who were now getting very agitated indeed said,

'Leave it Ted, if it is your old woman's piano and we take it without permission, we'll be in trouble, especially if she's got the receipt for it. (which she had) Is that it then?'

The Old Man replied in the affirmative, then went back into the room, took an envelope out of his pocket and placed it on the front room shelf. He then gave me and Ron one of his wet sucking kisses before turning to Maisie to give her his Judas kiss. The hatred in her eyes stopped him dead in his tracks. After taking one last look around the room, now empty and already lifelessly echoing, he left the house. He was never to enter it again.

As the furniture van turned the corner and went from sight, Maisie shouted, or rather screamed at us,

'Don't move, stay in the house, don't go away or I'll hit you,'

And with that, she dragged on her coat and burst through the crowd of neighbours, running off down the street with cries of,

'Are you alright me duck?' and 'What's the rotten bugger took your furniture for?' ringing in her ears.

Maisie ran all the way to where Mam worked and got the time keeper to fetch Mam out. To Mam this was all 'out of the blue' and she couldn't believe what she was hearing for when she set off for work that morning she had a lovely home and yet here was Maisie telling her it was all gone; she had nothing! He'd even taken poor Mabel's bed. (she must have been in the sanatorium again)

With permission from the factory Forewoman, poor Mam chased home, running all the way. The nightmare had ended in one sense, whilst another had begun. Did I say 'Home' because it wasn't that any longer; just an empty and echoing shell. Only the piano was standing forlornly alone in the front room and the letter was on the shelf where he'd left it. With dread in her heart, poor Mam took it down and opened it. If she thought it might contain terms for his return or similar, she was sadly mistaken, for the letter was addressed to 'Him'. It was from the city council housing department and in language leaving no room for misunderstanding, it said, in effect, that as so much rent was owed we now had to vacate the house; no appeal would be entertained. Mam had been turning the rent over to the old swine for months but he'd been pocketing it. That swine had deliberately withheld the rent and spent it on his fancy woman. What sort of a man would connive at a set of circumstances culminating in his wife and 5 children, one a hopeless consumptive, being turned onto the streets penniless, for that was what was going to happen! Even today I cry SHAME on the swine that sat on the Housing Committee and signed the eviction notice. You see, what it was really about was none of their visiting officials dare face up to the Old Man and warn him that if he didn't stop upsetting other people in the street HE, and not his defenceless family, would have to get out. Mam could've easily paid off the arrears and kept the rent up to date. She was working and so was Ted Jnr. The neighbours tried to rally round us whilst Mam pleaded with the council not to evict us. Petitions were got up and she was assured 'they'll never turn you out with five kids,' and Mabel a consumptive with only a year to live. Wouldn't they indeed!? Don't you believe it, for that's what those mealy mouthed hypocrites on the housing committee did! They didn't have the guts to tackle him, so they kicked us when we were down instead. What a pity when they were in church the following Sunday (for I bet they were all good churchgoing folk) that the roof didn't fall in on the bastards!

Most of what happened next went over my head but my mind, the mind of a six year old child, had taken so much, and could take no more. It closed down. I cannot remember any of the next few months but I know my Mam's sister took us in, only because I was told so. My uncle had a good job and was being sent to Australia by his firm (The British United Shoe Company) and their stuff was packed ready to go, otherwise they wouldn't have been able to fit us in and Mam would've had to take us into the Workhouse where, no doubt, we would've been separated, and I'm not kidding – these were the Good Old Days, remember!!

It was this Aunt's son who, in the days of the 'old' coal gas, used to hate to turn the gas off on the stove because coal gas always went off with a very loud 'pop' which frightened him. He was in the habit therefore of turning the gas down 'low' and then, after blowing the flame out, which didn't cause it to 'pop' he would turn the gas tap the rest of the way off. Unfortunately, one day after blowing the flame out (no pop) he forgot to turn the tap the rest of the way 'off'. An hour or so later, his mum, my aunt, came into the kitchen and, having a head cold and not smelling the seeping gas, struck a match. There was a very loud 'bang' and I understand the dent in the ceiling where the gas stove struck, could be seen for a long time after! (I'm joking of course; she only lost her eyebrows!)

I was told years later, that this son, after proposing to his future bride said,

'I do hope you understand that in marrying you I will be marrying below my station!'

In fairness to him though, when they returned from Australia several years later, I always found him pleasant and he was always kind to me; I quite liked him.

5: 1 Victoria Road East, Leicester

So, my aunt and uncle took us in, but they lived in a council house so our presence was kept quiet. We had to find somewhere else to live before they sailed to Australia. How long we were with them, I do not know, but Mam was still working and dashing around trying to find us somewhere to live, or rather rent. Not many working class families without a father, with no furniture, five children and no references were welcome at estate agents offices. How she did it I don't know to this day but my next memory (and it was like regaining consciousness after a long, nightmarish sleep) was of going into a dark, damp, evil smelling hall, with old whitewash flaking from the ceiling and silver slug trails over the broken brick tiles that oozed moisture as we gazed around. The living room wasn't quite so bad but the horror was the kitchen. Great chunks of plaster were hanging off over the shallow and filthy sink. The one tap dripped non-stop and fungus grew on all the damp spots, but the highlight piece was the old gas stove! It was red with rust from the damp, the top burners were in several small bits and the oven was lined with old newspaper on which were deposited small heaps of cat turds. We could easily tell from the smell where the moggies peed!

After being used to electric light we now found we were back to smelly gas mantles. We'd got lucky in renting the place simply because no-one else would take it on. We now had a roof over our heads, but what a roof!

Beggars can't be choosers though, and a start had to be made to clean up the filthy and disgusting mess to make it habitable. Young as I was, my heart sank when I thought of the lovely warm and clean home we were used to, and now this! Mam had managed to buy a few sticks of furniture; I'd like to say that our former neighbours had tried to help us, but they hadn't so I won't. What we had, had come from second hand shops and was rubbish, but seeing Mam fighting back tears as she surveyed the green mould, the stained and rotten floor boards and cracked windows, we made no comment and drew closer together. I think that occasion must have been the first time I heard Mam use the expression I always associated with her,

'Oh well, there are plenty worse off than us!'

Years later, 'Ted' told me that on that first terrible night in our new home, that he, worn out and sickened by what he'd found whilst trying to clean the worst of the filth off the walls and floors alongside Mam, had scraped a few coppers together and, going into the cheapest seats at the local cinema (The Shaftsbury) sat there and sobbed his heart out at the thought at what we'd been reduced to. We were, to all intents and purposes, at rock bottom. Little was he to know that worse was to come, far worse.......

The first full day in our new home, I was out in the back yard. Mam and Ted had to go to work although so much still had to be done in the cleaning line. Only Mam's earnings and Ted's board put food in our bellies. Maisie and Ron were at school and I was at home first as they allowed the younger children to get home before the bigger kids. I was in the yard because I was terrified of being in the house on my own. It may have been I was frightened of empty houses because Maisie had a vivid imagination and was a dab hand at telling ghost stories (you could dispense with the laxatives when Maisie was in full flow) or maybe I was sensitive to atmospheres then, as I am now, and was 'picking up' from that dump we were now living in, anyway, no way could you get me in there on my own! Suddenly, I had the funniest feeling I was being watched! It was only a small yard and my head was down as I played in the little bare earth that was showing through the rubbish we'd thrown out. Slowly, with my bowels already beginning to feel loose, I turned my head to the wall my back had been towards, and what I saw made my blood turn to ice with sheer bloody terror. Looking at me over the wall was the most hideous, contorted mad face I'd ever seen. It was an old woman; her hair stood up like a mop, her eyes were bulging in their sockets and the lids were pulled down and blood red. Her mouth agape had only stumps for teeth and, as spittle and drool ran down her chin she was making, what to me were the most grotesque, nonsensical noises. As I stood transfixed, too terrified even to run, she screamed with laughter and, with arm outstretched, made as if to come over the wall to me! The spell was broken and I ran! When the others came home, I was under the old table in the front room as far as I could get from the old crone. Like a tap turned on, it all poured from me. (Both ends, I suspect) How Mam made sense of it I don't know. I must have been almost incoherent. Then Mam explained......She'd known all about the woman next door and she was one of the reasons we had the house. Nobody else would take it because of 'Poor Lottie Blood' who was feeble minded. Yes, before God, that was the woman's name! Lottie lived next door with her old Mam and Lottie's brother. I suspect it was only the love and devotion of her Mam and brother that kept Lottie from full committal into the asylum for lunatics and the simple minded! When the mood took her, Lottie would lock the old lady in the toilet, and when the brother came home from work at dinner time he would 'paste' Lottie for locking their old Mam out of the house all morning!

Lottie even came over into our yard one day when we were out and tried to lock poor Mabel in our 'lavvy.' Poor Mabel, she'd discharged herself from the

Sanatorium to save Mam expense, even though she knew it meant her end would be hastened!

Mam explained it all to me with the compassion and sympathy she could always show for the underdog and those with problems that would cause them to be shunned by others; in such a way that I lost the worst of my fears and began to think of that poor deranged woman as 'Poor Lottie!' I was instinctively aware that my fears of her had to be suppressed as we had nowhere else to go. I still wouldn't go into that house alone and could never think of it as home. Often, as we sat around the table for dinner we would hear the screams from next door as Lottie's brother tanned her for being cruel to their old Mam. She never learned and was still locking the old lady in the bog by jamming the sweeping brush against the door!

Once I got used to the routine I became quite blasé about the screams, in fact I'm quite proud to say that for the short time we remained in that house, Lottie grew quite fond of me, and whilst I was in the yard would stand peering over the dividing wall at me as I played my make believe games. She would stand smiling, mouthing gibberish and making drawing in motions with her arms to me, however, don't let's kid ourselves, I would still have been 'off' if she'd made the slightest sign of getting over the wall to me! Our stay in that house wasn't to be a long one. Even without the presence of Poor Lottie hanging over the wall, we could never have settled. The smell of cats and damp in the walls was impossible to remove. There was also that 'something else' I could never put into words, but it was always there!

One day, Mam came home waving a new rent book in her hand. Once again we were on the move, leaving Poor Lottie gazing forlornly over the wall for the little boy who didn't run away from her anymore; the little boy who didn't call after her, 'You're daft, Lottie Blood!'

I never saw her again!

How had Mam managed to get another house for us to rent when even complete families were being turned away by the house agents? Simple, she'd turned that dump into a clean home and she paid the rent every week without fail. Never ever did she let a week go by without paying the rent! Sometimes she went hungry, and the already miserable portions on our plates got smaller but, with only her bit of wages plus Ted's board coming in, I can never remember being without a fire when it was cold nor being inadequately clothed. Never, never were any of us lousy, verminous or dirty, and we still had a long way down to go yet! No charity for us, no state aid, no social workers. Our Mam must have been a giantess compared to the 'we can't manage brigade' we have sponging off the state today.

6: 1 Moreton Road, Leicester

Our next house was also a terrace, and an end of terrace the same as the one we'd just left. It also had a small front garden although nothing ever grew there, three bedrooms and the usual 'out offices', which meant going outside to sit on the lavvy in the cold weather. This took a lot of courage unless you wanted to be chronically constipated. The back garden was quite long and enclosed on three sides. On one side lived Liz and Den, the other side was the railway embankment and at the bottom of the garden was the dilapidated rough brick side of a local butcher's slaughter house. The new area was poorer and the houses older but in a sense the move was an improvement. The neighbours were the salt of the earth; really caring and compassionate people. That slaughterhouse was the only real drawback; the squeals and screams of the animals, especially the pigs as they were driven in to be slaughtered, was heart rending. It was if the poor brutes knew! Someone said the pigs throats were cut to dispatch them whilst they were still alive! Others that they were put into vats of boiling water! We only knew that they screamed like human beings in their death agony. I think the bigger animals were shot as there would be a god almighty 'bang' and a terrible clatter of kicking feet as they went down. If you think that was savage I remember the sign of a man a few streets away that put horses down. Hanging outside his house was a sign showing just the head of a horse and a man's hand holding a cold chisel to its forehead whilst the man's other hand held a small lump or sledge hammer which was to drive the chisel into the horse's brain! Horrifying but it didn't seem to put people off – we were too busy surviving!

We kids had a bit of a joke about the horse to be slaughtered! You see, on the forehead where the chisel was placed, was a white, clearly to be seen, spot, and passers' by were asked,

'What do you think that horse is called?'

Invariably, the reply came back as, 'spot' or 'patch' or even 'Dobbin' to which we would reply,

'It ain't called any of them; it's called dead!'

Not funny at all, but we laughed. We had to find something to laugh at or go stark staring bonkers!! Poor Mabel, for as she began to get weaker and weaker, and spend more and more time in her bed which was in the small back bedroom, she had to listen to those horrendous noises.

Besides having the small iron railings at the front of our house, we had the pavement such as every street or road had and, at the edge of the said pavement, iron posts and horizontal bars to stop people falling over the edge onto the road below, for there was a drop varying from about three feet outside our house, stretching about twenty yards one side to approximately forty yards on the other side where it gradually sloped up to meet the level of the rest of the road. At the deepest part of the dip, the road passed under the railway bridge next to our house. I suppose when the railway was first built the bridge height was alright, but now, or at the time the house was built, it was too low a bridge, so possibly the road was scooped out for extra clearance. The railings were great for 'tissing over' or 'tightrope walking on' but I imagine many a small boy almost ruined himself for life by slipping and doing the splits across the bar! (Ouch!)

One of the sights, and I suppose thrills, for kiddies in those days of the thirties was to see cows, bullocks, sheep and even pigs, being driven through the streets on their way to the slaughter houses which, until centralisation, could often be found at the back of butchers' shops – as at the end of our garden. The drovers were big, red faced men, often in cord breeches that laced just below the knees from whence the breeches went into turned over long stockings. The feet were shod in strong boots which were well splattered with the shit of whatever type of animal was being driven. The whole being was topped off with a filthy flat cap squashed flat to the head and often removed to mop the drover's sweaty brow. Armed with a thick stick with which the poor terrified brutes were beaten without mercy, he might be afoot but most often was on a bike. To aid him the drover had several small boys whose number increased as they proceeded along, herding their terrified charges by digging them in the ribs and flank, which seemed to set off a chain reaction of more lowing and rolling eyes etc. Frightened and bewildered, the herd stared in fear at the clanking tram cars and yells of the most staid and respectable passers' by. The song, 'I'm an old cow hand' had real meaning to us. The adult drovers only seemed to come to life when a particularly difficult animal tried to bolt the opposite way to the rest of the herd. All other times he left the herding to his young apprentices, calling across to those seeming young dynamos!

'Come on now me lads, send that old bugger back' or

'Watch that bleeder, son, he's going to bolt.'

However, as much as the man's language seemed to be bad, that used by the boys was far worse and they didn't hesitate to direct it at us, the crowds of neighbourhood kids who tried to join in on the seeming 'free for all'.

Consequently, many of us aspiring herders (small boys who would run for miles to get into the act and yet moan like hell if asked to run to the corner shop) picked up the expletives that were used so freely. Those self-same swear words, if accidentally or inadvertently used later in front of our families, swiftly brought down the wrath of our elders around our necks!

News of the onrushing cattle or whatever, would spread in front as though by bush telegraph; sometimes, even a front runner would storm ahead screaming and shouting,

'Shut your gates and get the kids in!'

Anyone who didn't get the message then soon did when, hurtling around the corner would come first a man on a bike, closely followed by the mad eyed, heaving flanked, tightly bunched together herd; heads back and chins lifted, pouring out steam like a steam locomotive. On they came, at times so bunched they were climbing up each other's back! All it seemed, suffering from a chronic looseness of the bowels as the runny droppings in the road and their shit caked flanks clearly showed as they hastened to their doom! Steaming, wild eyed, muzzles dripping; great lethal horned heads swinging wildly from side to side, looking always looking (as if they knew what awaited them) for a way out. Even charging into a hall or passageway where doors had been insecurely fastened. It was a brave man who stood his ground when faced with the herd! Usually, he would dive into a passageway, slamming the door shut in other slower mortals' faces; even pounding on the doors of total strangers, shouting for sanctuary! In just a few short moments it was all over and the street was clear again. All that remained was the stench and runny dung, green and slimy on the footpaths.

Mr Townsend who kept the local sweet shop, had just cleaned his window one day when a steer running by stopped and, half turning in its panic, began to empty its bowel of runny contents. At the same time it gave an enormous cough and in a second the newly cleaned window and half the shop wall for six feet up, was covered in shite!

Before leaving the subject of the cattle drives, in these times it was regularly reported in the local papers that whilst a drive such as I have described was taking place, one of the poor beasts would run amok, attacking and running down any passer-by. If lucky, the drover or police would trap the animal in an entry or blind alley and bring it under control. However, in extreme cases this was not always possible and so a gun was sent for from the nearest abattoir and the maddened animal would be 'put down' in the street. Mam once told me that as a little girl at school around the turn of the century, the whole school was forced to 'stay in' after the bell had gone because a mad steer in the playground had resisted all efforts to remove it, so was 'put down'. When the kiddies were eventually let out the overwhelming impression was one of 'stink' that pervaded the yard well into the next day. Visitors to cattle markets will know the smell well.

With Mam and Ted at work all day apart from their dinner hour, Mabel was spending more and more time in bed as the 'Sanny' could do no more for her; it was just a question of time although no one could say with certainty if it would be a short or long time. Mabel had received her death sentence in this way: Mabel and her close friend from across the road, who was also a consumptive, had gone to the 'Sanny' for a review of their disease; a progress report if you like. The senior chest physician, after scrutinising the latest set of X rays had addressed them thus:

'You can both go home and there isn't much point in your coming back again; we can do no more for you; it's just a question of time!'

Is it any wonder both girls were hysterical when they arrived home?! Neither one was yet twenty one years of age!

Ron and I were always left to the tender mercy of 'Our Mais' (13) when Mam and Ted were at work. From an early age Mais wore spectacles which were provided by the school optical service for a small charge. Nothing was free in those days. Free school dinners for the children of the poor? Don't make me laugh! Mais, like so many other kids of the time, was absolutely smothered in freckles. Not to put too fine a point on it, she was bloody ugly with a short fuse temper to match. In retrospect, and she would be the first one to agree, the uncertainty of our lives didn't help things, with them hitting her harder than it hit us. For example, we took the bit of food on our plates for granted whereas Maisie knew how hard it had to be worked for. Puberty was also in the offing for her.

We lived with Maisie's, 'Wait till Our Mam gets home' and 'I'm going to tell on you, I am!'

Poor Maisie, her threats frightened us not one bit, for 5:45pm when Mam and Ted came in, was far away, and not having the shadow of the Old Man hanging over us gave a feeling of freedom that none of Maisie's threats could undermine.

The end of the street on which our house was situated was about one quarter up of the whole street, with the division being where another street cut across. Poor as we were we felt our end of the street was a better end to live than the larger section. Why? Don't ask me, we just did! Certainly, income wise, we must have had less than most. Anyway, Ron and I soon made friends with a few kids who lived in our section of the street of about 10 houses. Four doors away lived George and Eddy aged about 12 & 14 years respectively so, to our eyes they were quite big boys. These two had the reputation of being naughty but as the naughtiness was mainly due to high spirits and they never hurt anyone, they were ok with us! Maisie regarded them with a jaundiced eye though, for George was in her class at school and was often in trouble. Early one Saturday evening, Ron and I went to their house to try and scrounge some comics and were invited in with the assurance,

'It's all right Mam and Dad have gone out for a drink.'

In we went, knowing full well that had the parents been in we wouldn't have got our feet over the back door step as their Mam was very, very house proud, even to the extent of putting old stockings on the legs of her table to stop them from being scratched...... but now the coast was clear so in we went! It was dark outside; the curtains were open and the light was on. They had electric; we still had gas. Ron and I soon sat down and were reading comics (of which they had plenty) whilst Eddy and George, with much whispering & giggling, disappeared upstairs, bumping & banging around. Then quiet. No noise from them; what was going on? Then the stairs door suddenly burst open and the pair of them pranced out, dancing like dervishes, whirling & twirling about, stark bollock naked except for a piece of card about 8 inches square covering their 'tackle' in which they had cut a hole and through which they'd poked their 'dicks!' Ron and I were screaming with laughter; we were doubled up. It was hilarious, and the more we laughed, the harder they danced with their dicks flopping up & down! In the middle of this jollity, HORRORS, a loud banging on their back door and Mam's voice screaming,

'Ronnie, Norman, come out here at once!'

Panic stations! Eddy & George nearly knocked the stair door off its hinges in the rush to get upstairs again to dress! When Mam spoke like that we obeyed! Outside we were grabbed by the ears and 'Home James!' Phew, she did go on! Once inside she was shouting and telling a goggle eyed Mais that those two dirty little buggers up the street had been dancing around with no clothes on, but completely omitted to tell her what I considered the best bit! Namely, of course, that our heroes had got some squares of cardboard stuck over their 'Tally Whackers!' Ron and I denied it had ever happened and got a whack over the ear for our pains. You see, we didn't realise that if you're in a room with the curtains open and the light on and it's dark outside, you can see in, even though from inside the room you can't see out! Mam had seen everything. I don't think she told their Mam and Dad but in any case their dad bought his own house soon after. A semi-detached with bathroom, the lot! We weren't encouraged to visit and we never did.

Wag:

We made a new pal, Wag. This was his nickname, his real name being Charles. We all had nicknames, even me. I was Bill Bloggs for some reason I was never able to discover, whilst Ron was always 'Titch' because he was small for his age. Other common nicknames were Paddy, Nige (Nigel), Dog Eye (he had a drooping eye lid) and a boy called 'Curly' who was as bald as a coot! Wag was addressed thus, even by his mother, to distinguish him from his father, also called Charles. Wag's family were Catholic, and lovely kind people. They consisted of Dad, Mam, big sister Kathleen and Wag himself. My first impression of Wag's Mam was of a fierce sort of woman, small with very wiry hair – the sort who would bite before she barked, but first impressions were very, very wrong because underneath the no nonsense exterior beat a heart of pure gold. She adored her family but undoubtedly the one who was king in that household was Wag! I'm still amazed that his Mam could be absolutely raving at him and yet even I could see her eyes were telling him,

'Wag, you shocker, I love you!'

The Dad was a balding, bandy legged man who wore hard wearing whipcord riding breeches, steel rimmed spectacles, and he stood market or drove round the streets selling vegetables from a horse drawn flat cart, the side on which he perched as the horse trotted up the street. Wag's dad was a good, kind man and one knew instinctively that he liked boys for his eyes always twinkled, even when he was telling us off for putting tadpoles and minnows in the green algae lined barrel of water that was kept outside the kitchen window for his horse to drink from when they returned at the end of the day from the round. Their yard was wide and cobbled with high double entrance gates. On the left were the usual 'out offices' and at the bottom of the yard itself was a stable for 'Tommy' the pony with a tack room at the side. Over these was a loft, from which access was gained by climbing a wide wooden step ladder at the side. This loft was an absolute dream of a child's play room; raftered ceiling showing the underside of the roofing slates, filthy & dusty with the years but with a smell all of its own although predominately smelling of the stable below. (More of the loft later)

Kathy, Wag's big sister, was a lovely sweet girl, who, like his Mam absolutely doted on Wag. She was tall and well-built, with peaches & cream complexion and the sweetest smile I had ever seen.

I got my first introduction to Wag in this way. Outside our house was a cast iron lamp post. On this particular day, I came out of our house and stood looking up & down the street for someone to play with. As I stood there I heard a voice, seemingly coming from thin air,

'Hello, who are you then?'

I looked around startled and then looked up. Hanging by the arms from the small horizontal bar jutting out from just below the lantern against which the lamp men leaned their ladders, with his legs wrapped tightly around the lamp post itself, was a red, heavily perspiring boy who, years later when I read the 'Just William' books fitted the description of William perfectly. Politely, I told this strange boy my name and that this was my house. Besides the fact he was, as I have already said, sweating heavily, I noticed he had the clearest most honest eyes of any boy I knew. In fact, in all the time I was to know him, I never ever knew him to do or say anything mean or petty. Also, he put so much energy into everything he did, invariably his face was brick red and sweated buckets. With introductions made, we weighed each other up for a moment or so, and then in the way of all boys once we were satisfied, were immediately at ease with each other. He was still up the lamp post looking down at me and got on with doing what he had been doing when we met, that is, he was pulling himself up by the arms, his legs wrapped tightly around the post all the while. When he could pull himself up no further he let himself slide down again until arms stretched to the limit, he again pulled himself up again, his crossed legs working all the while. His face got redder and redder and he needed to pause for rests more frequently. Finally, in one of the pauses, I could contain my curiosity no more.

'What are you doing?' I asked.

'It's called the Tickler' Wag replied, volunteering no more information than that.

'Oh' I said, and then a few moments later, 'What's the Tickler?'

Wag looked at me.

'Come here' he said, and in a few seconds flat he'd slid down the lamp post and was pushing me up to hang on the bar as he'd been doing! I was looking around all the while to make sure no policemen were around as climbing lamp posts could get you and your Mam in trouble, and Our Mam had plenty of trouble without me running foul of the law. All clear! I could feel the warm post through my shorts – you didn't wear long 'uns until you were nearly ready to go to work. Wag had warmed the post nicely!

'All set?' he called, and when I answered in the affirmative, my instructor said, 'Now pull yourself up by your arms and squeeze your legs tight around the post as you do, then let yourself slide down again and start again!'

I very quickly caught on and went up and down the lamp post like one of those monkeys on a stick that you got at fairgrounds. The exercise didn't do a blind thing for me although Wag kept shouting, 'are you getting it yet?' I didn't have a clue as to what it was that I was supposed to be getting, but not wishing to offend my newly found chum I assured him that indeed I was. Eventually, feeling as though my arms had been pulled from their sockets, I gave it best and came down but my curiosity was aroused and so for the next few weeks I was to be found going up & down that bloody lamp post like a 'YoYo', and then one day I did get it! In the meanwhile, other kids in the area, drawn by the sight of me and Wag in turn going up & down the lamp post were drawn in to try for the elusive 'Tickler.' Honestly, that post drew more kids than a bitch in season! They in turn were hooked once they 'got it!' What was the ticker? Quite simply, it was a form of masturbation. The friction of the post on our privates, plus the squeezing of the legs & thighs as we pulled ourselves up & down, made it pleasurable. Hand on heart it was years later before it dawned on me what we'd been doing, probably because the effort to keep going so as to reach a climax was more than our children's arms could cope with. Consequently, all we ever got was a tickle, hence the name. With today's lamp posts being rough concrete, countless numbers of small boys have been deprived of the simple pleasure of 'mounting a lamp post.' City Highways have a lot to answer for!

About this time, I got the 'Twitch' which was diagnosed as St Vitus Dance by the doctor! However, a proprietary medicine called 'Parishes Food', so full of iron that when taken caused the mouth to purse in so it nearly turned inside out, seemed to soon put that right, in the same way white ointment called 'Indian Cert' (Engine brand mind) used to pull chunks of gravel out of a badly grazed or septic knees.

Wag's dad, as has been remarked earlier, had a pony called 'Tommy' to pull the vegetable cart through the streets on his round. In the evening, after first being allowed to suck up long satisfying gulps from the aforementioned barrel of water, the rough coated pony, with bits and pieces of leather harness hanging from him all ready for the final disrobing in his stable, would clatter down the cobbled yard, hind quarters swaying like some exotic dancer. Hunger satisfied but still chewing with a most satisfying crunch/ munch, he would manoeuvre himself around in his stall, poke his head over the half gate and, with a wicked gleam in his eye, would wait for us to rip chunks of water cress and other goodies stored in the wickerwork skips that were hosed down regularly twice a day to keep them fresh for the customers. These titbits were accepted with relish as his (Tommy's) due. Watching his profits going into the belly of his already well fed horse didn't exactly endear us to Wag's dad but, as I said, he was a lovely man and didn't anger often. Tired of spoiling the horse we would climb the outside wooden stairs into the loft where in the past harness and tackle had been stored. We were met with an untidy mess of old tables and chairs, pictures and household junk that today would be worth a small fortune. Round the walls were cages of rabbits, mainly black and white 'Old English'. Each had its own name; several had litters. Noses rubbing against the wire mesh, pink & twitching, they waited to be fed. Down the years, I remember one was called 'Scabby' due to a sore that never seemed to heal due to its constant gnawing at the wound. Often, a doe would break out and when returned to her hutch would go frantic to break out again. Given this clue we would search among the litter and 'Eureka' a litter of young would be found in the innards of an old chair or sofa where some primitive instinct had driven her to give birth unfettered by a cage. It was often difficult for us youngsters to tell if they were baby rabbits or rats we had found. Decision making was left to young Wag; his dad didn't interfere. Pride of place in the middle of the floor was Wag's old rocking horse. It was a monster – a beauty. The rockers were intact on great steel bars. It had a perfect mane and tail of long flowing horse hair, a near real saddle & harness, great artificial but lifelike eyes and a body of white with black & brown patches. He was beautiful. Mounted on a solid frame, the feet attached to the moving slide bars of steel. He was so perfectly balanced that only the slightest pressure was needed to set him going back & forth, back & forth. God knows what the kids of today wouldn't give to ride on him! The leather creaked and the loft floor protested as the kids in turn mounted & galloped that wonderful horse into the dreams & fantasies of our minds. We were in a child's paradise as we played amongst the bric a brac in the dust and cobwebs within those old, once whitewashed walls, with the smell of hay, straw and horse dung wafting up from the stable below. This half dream fantasy world for Ron and I got us away from the harsh and bitter reality of the world outside. We wouldn't have changed those sanity saving moments for anything as the poverty of the outside world was being experienced to the full and added to that was the poverty in our home.

Into that once again came the threat of violence; the hammering at the front door or windows for, having reduced his family to poverty so that real griping hunger lived with us daily, the Old Man came night after night screaming filth and abuse at Mam and, indirectly at us. We would huddle together in terror lest he kicked the door down and got to us before the police arrived to drive him away. (Until the next time) After seeing the Old Man screaming and raving again, a policeman once ventured the comment to Mam,

'He's mad missus, he's stark raving bloody mad!'

Wag had nerves of steel and, even though he knew full well his escapades would land him in the mire right up to his ears and get him a wallop from his long suffering dad into the bargain, (when really pushed Wag's dad didn't spare the rod to spoil his child) Wag Jnr just pushed on with whatever devilment he was engaged in, regardless. He was naughty, yes, but never wicked, vindictive or spiteful. That boy was secure in his parents and sister's love.

It was the school holidays and we were stuck for something to do. Wag's parents had gone into town shopping and Katy was at work. Bored, we discussed what we could do, rejecting each proposal in turn. Wag was red faced, hot & sweating as usual when he came out with an idea which turned me white with its sheer audacity.

'I think I'll get Tommy out and ride him in the street', he said!

'No Wag; don't Wag! said I (ever the first to chicken out). 'Your dad won't half hit you Wag', I continued to rabbit on.

Ron, of course, was on Wag's side but all I wanted was the quiet life and could see that this could end in disaster. Of course, I was outvoted and being two years younger anyway meant I was ignored. I can see it as though it were only yesterday. Down the cobbled yard we went, me moaning and whining all the while. Wag stopped only to pick up a piece of rope and an empty potato sack then, reaching up, he unlatched the bottom door of the split stable door. Tommy, whose head had been poking out, rolled his eyes wickedly as though he knew the young master was up to no good and wished to be part of it. Tommy backed up to let Wag enter and the bridle was slipped over his head and bit put between his teeth. Backed into a corner, Tommy snatched at wisps of hay from his manger as the halter and strap were pulled tight and the sack put over his back and tied in place with a bit of string from one of the bales of hay.

With Ron cheering him on, and with me still mouthing,

'You won't half cop it when your dad finds out, Wag,' the little procession formed up and, as Tommy clip clopped past me I swear he rolled his eyes and laughed in horse devilment in as much to say,

'Why don't you stop moaning; the young master won't come to no harm with me!'

Into the street we went; two small boys and one pony with Wag astride his back. Ron ran up ahead and I brought up the rear. Wag sat bolt upright and Tommy, with no prompting needed, set off at quite a fast trot with Wag holding on and being bounced around all over the place. Unfortunately, the piece of sacking being used as a saddle kept slipping under the pony's stomach and so Wag untied the string and threw the sack away. Wag was now riding bear back wearing short trousers ON A PONY WITH A SHORT HAIR! A half hour later Tommy was reigned to a standstill. He was blowing hard (so was I) and Ron was invited to ride. Now Ron hadn't been on a horse before so Wag led him. Wag, I noticed, was limping noticeably. In fact, not to put a too fine a point on it, I thought he'd 'done IT in his trousers!' The limp got worse and finally poor Wag was forced to stop. He pulled his short trouser legs up nearly to the crotch and, Oh my goodness, what a mess! Tommy's short coat hairs, as sharp as needle points, had rubbed a great raw patch off the inside of Wag's thighs! They were red raw and by now he could hardly walk. Seeing the gory mess, Ron hurriedly got down and I was invited to have a turn on Tommy. I declined with thanks and we finally led Tommy back with Wag sitting side saddle on the by now steaming and foam flecked pony's back.

Wag's parents were still out shopping when we got back so, whilst Wag pulled the bridle from Tommy's head, Ron & I rubbed his coat hard with handfuls of hay and straw to remove all traces of the beast's rather hectic exercise. Satisfied that all traces of our misdeeds were removed, we went off for our tea leaving Wag, trouser legs pulled right up whilst he rubbed the by now sore & weeping thighs with ointment, watched by an interested pony whose head poked over the top of the stable door. Wag was anointing himself in the fresh air because the ointment used was rather pungent and his Mam & Dad would have smelt it indoors! (We didn't miss a trick in those days) Going back after the bread & dripping which was what we had for tea in those days, we arrived to hear the following conversation between Wag and his dad:

Dad: Tommy hasn't been out of the stable has he Wag?

Wag: No, I'm sure he's not dad.

Dad: You seem pretty sure of that Wag!

Wag: Certainly dad. I've been here all afternoon. He's not been out!

Dad: I must be imagining things then, wouldn't you say Wag?

Wag: I reckon you must be dad.

The next thing that happened was Wag letting out such a yelp, and Ron & me being treated to the spectacle of young Wag dangling by the ear from his father's fingers!

'Oh yes?' said the irate father, 'and I suppose I'm imagining that am I?'

As we looked, there, leering up at us all from the cobbled yard was a pile of dung that Tommy must have voided as he was being led down to his stable after our afternoon adventure. Perhaps it would be kinder to draw a veil over what happened next............!

Summer Holiday Adventures:

In those days of yesteryear, every day of the long August school holidays seemed to be filled with long hours of adventure & golden sunshine. The fresh clean scent of grass & hay along with the muted sounds of bees, wasps and other insects, were not drowned out or the scent quashed as they are today by the noise & exhaust fumes of motor cars as they pollute the air we breathe.

Another memory I have is of a gang of little boys, the eldest no more than 10 years, like the pioneers of old, setting off in search of adventure! The only supplies we carried was a round of bread & marge wrapped in old newspaper which gave the bread a taste all of its own. One of us would be carrying a bottle of tap water that was quickly consumed by little boys who were always parched. So, a start was made, drinking & sipping before we had even left the street. In the afternoon heat we swung, or rather swaggered, along the rough cart track lanes that were edged with dense thickets & spinneys on either side, each having a scent of its own and adding to the rustic scenes of 'ago'. With no verbal exchanges, we each took it in turn to push the push chair in which sat Our Jimmy, the little brother of one of the group. He'd been forced onto us by his Mam in the vain hope that having him along with his perpetual whining and needs, would keep us out of trouble. (Vain hope) He kept losing his 'tit' (dummy) and we had to retrace our steps to find it time & time again! We began to sing; it was something the bigger boys had learned at school, or part learned, for they could only remember the last two lines. (I've since learned it came from 'A Midsummer Night's Dream') I've only heard it sung once since and the memories it brought flooding back filled my eyes with tears as I remembered those days gone, bad as they often were, and those friends & loved ones with them. How did those little boys, most of us from the poorest and most deprived families, latch onto a song with words that fitted our rural setting so aptly? For the words we chorused again and again until we were hoarse went:

'Merrily, merrily shall I live now, under the blossom that hangs from the bough.'

The new Garden City through which we passed, seemed terribly posh, then the houses get fewer and fewer. Each of the gardens we saw were a blaze of colour but not for us the marigolds, roses and pansies. No, indeed our eyes only saw the orchards and lone fruit trees laden with still unripe fruit: apples, pears and other seasonal fruits, still bitter in their immaturity but never the less, highly desirable to those of us who rarely had access to fruit unless one of the better off kids (and they were rare birds indeed around our way) gave us a 'bite' or, to the plea of 'save us the core', did just that. I used to think it was usual practice to pick up discarded cores and clear them of any remaining flesh. Unable to resist what was really forbidden fruit, one of our band climbed through a hedge surrounding one such garden and began to tuck the fallen fruit on the ground down the front of his jersey, all the time looking furtively around to see if the 'bloke was coming!' Panic stations!!! The bloke IS coming. We all scattered, running as hard as we could! The erstwhile gleaner of the fruit somehow got a head start and flew down the road scattering unripe fruit as he went. Unfortunately, Kenny, who had charge of his little brother Jimmy, whilst getting a good start, lost one of the wheels off the pushchair in the process! Initially, Kenny abandoned the pushchair with little Jimmy in it, but with no choice, and common sense prevailing, (he could hardly return home and tell his mam he'd lost his little brother) he turned back. On looking backwards we could see the bloke had the pushchair and little Jimmy hostage whilst Kenny was demanding the return of his little brother. Edging back, we picked up that the bloke was demanding names & addresses. Kenny was mumbling, but what exactly we couldn't tell, but by lip reading we knew the bloke had used the word 'police!' With Jimmy, by now thoroughly frightened and screaming his head off, Kenny was released after being given a parting clip around the ear and, with his head down in the traditional way of contrition, he pushed the pushchair which had acted as a brake on our escape, to re-join us. Dejected, and with visions of the police coming around to our homes, and then being taken to the juvenile, and knowing what our parents would do to us when they found out what we'd been up to, we moved away. Then joy of joy, we heard Kenny talking out the side of his mouth like the gangsters on the films at the 'tupenny rush' on Saturday afternoons,

'It's all right, I gave him all the wrong names and addresses! The coppers won't be able to find us!'

Good old Kenny, we could have kissed him but we repaid him the only way we could, that is for the rest of the outing he didn't have to go back once to search for Jimmy's 'tit!'

'Merrily, Merrily, I shall live now!'

The Black Pad:

I think every hamlet, town and village in those days had a 'Black Pad'. The name probably derived from the local council's habit of using boiler ash or clinker to lay on the muddy churned up surface of what had once started off as a cart track but over the years had been used more and more as a regular road by pedestrians and pedal cyclists. The 'Pad' was often skirted by allotments and small holdings dating back to the days when so many people would have a pigsty with the occupant fed on swill & waste for which no other use could be found. Without pigs what else could be done with the unusable scraps of fish generated by the local 'fish & chip' shops, left out and crawling with maggots, other than to boil it all up and feed it to the pigs!?

The heavily rutted wheel grooves that had been there for centuries probably, in winter became a churned up quagmire; sticky and gooey enough to suck the shoes from one's feet. The gritty clinker dross, waste from the factory boilers, was widely used because of its cheapness and availability before oil became so widely used. It was taken by horse & cart to the site where the carter and his mate would shovel it off the cart and spread it evenly, thus making a compact and perfectly usable surface for the light traffic which was all the 'Pads' had to carry. In fact to stop any heavier lorries which were just beginning to appear in numbers, the ends of the 'Pads' would, more often than not, be sealed off with chunks of iron girders which were sunk into the ground and stuck up like rotten teeth barring the way to all but pedestrians and cyclists. Unfortunately, and to this day it remains a mystery as to how they did it, bands of Gypsies with caravans would get through and park on what little grass verges there were, and then free passage would be a nightmare as people tried to dodge the packs of dogs belonging to the 'Gyppos', snarling and feigning attacks on people going about their lawful business.

The Gypsies, and I mean the Romany people and not the Irish Tinkers who are such a nuisance today, would sit outside their beautifully decorated and ornate caravans, swarthy and dark eyed, many still wearing the kerchief on their heads, smoking; the men with cigarettes and some women with pipes, plaiting baskets or carving wood into clothes pegs whilst around them tumbled fat, swarthy, snotty nosed children, thriving, or so we were told, on hedgehog pie. As quickly as they appeared, they would disappear, and all that was left would be a few bits of old rag or a tin, and grey fire ash. Not even a few half burned sticks of wood on the camp fire! These people wasted nothing.

On entering the 'Pad,' the entrance of which was just around the corner, one of the first things noticed was the sweet sickly smell of poultry that many of the allotment holders kept on their allotments which ran down one length of the 'Pad'. This was quite against the local bylaws as the allotments were for growing vegetables only; it was widely known after all, that poultry drew in the rats which infested the tall, three storey tenement houses that ran at the bottom of the land. However, it was a very brave (or foolish) council official who would tangle with the poultry keeping allotment people – many of which who were embittered, old before their time ex-servicemen of the Great War of 1914-1918. These men, unemployed in the aftermath of the Great Depression, unable to keep a wife or children on what little dole was available to them, with only the hated 'means test' to fall back on should their dole be stopped, as it often was........These men had lain in the mud of Ypres and Passchendaele and the Somme, surrounded by the rotten corpses of their comrades, and they'd mounted attacks across the bodies of the slain. These men had drunk deep of the cup, and no petty fogging council official was going to stop them raising a few chickens that would lay eggs to put in the belly of their always hungry family.

The allotments were separated from the 'Pad' by high iron palings. They had to be iron because had they been wood, in the cold weather these would have ended up on the fires of the destitute, and that meant nearly every family in the district.

The aforementioned Gypsies were pretty well detested. We, who had next to nothing, would have lost even the little we had to these thieving itinerants who knew only loyalty to their own group. Even our few worn rags of clothing would be stolen from the clothes line if these people managed to get near them, and yet compared to us, these vagabonds were well off! They paid no rates or taxes, the fodder for their horses was growing at the roadside, and even the boiler ashes on the 'Pad' if carefully sorted through, gave up little nuggets of coal & coke, yet still our few miserable possessions were fair game to them. We heard the 'Gyppos' even stole babies but, even so, you were pretty gullible to swallow that one!

When the Gypsy women in shawls and brightly coloured headscarves came silently around the backs of our homes selling clothes pegs or offering to tell fortunes, they were quickly told to 'clear off' and watched until they did so, lest even the most worthless of our 'gewgaws' ended up in their voluminous pockets.

Princey:

From somewhere, I don't know where, we acquired a pet; a little mongrel dog. Not for us a proud pedigree of the canine world, no indeed, our dog had to be a 'survivor,' so what we had was a squirming, squealing, face licking, tail wagging bundle of joy that was so in love with the world he would piddle down you at the drop of a hat. Coming as he did to share our lives, Princey, for that is what we named him, was in for a pretty rough time. However, even the poorest households had a pet and this is a true today, the pet usually being a dog. Cats or kittens were rarely kept, and kittens were drowned in buckets of water as soon as they were born. Nobody wanted them. People weren't intentionally cruel but with a house full of hungry kids, they had no alternative. I think keeping a dog is a throwback to 'Man, the hunter.' Most of the poor things had to forage for their own food because any food on the plate was considered too good for a blasted dog and devoured. It was a common sight to see dogs eating horse droppings on the street, and they soon became cringing curs who would bite at the drop of a hat if the back was turned. As for their coupling habits, well, it was common to see a dog and a bitch locked together in the mating embrace, and unlocked with a bucket of cold water; a freeing that must have been painful in the extreme!

Princey was a small mongrel dog of uncertain parentage. He was white but with the odd patch or two of black on his face and body. When he was feeling on top form, and I'll say this for him he usually was, he was the happiest dog I was ever to know. His tail would wag so hard that within the close confines of our house, if his tail was going back and forth like a flail and caught you on the leg (as it so often did) you were left with a very nasty bruise indeed. In fact that 'rudder' as we called it, became such a menace Ted was given the task of finding a 'tail biter' in the district to sort out the problem. No, this is not a spoof! The operation was called 'docking' and if you can't see the need for the services of a 'docker' then think on! Our homes were, in the main, small and cramped. A family might consist of Mam & Dad and perhaps seven kids so, madly wagging tails of family pets had to be, so far as was possible, eliminated; either the tail or the dog had to go! I was told then, and I can see no reason to doubt it, that the tail biter held the puppy in his hands and, grabbing the offending tail in his teeth, bit hard, leaving several inches of the tail between his teeth whilst the by now highly indignant and squealing with grief pup, was left with just a small stump. That was how Princey was done; no instruments were used. It was a very sad eyed and subdued little dog that was brought back to us; feeling very sorry for himself and sporting a bit of old rag around the end of his stump. The improvement was immediate. Sore shins became a thing of the past and, like all young animals he soon got over the shock. The added bonus was that with no tail to chase he no longer sent us giddy watching him fly around in tight circles trying to catch his tail, an exercise that knocked chair and children over indiscriminately. The little stump stuck straight up in the air at a right angle to his body.

We were playing with Wag in his yard, all the time with our ears cocked for the sound of his dad driving 'Tommy' home at the end of the day, so we could pat the pony as he sucked up the water from his barrel. Princey was with us. His tail had healed and he was a firm favourite with us all. He loved being with us boys as he demonstrated what a grand fellow he was; everybody and everything was a friend and presented no danger, or so he thought! On a box close by lay a large old cat, kept to keep down the vermin that abounded in the district. Everybody, and I mean everybody, also had spring loaded mouse traps to keep the pests out of the pantry, although what they found to feed on in ours I just don't know! Anyway, the cat lay, seemingly taking no notice as Princey devised a little game of prancing towards the cat, yapping with glee and, just before contact was made, he would stop dead; front paws down, rear poking up in the air as though bowing. He would then retreat to do the same again. The cat all of a sudden stood up and through narrow slits of eye, regarded our little pet disdainfully as he dashed in again to play his little game. In a flash, so quickly that the movement was a blur, the cat's paw shot out, hardly seeming to make contact as it patted Princey's face, almost caressingly, or so it seemed. Princey gave one loud yelp then ran off, screwing his head down and around whilst trying to touch his eye with a front paw. When we finally caught up with him he couldn't open his eye. We had no money for a vet and so we tried to make it up to him by being especially kind. We also bathed the injured eye and put in some ointment. For the next few days he was treated like royalty and given lots of fuss and attention. We even managed a few tit bits but it was clear the eye was damaged because for a week he couldn't open it. When he did manage to get the lids apart we saw to our horror that the whole eye ball was a horrid milky colour. It remained that way for the rest of the time we had him; the sight was gone. I've detested cats ever since!

It says a lot for his great little heart that the blind eye never bothered him in the slightest except anything non-human was forever a mortal enemy and that made him feel he owed it to the world to exterminate all non-humans! Perhaps next to cats the thing he hated most were the trains that belched and puffed steam as they chuffed along the lines of the 'rally' at the side of the house. To his eye (no pun intended) the brick wall between us was no obstacle at all. He would go at it like a steeplechaser, one God Almighty bound and, front paws skittering on the top bricks, he would pull himself over. The slightest vibration of those train lines as the loco steamed out of the station half a mile away would be enough to set him in motion. Even in the deepest slumber he would jerk, spring to his feet in a single movement, one ear would cock, first to the left and then to the right, just to confirm his mortal foe was really coming, and then, if the window was ajar, and mad to all else, he would jump onto the chair backing on to the window. Heaven help anyone who was on it as his claws would dig in to get a toe hold and 'off.' It was every man for himself as we hastened to get out of the way as, feet skittering and sliding on the linoleum, he would go through the kitchen door like a flash into the yard, and on his good days, over the wall like a rocket. Many a plate of our pitifully small dinner landed on the kitchen floor, to be scooped up (nothing was wasted) after the plate was up ended by that mad headed little bugger. Up the embankment he would hurl, his little legs going like pistons and there between the rails he would stand, lips curled back, loins girded for the fray, just like Horatio on the bridge. What happened next had us absolutely in hysterics, for as his mortal foe the great steaming, hissing monster came blowing nearer and nearer to him down the line until it seemed he must be run over and killed, his great little heart would fail him and with one great leap he would jump aside as an invisible audience cried, 'OLEZ' in the best tradition of the bullring and the great beast, invincible victor, would rumble by, leaving momentarily a disconcerted Princey standing there, all stiff legged and body aquiver, bested again. Most of the local drivers of the trains along with their firemen knew our Princey, and with the guard at the back of the train would hang from their respective ends of the locos and shout encouragement at our hero. If that didn't set him off they were not above pelting him with small cobbles of coal from the tender, which we quickly retrieved for our fire! That did it though, this was the final straw, and Princey the giant killer would go stark raving mad. With a shriek of fury that seemed to start at his toe ends, (it definitely wasn't a bark) he would catapult his tiny frame forward. Princey would never be a big dog, nor old bones either if he kept on like this, and with no thought for those great pounding drive wheels thundering past his shoulder, he would throw himself forward after the hate of his life. KILL, KILL,KILL! The driver would be waiting for just such a chance as this and, hand on a certain lever until our Goliath Mauler was just in the right position, he would operate it causing great clouds of white hissing steam to envelope him in its damp embrace. Our Princey hated to get wet. This then was the final indignity. Our Prince Valiant would stand the verbal abuse, the chunks of coal even, but oh dear those clouds of wet hissing steam! Was it the hissing noise that broke through the kill madness within his brain, reminding him of the hissing cat that had so cruelly taken the sight from one eye? Whatever, in he went, the magnificent brave heart in his tiny body driving him in for the kill! And so, the last we would see of our brave little mutt, sometimes for hours, would be his rear end, back legs just a blur, pounding up the ballaster track after the monster. I remember one old chap who, having witnessed the whole of the performance from the road, saying to our laughing Mam,

'By God Mrs, he's a fierce little bugger ain't he. What would you do if one day he caught it and came running back with the whole caboodle in his mouth?'

I was in the street, not doing very much at all, when an elderly lady passing our front gate was nearly knocked flying by Our Princey as he hurtled out of the open front door at a speed that all but took your breath away. From the front door to our little iron gate was a couple of yards, and shooting across this patch that fool of a dog was just a blur. Thank goodness the gate was open or he'd either have broken his neck or taken it off its hinges. Scattering and scrambling, yipping and yapping, helped on his way by a vicious swipe from the lady's handbag, Princey disappeared again into the house only to re-appear a few moments later looking like a November 5th rocket! What was going on? Draw a straight line in your mind which starts at our front gate, goes through the front door, continues along the stone flagged hall passageway, straight up the stairs, ending at the miniscule landing outside Mabel's sick room door. Right! Now, at the bottom of the stairs was a small rag slip mat, and this was the game our daft dog had devised, with no help from any of us I might add. Princey would stand at the top of those stairs, tail wagging 90 to the dozen; he then hurled himself into space, taking those steps 2-3 at a time. Four steps from the bottom, he launched himself hard forward landing plonk, smack on top of the slip mat. His forward momentum then shot the mat with him hanging onto it for dear life, along the stone passage until the mat's forward movement came to a dead stop by hitting the front door draft excluder. Smack! Nothing between his bottom and the slabs outside our front door, Princey would try to break hard, but no way could his hard little claws get a grip. And so, skittering and scattering out of the front gate he would hurtle, causing pedestrians to risk life and limb should they pass by on our side of the road.

Equilibrium restored, that daft dog would restart the sequence. Snarling, yapping, yelping, he would push, pull, heave and tug the mat back to the bottom of the stairs and off he would go again. I reckon that if during his run, a breeze had got up and blown our front door to, he'd have knocked his own doggie flap through.

Dear old Princey. Eventually he had to go, for Mam could hardly afford to feed us as a family, let alone him, even though his good nature would allow him to go along with any con we tried on him, such as 'this piece of stale bread is really a huge juicy steak'. The deciding factor was him turning up one day with a huge, well chewed over, joint of meat. We knew that if the thieving culprit was identified as our dog then Mam would be expected to make good the damage, and no way could we. And so on this certain day, Ronnie and I, with our faithful little Princey on a piece of old cord, set off to a very nice house in a very nice district, to some people Mam said would give Princey a new home. I'd like to say he fought, whined, and pleaded with his doggie eye not to be left, but he didn't, so I can't. After a good few sniffs around to see if his luck was in and there might be a bitch in season in the vicinity, he peed up the new owner's back gate and got stuck into a dish of goodies put there for him. That's the last time we saw him. I like to think a new home was what we had taken him to, or was it just a made up story, and as soon as those two little boys fighting to keep back their tears, had left, was our Princey taken along to the vet and put down? After all, who in their right mind would want one eyed dog that chased trains, converted halls and stairways into helter-skelter rides and, having just discovered the joys of sex tried to use his young masters' legs in the same self-same way the young masters used the street lamp post? Whatever, where ever you are Princey, I salute you. You truly were a Prince among dogs.

The Good Old Days:

Lest anyone be taken in by the phrase 'the good old days', then let me assure you that 'good' was the last word to describe them. 90% of those in the area where we existed must have been on the bread line, and even then our bread was decidedly stale.

Industrially, the picture was bleak and we'd hear harrowing tales, perhaps a 'hodge pot' of different stories, of lines of unemployed men and women being subjected to an auction type bidding process for any vacancy. The Boss or Foreman would come out and address the poorly clad, often hungry applicants thus:

'I need a packer! Who among you is a packer by trade?'

Hands would shoot up whilst eyes, dull with lost hope from years of the most appalling and grinding poverty after those terrible years spent in the trenches of France and Belgium, would light up with renewed hope.

'Me Sir, I'm a packer Sir! I fought with the 24th Leicester's Sir! I'm a good worker Sir, even though I was wounded at 2nd Ypres, and gassed at Villiers Bretonneau Sir! My lungs are as good as new Sir! I won't let you down Sir! I've got a medal Sir, I have, well, I would have had it still but I had to pawn it to get a few coppers to buy food for the missus and kids; they gave me the medal for standing and fighting when the rest of me mates lay dead and dying around me, so if I didn't let them down, I wouldn't let you down, now would I Sir!' ....

And then that man, grey of face, worn with worry and distress among that small crowd of men, fatigued and hungry, smoothed down his ragged clothes or tried to dust off his old khaki great coat, army for the use of, as he desperately tried to stand straighter so as to catch the eye of he, who with just a simple nod, could change the whole future for that man's family for the better. These men then, who some few years before had been cheered as the Nation's saviours, had marched so proudly back to the land that in the first few halcyon years of victory had hailed them as heroes, fit only to receive the best that a grateful country could offer, were now to have the cup pressed to their lips.

'How much do you think a job with me is worth in wages?' he'd be asked.

'£2 a week seems fair!' he'd answer, even though he knew £2 a week was near slave labour.

Another hopeful would be asked the same question and, with eyes downcast, he'd reply '£1 17/ 6pence'. At this, the first man would desperately butt in....

'Please Sir, he can afford to work for that much even though it's well below the union rate, but I can't afford to take less than two quid for the job even though that's five bob below the union rate. I'm behind with the rent and the landlord's threatening to put us out on the street. One of my kids has consumption; he caught it off the missus. She's in the Sanatorium and not expected to live!'

If he'd expected mercy or compassion he was to be disappointed. There were thousands in the same desperate strait as he, and many even worse off! The

Boss/ Foreman would nod to the second man who jubilantly followed his new employer into the works. The rest, near in tears, would turn away.

Someone else would say,

'I would've taken less but the missus aint too good and the 'babbies' need me around to take the strain so I can't leave her. Still, ner mind, eh! This way we can all starve together! What a bleedin life!'

Mam's health wasn't very good; Ted would demand better food because 'I pay my board,' and Mabel was getting progressively weaker with that terrible cough that echoed around all the rooms, night and day. Mabel's own cutlery had cotton tied around the handles to warn us not to use it, and the smell of the Lysol in her metal sputum mug which had to be carried down stairs to the outside lavatory was overpowering; nothing was left to our imagination because we knew of its terrible phlegm/blood stained contents which she brought up. God knows what percentage of it was lung tissue. The Old Man was still stirring things up for us and threats flew back and forth. It wasn't funny going out into the street knowing that at any time his face might appear around the corner or from an entry and the ceaseless 'pumping' would begin again.

'Did the old woman go out with her fancy man last night?'

'What time it did she come in last Saturday?'

It went on and on. It was no use pretending she didn't have a fancy man although I didn't know what the expression meant. What I do know however is I began to fear him even more than I did before, and it didn't help when people around us began to describe him as mad. Mad he certainly was not but I knew what mad was. If adults said 'your dad is mad' then mad he must be.

Each and every day a grim procession of people who lived or existed in the next street passed our front door and today it never ceases to amaze me that although our plight must have been far worse than theirs, I always regarded them as the poor. Perhaps the difference was Mam had a job in the 'shoes' (shoe factory making shoes) and they mostly had no jobs. So, Mam's wage plus Ted's board, pittance though it was, kept us off the parish. We knew from the sights we saw and the yelling we heard at pub chucking out time, that so much of the dole or relief paid out to families, mainly in the next street which was really an 'abandon hope all ye who live here' place, went into the local publican's pocket. The sobbing of women and hungry children was loud in the land. What a tragedy that within 10 years we had full employment, a welfare state, in fact everything going for us after decades of poverty, and yet the politicians gave it away to ingratiates who then promptly turned around and bit the hand that fed them. Mam's usual greeting to any friend, relation or acquaintance she might meet in the street was invariably the same and this reflected the shaky state of the industries in the city, for she would say 'have you had to have any short time working lately?' This referred to the sending home of employees by the foreman or woman (the boss always got them to do his dirty work) because there just wasn't any work or orders in the factory. Being laid off was a tragedy, for no wage was forthcoming for days, and in homes where every penny was spoken for, this meant a drastic reduction in diet.

Mam being able to go in on a Saturday morning was a luxury, although with many firms this was part of the working week. Extra time? Double time? Don't make me laugh! Often we kids would arrive home from school to find Mam already there; the table laid and Mabel's needs taken care of. For Mam to be at home to greet us was a luxury we could well do without..........

'I'm on short time' she would say brightly, 'Ah well, there's plenty worse off than us.'

It was high summer, and my memories are that every day was bright and sunny 24 hours out of the 24. I can only remember the rain coming on the Saturday afternoons whilst we were in the local cinema (or as we called it, the pictures) the Shaftesbury, known to one and all as 'The Shaz'. The children's matinee was always called 'The Tupenny Rush' and that was what it seemed like with all the big kids jostling the smaller lads in an attempt to get a seat at the back so as to kid all and sundry they'd paid threepence for their seat. In those early days silent films were still around and it struck me that with the type of make-up used nearly all the women looked as though they were desperately ill. After sitting fascinated, watching the image on the flickering screen, each boy came out from the cinema at a rate of knots, and because invariably the film or serial shown had been a cowboy picture, we would go flying down the street, pasting our own bottoms with our right-hand whilst holding on to an imaginary rein with our left, imitating Tom Mix or whichever star had taken the leading role. One silent film was to do with a lovely young lady being put into a tomb whilst her sweetheart held his head in his hands. However all was not lost as, for some reason that time has denied me, she came back to life. Another favourite was a serial, the tune of which held me as much, if not more, than the action. The tune was 'poet and peasant.' Invariably after arriving home from the film, we would find Mam doing the ironing on the living room table which she would cover with an old blanket. Within 10 minutes of getting in our Ronnie would have a sick bilious bout. Mam said it was because he didn't blow his nose properly, but I think it was coming out of the dark cinema after watching the flickering shapes into the afternoon light that made him 'bring up.'

As the sun on most of those glorious summer days that I remember so well, seeped oh so slowly away making room for the twilight shadows, the still warm comforting air closed around us and our little family would, as so many other families were doing, sit outside on or around our doorstep, front and back doors plus windows wide open, trying to draw the cool evening air through. The warmth around us fought hard to remain but at times it was so sultry we found it hard to draw breath into our lungs. Poor Mabel must have been in agony, although she rarely, complained. God knows, she had little enough of her lungs left to draw upon. Gradually the sky would grow dark and great threatening storm clouds would gather, and as the first wisp of cooling air touched our cheeks we would hear in the distance the first rumbling of the approaching thunderstorm. Looking into the blue/ black threatening heavens, we would see dozens of those little black fluttering mammals, so rarely seen today; Bats. It would be impossible to hazard a guess as to how many there were as they poured out of the holes in attic brickwork or through gaps where slates were missing. Bats, whose swooping and fluttering and lurching seemed to take them all over the lowering sky. How did they avoid one another I wondered? Legend had it that if a bat got itself tangled in a woman's hair, she would have to be shorn bald. Then the chill in the air deepened and the first great spots of rain dappled the ground. At once a new smell could be discerned as the dust was laid in those spots at least. Passers-by hurried their steps and those who didn't seem to be aware of what the flickering and rumblings presaged were called to by those standing in their own doorways.

'Hurry home Mr/Mrs or you'll get soaked!'

With the dust laid, and as the last distant rumblings of the retreating storm faded away into the distance, gas jets were lit, and we were prepared for bed knowing that with the heat gone from the day, we would all sleep easier and not be disturbed too much by that terrible coughing from the back bedroom!

The winters were pretty awful and we hated the cold, icy mornings. We would get up to find the ice on our bedroom windows was inches thick. Sleeping in the middle of the bed at winter time wasn't such a bad idea, as up to having to get up I was nice and warm having Ted one side and Ronnie on the other. Ted was still complaining to Mam I was using his legs and lower regions as a football in the middle of the night, and in fact several times I was wakened by him pasting me for kicking him in the short and curlies.

Dressing was done in the dark of the morning. It wasn't too difficult for we used to sleep in our shirts for extra warmth. There was no way the gas pipe that didn't have mantle could be lit, and Mam wouldn't let us have the bare flame of a candle, even if we had a candle, which we didn't. So that was that! I must confess though it isn't easy trying to identify a pair of socks in the near pitch dark. We often found we had odd socks on when we got into the lighted living room downstairs.

Mam always lit a good fire for us in the morning. I say for us although of course it was for when poor Mabel was able to drag herself down the stairs. Ted would be in the kitchen having a wash at the sink which we would all have to use in turn. He would, more often than not, be moaning and groaning that he wanted bacon for breakfast instead of the bread and dip (dripping) which was all Mam could afford but he, better than all, knew the mess we were in and Mam's struggle to keep our heads above water.

Ted was one of the best and smartest dressed chaps in the street and only contributed a small amount to the family's float. Mam did her best, but we all rose from the table hungry. It wasn't any use asking for more food, there just wasn't any unless we were prepared to take some of Mam's meagre portion, for most certainly had we asked she would have passed it over to us and gone to work with an empty belly. Years later, in fact a month before he died, I asked Ron,

'Do you remember when Our Ted and Maisie were working, them ever giving us even a penny?'

He thought for a moment then said,

'No, they never ever did!'

Our living room, for that's what the most used room in the house was always called, boasted two or three old dining chairs around the wall whilst dead in the centre was an old, rough topped, well-scrubbed table. That old table really earned its keep. If we had visitors, we kids used it as a seat, and I can still feel those rough planks against my legs as I sat on the table looking at myself in the mirror. Once, I took the kitchen scissors and sliced a chunk out of my hair. It was noticeable for months after, and people and kids in the street would stop me and say,

'You've been chopping at your hair, haven't you?'

It was used when Mam gave us a wash down, and even today I can feel myself sitting on it, close to the fire, with heat upon my bare legs as I was given the cleaning treatment. How I hated it when, coming to my ears, the flannel was first screwed up, and then screwed into each ear in turn. I swear she pushed and screwed that old bit of rag so hard (did I say flannel!) first into one ear so the dried up wax and dirt came out of the other!

The table was also a games table: Ludo, snakes and ladders, games which for me ended when I burst into tears at losing, and which brought the charge from my peers, after first checking Mam wasn't within earshot,

'You're a Mardy Arse!'

Maisie was a jigsaw addict and the table was big enough to take any size of puzzle, but by far the favourite past-time in those long, dark, winter evenings, was painting paper doilies. To get these we would scrounge around the streets and tips to find a long discarded beer bottle and return it to the outdoor beer license for a penny. How those publicans would curse us for returning the bottles in such an awful state, often with the dried up dregs still in the bottom. With the coin we'd buy a packet of lacy paper doilies which we'd then paint with water colour paints. On completion, some of the better off women Mam worked with would buy them off her out of pity. Even half a penny profit was better than nothing as half a penny had some purchasing power in those days.

All our furniture apart from a small black, ebony, thin legged table which stood in the hall was second-hand or other people's throw away, but they were regularly dusted and that old table was scrubbed to a pristine whiteness using bar soap and bags of elbow grease.

Dining tables were usually left 'set', that is as one meal was cleared away the cloth was taken off and shaken then replaced, and the tea caddy, sugar bowl, milk bottle, in fact all the everyday items including salt in its packet, were returned ready for the next meal. There were no fridges in those days and in hot weather we used the cold pantry floor and a bucket or bowl filled with cold water to stand the milk in.

Every Saturday morning, we kiddies were hoofed out by Ted with a loud and often repeated threat as to what we would get if we dared show our faces indoors for the next hour or so. With us safely out of the way, he would pile every portable item of furniture from the room onto the table (and it was big enough to take all our meagre possessions). Hot soapy water in a bucket, well laced with disinfectant and soda, was then brought in and every inch of our old lino floor covering, left by a previous tenant, was attacked by Ted and his scrubbing brush. Honestly, anyone would've thought he had a grudge against it. I was surprised the already faded pattern, hardly discernible on the lino, could stand up to his seemingly venomous attack without being scrubbed off completely. Finished, the surface was scrutinised carefully and once satisfied, sheets of newspaper were spread over the by now rapidly drying floor. I'll say this for Ted, he never ever did half a job! Peeping in through the door to see if we could now get back to our favourite past time of reading comics, we would be greeted by Ted using those words that I swear I will carry ringing in my ears to my grave,

'If you buggers dare dirty this floor after I've scrubbed it, I'll give you A BLOODY GOOD HIDING!' (Amen!)

Under the window of our living room was a huge, old fashioned, overstuffed armchair, which had been donated or obtained from someone kind and much better off than we were. I say it was overstuffed for much of the stuffing was poking out of the arms. When Mabel was well enough to come downstairs, she had first call on its size and comfort. Seated upon it, it seemed as though that old chair, with its stuffing and springs sticking through, wrapped itself around her tiny frail frame, comforting and warm. None of us begrudged her that bit of comfort, getting up if we were already in it without needing to be told or asked, and sitting ourselves instead on one of the straight backed, uncomfortable dining chairs. Let her move though, even only to go to the outside lavatory, then we'd dive in, sometimes two bottoms wedged into the one seat pushing and shoving, before scrambling out again as Mam helped poor Mabel, near to complete collapse, back into that little haven of comfort. Next in line for that armchair was Our Mam; after Mabel, Mam always had priority. Do you know, I can never remember Ted sitting in it which is surprising really as he would never usually relinquish his right to anything. Maybe he was afraid it would spoil the creases of his trousers, after all he was very conscious of being smart, but Ted wasn't daft and knew better than any of us, that the only person standing between us and the Workhouse was Mam.

Always when the weather was cold, we would have a fire in the morning to warm us and our clothes before we went off to work or school. It was then allowed to die down for coal cost money, and more often than not Mabel was in bed. Around the fire was a huge, old-fashioned, fireguard, which was ideal, not only to stop us kids falling in when we were falling out (and we did fight a lot) but also perfect for spreading the drying clothes to air after being washed if the weather was inclement. In our day, clothes had to be dried quickly or how else could you get out. We had little in the way of clothing. Everything was used, nothing was wasted. Even the heat contained within the old cast iron fire range was taken out via the iron oven shelves, wrapped in thick brown paper or, if that wasn't to hand, then newspaper did just as well to wrap the shelves. Too hot to handle, these were placed between the cold bed sheets to warm them, a job they did beautifully. Far better than the hot water bottles which we knew of but didn't have. In those days hot water bottles were made of aluminium or thick pot. Later, much later in that state between dozing and deep sleep, we would be aware of the soothing warmth being slid from under our feet, as the shelves were taken to be reheated in the still hot oven, ready for Mam and Maisie's bed. We'd already warmed Ted's side for when he came up. Three in a bed; me in the middle!

Mornings followed the same pattern as, in between making sure the fire had caught, preparing our breakfast, getting her hair combed before dashing off out to her work, Mam would be taking special pains over the few little extra tit bits she'd managed to set aside for Mabel's breakfast.

Mabel's terrible cough was now echoing around the silent, sleeping household, often disturbing our sleep no matter how much she tried to suppress it. Time after time, night after night, desperately needing the sleep denied her, Mam would get up and go along the cold, draughty, passageway to Mabel's room. There she would try to comfort Mabel as, coughing and choking, she would near fill her sputum mug (stinking of Lysol) with blood stained phlegm and lung tissue, praying all the time that the attack wouldn't presage a full scale haemorrhage.

At always the same time those work day mornings, the factory hooters would sound in set sequence. With so many households in our poor district having no reliable clocks, the hooters had to be sounded, and sounded accurately. Each had a different tone: each was Greenwich Mean Time accurate. Once ours had sounded, Mam and Ted set off at a run. Come to think of it, Ted had a bike to get to work; poor mam had to race the whole way and it was well over a mile. She always seemed to be dashing. One minute late and wages were docked. If very late, the gates were locked and they were 'out' for the day. Every child from the working class homes knew what a 'lock out' meant.

With the elders out to work and with Mabel upstairs, Ron and I were now left to the tender mercy of our Mais who now exerted her authority by chivvying and chasing us around. Before escaping off to school we had our chores to do. The pots from our meagre breakfast were cleared from the table which was at once reset with the dinner plates, salt etc. The breakfast dishes were washed and put away and we would consume our round of bread and dip out of our hands. The room was then tidied and the fire guard checked for safety, all this to our Maisie's,

'You wait till Our Mam comes home; I'm gonna tell on you, I am!'

This was a threat bawled at us so often that nine times out of ten we'd close our ears to it, but sometimes the sound of our careering around would penetrate up the stairs until Mabel hammered on the floor with the dolly stick placed at the side of her bed to draw attention to her needs. Then off to school we went, always within me a horrid gut feeling that one day I would return back to find my home gone. Years later I was to find that children from broken or deprived homes experienced that same rotten feeling!

Being the eldest, Maisie was permitted to leave school early so as to get the dinner cooked and ready for the adults dashing in about 12:50pm. Each of us in turn performed this duty as first one and then the other, was eventually going out to work, which meant the last one left at home did all the work formally done by three, then two, then one...... ME!

Dashing in at 12 noon, a light was put under the gas to heat the saucepans containing the few potatoes we could afford, so that by the time Mam and Ted arrived home out of breath (they had less than 20 minutes before racing back) the spuds were cooked and ready for the slice of corned beef to be beaten up in them. Many times this constituted our mid-day meal.

Mabel was upstairs, too ill to be brought down. I can still remember the looks of hatred, even contempt, that were thrown in my direction by my brothers and sister when I whined,

'Mam, I'm still hungry!'

I cringe when I think of how I wolfed down that portion of her own dinner she'd slide onto my plate. I could cry when I think of how many times our poor Mam had to go back to work on a near empty stomach. Since those awful times she's told me that in those days her priorities were, rent, insurance (to bury Mabel when her time came), and food, even though she knew that having been paid on Friday that by Saturday morning, having purchased the food for the week and after setting by money for the other two essentials, she would often only have sixpence left (three pence in today's money) to take care of any emergencies. I feel sure that only the poverty she'd undergone as a child herself gave her the strength, wit and wisdom to carry on, otherwise I'm sure we would have gone under.

I always felt Sunday breakfast was the best meal of the week. I realise now of course that this was the one day the pressure was off and as a family we were together. Always, always, on Sunday we kids got an egg. NEW LAID! Mam never ever purchased anything other than new laid eggs, and the good Lord have mercy on Mr Warren at the corner shop if he ever sold us a single egg that was found to be 'OFF!' Back would go the egg 'tout suit' and an explanation demanded!

'I paid for NEW LAID!'

The egg would be exchanged, no questions asked!

On the question of shopkeepers, it is well to remember that before the days of modern supermarkets, and with the prices of the in town shops being well outside the ranges of what most ordinary folk could afford, (they couldn't spare the time for going into the town let alone the tram fares) the most popular and used places for the family groceries was always the corner shop, and rightly so. The shop was a delight visually and the aromas....... ham on the bone and cheese; Cheese in blocks cut with a very thin wire attached to what looked like a duffle coat toggle. Then there were the great sides of bacon suspended from the ceiling by shiny 'S' books which were screwed into the supporting rafters of the rough & uneven, plastered & whitewashed ceiling. Every sort of household need was catered for from clothes pegs through to mousetraps, loose sugar through to milk and bread. The shop was stacked up to the ceiling and yet the size of the room where business was conducted was miniscule, no larger in fact than the front room of an ordinarily terrace house. (Which they often were) Most folk who traded with the corner shop were 'on the book' or, to put it more politely they had their groceries etc 'on tick'. Under this system items purchased were entered into a ledger kept by the shopkeeper. The customer had a duplicate book, much smaller obviously, and sold by the shopkeeper to the customer as nothing was free in those days. A duplicate of all purchases was entered in the book and at the end of the week the amounts were totalled up. If the balances were the same then the bill was paid, usually on the Friday evening. I reckon over 90% of the workforce were paid on a Friday in cash or, on the Saturday morning when the rest of the groceries to last the week were bought. It is also a matter of record that when squaring up time came many rows broke out when the amounts were questioned by irate mums who'd little enough money to get by on anyway. It's also a matter of record that the reason, or main reason for such a discrepancy, would be the husband. During the week he would go into the shop and ask for cigarettes 'on the book' which he would declare could be entered 'on the book' later! The shopkeeper would subsequently forget to enter the amount the next time the wife came in and so all hell broke loose later on. The forerunner of 'putting it on the book' was 'putting it on the slate'. This system was discontinued for the simple reason there was little trust on either side and of course, chalk on a slate rubs off too easily or can easily be altered. A bad or 'welcher' payer was 'blacklisted' and the only thing left for them to do was to leave town or pay cash. It was so pathetic to see the poor wives of the creatures without conscience who'd spent 'the dole money' on booze, going from shop to shop, trying to get essentials for their children and babies 'on the book.'

Our local shopkeeper was Mr Warren. He was a slim and very smart man, aged about forty. He often wore plus fours, which in those days was associated with male golfers we all knew, but only from 'fag' cards. (Cigarette)

Mrs Warren was a very handsome woman, beautifully spoken and with jet black hair, who was usually cuddling a snub nosed, snuffling, Pekinese dog named 'chummy.' Rumour had it that when 'chummy', who I can never ever remember being out in the street, squatted to do its 'business', its bum was wiped afterwards by Mrs W! It was also alleged that when the Warren ladies washed their hair that an egg was massaged into the scalp. How true this all was I don't know. What I do know is that Mr and Mrs Warren had three daughters: Myrtle, Hazel and Nina, and to me aged seven years, they were all grown up. Myrtle was known to all and sundry as 'wee Myrtle' and her height told us why. She was a lovely, lovely, tiny person, who was something on the stage. I didn't see her very often, but when I did, it made my day. This sweet lady, who was likely in her late teens or early 20s, would come bustling into the serving area of the shop, and it didn't matter if you were the poorest of the poor, to her you were always 'darling'! Nothing was too much trouble. Next was Hazel. I confess I was in awe of Hazel, but to be fair, like the rest of her family, she was kindness itself. In looks she was like her mother; very dark, ladylike, cultured and sweetly spoken. That just left Nina. Nina was Nina; she was obviously her father's daughter! A little bit tomboyish, not dark like the other women of her family, and Nina wore spectacles. This then was the corner shop family who wielded more power in the area than the Lord Mayor had they but known it. BUT this family commanded more respect from being so humane and kind.

A Sunday dinner meat course would be rabbit purchased the night before at the very last minute before the local town centre market closed for the weekend. In those days there was no refrigeration and so stall holders had to dispose of any game that did not improve with 'hanging.' Rabbits went very cheaply indeed; for a few pennies in fact, as did fish which, having been bought at the very last moment, would fill the homeward bound trams with a very penetrating smell. One always knew who was taking overripe fish home! 'Specs' (damaged or bruised fruit) were sold off very cheaply too. These were usually apples or pears which, once the bad bits were removed, were our sole intake of fresh, or rather slightly jaded, fruit. Half a dozen or so of these items would be sold off to the eagerly awaiting housewives who stood shivering in the cold evening air, for about tuppence. (One new penny)

With Mam in the kitchen preparing Sunday dinner, Ted, in his best clothes, and he always did look immaculate, would come downstairs, open the lid of that lovely piano which had gone through the mill with us since the Old Man's desertion, and play all those songs we'd grown up with:

~ When the moon comes over the mountain

~ Carolina Moon

~ Oh play to me gypsy etc, etc.

With the lovely warm coal fire in the hearth, the delicious smells of rabbit cooking wafting in from the kitchen, Mam would call for Ted to play this, or play that!

Then we would forget, for those precious few hours, our pitiable plight and sing our hearts out. These were times we wouldn't have traded places with even the King of England.

But still, the Old Man would not, could not, leave us in peace. What devil drove him on, I know not, but devil it surely was. Many of our nights were made hideous by him shouting and screaming outside in the street or shouting and raving through the front door letterbox. Drunk or sober made no difference.

Sometimes his tone would change and he'd shout through the door begging Mam to take him back, but too much water had flowed under that particular bridge. He'd had his chances again and again. No money was sent to support his children, and even if occasionally some was sent, then the envelope would be covered in the filthiest most abusive language, so much so the postal officials warned him that if he didn't stop writing the filth, he'd be in trouble. Postal orders if sent would be crossed. He knew this way they could only be paid through a bank or similar, yet he knew full well Mam didn't have a cat in hells chance of holding a bank book. He'd do anything to make our lives difficult or near on impossible.

One night the shouted filth, abuse and neighbourhood disturbance got so bad, Ted, who at the time was still only a slightly built teenager, had no choice but go out and remonstrate with the Old Man. He then set about Ted and smashed him all around the street; the marks of the beating showed clearly on Ted for days. Afterwards, Ted joined the local YMCA taking up gymnastics. He never carried any spare weight, and in less than a year he'd became little more than sinew and whipcord. The day of reckoning finally arrived for the Old Man and, coming to our house about a year later, the old devil again came face-to-face with Ted. That fight in the street was spoken about by those who witnessed it for long, long after. At the fight's near conclusion, the Old Man was flat on his back, his face blue with the effort of trying to get air into his lungs whilst Ted lay on top of him trying to throttle the last bit of life from his body. Realising this youth was in danger of throttling his own father, bystanders dashed forward to drag him off before the Old Man's face, which was now a rich plum colour, went black. He never returned to create a disturbance, although we would often spot him lurking around trying to catch Mam out in God knows what!

The young bull had bested the old bull, and from that day on Ted was never afraid of man nor beast..... and his fists were lethal!

Lizzie & Den:

Our next door neighbours were Lizzie and Den, a childless couple in their late 20s come early 30s. Lizzie worked at a local factory and Den for the local council. So all in all for those hard times, they were pretty well off. These were good folk and as neighbours, excellent; they must have been for they put up with me and Ron! To be fair we weren't bad lads, just noisy and always fighting; we'd fall out at the drop of a hat. I remember one incident well.

Ron and I were skimming a rather tatty, but hard piece of old shoe leather, to each other. As always happened, we threw harder and harder, until it finally finished with me in our entry and Ron outside in the street, throwing really hard. Unfortunately, the two front doors abutted the entry (one on each side) and the upper door panels were GLASS! Ron let fly. I can see that thing skimming towards me even as I write, and I ducked. No need to have done though, for the skimming piece swerved to one side and crash, careered straight through Liz and Den's glass door panel. It was a work day and so both of them were at work, as were the adults in our family. More importantly there were no witnesses in the street! By golly, we sweated for the rest of the afternoon until the adults from both sides came home, and still we said nothing.......That night a knock came at our back door. Lizzie.

'Do your Ronnie or Norman happen to know who it was that broke our front door window?' she asked.

We pair were called forward by Mam.

'Where were you this afternoon?' was the first question.

'We went on the park all afternoon, Mam' we said. (This had been agreed as our cover story)

Mam wasn't satisfied and she pressed us hard. It was Lizzie who got us off the hook.

'Leave them Mrs Hastings' she said. 'If they were on the park then we know they couldn't know anything about it.'

Both Ronnie and I would've loved to confess. We didn't though for we knew Mam would've insisted on paying for the glass, and had she done so, our rations would've been cut that week, and God alone knows we had little enough as it was. In retrospect, I think Lizzie probably guessed it was us boys, but she didn't press it, and so we were let off the hook. Wherever you're resting, Lizzie and Den, THANK YOU!

Liz and Den were the proud owners of what must have been one of the earliest radiograms invented. It was a monster! A great wooden cabinet thing that lit up like Blackpool illuminations when switched on - they had electric whilst the rest of us had gas. So proud of it were our neighbours that all our family were invited to view its pristine magnificence. Volume, tone, wood and quality, were all admired, and the price hinted at! Now, let me say here that Liz and Den rarely conversed in a normal voice level. Instead they spoke as though they had their own volume turned on 'high!' Our Mais told me years later that because the dividing wall between the houses was so thin, when she and Mam were lying in bed they used to be in hysterics at some of the pillow talk emanating from next door. In fact sex education was free with Liz and Den as neighbours. But I continue.........that radiogram was turned up to play as loud as the pair of them spoke. I can personally swear to the volume peaks that instrument reached, thereby enabling the whole of the neighbourhood to enjoy the music. All through that marvellous summer of 1935, with doors and windows left open, the whole street was entertained free of charge, the music only being interrupted by their voices pitched higher than the highest peak of the radiogram as they congratulated each other on their 'good buy'. Even today, I cannot hear the strains of 'Oh Play to me Gypsy', 'The Isle of Capri' or 'When I get too old to dream,' without tears flooding my eyes.

The back gardens of those houses were a reasonable size, in fact I remember we even tried to grow a few potatoes to supplement our diet. Unfortunately, the slugs etc had a field day and pesticides, if any, cost money and so we didn't try the next year, following the adage,

'If at first you don't succeed....give up!'

Anyway, Den next door decided he would raise chickens and, give him his due, he worked hard at building a six foot high wire mesh pen to keep cats and rats out, and the poultry in! Everything got off to a flying start, and even Ronnie and I got interested, digging up worms from our garden and throwing them high into the air over the fence, just to see the hens scrabble for a protein addition to their diet courtesy of the little boys next door. Great!

1935 saw really lovely weather as I've said before and this evening was hot and muggy. The front and back doors were open to admit a cooling through draught and Mam, Ronnie, Maisie and myself were sitting just outside our back door, with Princey facing away from us in rough vegetation further down the garden.

We weren't overlooked from either side for we had the railway embankment on our right and Liz and Den's back garden was shielded from us by a little 'outhouse' that used to be the toilet cum wash house. Signs of activity came from next door, followed by the clump and then lighter patter of feet down next door's garden path.

Den's voice: 'Are you sure you only counted 11 hens, Liz, because we've got 12 and they can't get out!?'

Liz: 'Well, I counted them Den and I only got up to 11, but there might be one sitting in the laying box!'

Den: 'Tell you what, Liz, I'll go into the pen and as I drive them out, you count them.'

Liz: 'All right Den, in you go!'

Then we heard,

'Right Lizzy, here we go!'

Lizzy began to count: one, two, three......until she got to 11, and then she stopped.

'Is that it Den, because only 11 have come out?'

'That's funny Lizzy, there ain't no more in here, and we definitely have 12!'

We listened with baited breath! Was the mystery of the missing chicken going to be solved? IT MOST CERTAINLY WAS for, disturbed by the activity next door our faithful little pooch roused himself from the nettle patch, stretched his back to the full extent, turned and trotted along the garden path towards us. Even as our neighbours were debating further,

'Could it be a rat that's got our chicken, Den?'

'I doubt it Liz or it must have been a bloody big rat to climb or jump over a six foot wire mesh fence and then jump back with our chicken in its mouth!'

Princey was the focus of all our eyes. Thank goodness that even as he stopped to scratch himself with his back leg and then, in spite of our silent pleadings, stop again to sniff at, and then pee up the line post, our neighbours had their backs to our yard, else they would have seen what we were seeing as we grabbed our surprised dog and dashed him inside! Namely that his face and neck was covered in blood and feathers which stretched right up to his ears. No wonder he was too tired to chase the 6:45 to Peterborough!

Wireless:

We had a wireless set in the days when not many people in those mean streets around us did. It was our pride and joy although God knows it was enough trouble trying to tune it in. It was contained in a faded and battered wooden case, operated by a battery. In the centre of the said case was one very large, Bakelite knob, each side of which were two smaller knobs. There were no other controls. Tuning in was a very time and nerve consuming exercise, and I must have got the station 'off tune' more times than I care to remember for I loved twiddling those knobs whether the set was on or off! I was up on all the technology of those days to do with wireless sets. Battery, battery charge, accumulator, oscillator etc. etc.

Radio was very much in its infancy and radio repair shops in our district were very few and far between as there were no more than forty decent sets in the streets around us. Most houses had gas only and I doubt if anyone had come up with gas radio!! So, electric was the only thing that would power the brutes via a battery wired into the radio innards. Unfortunately, batteries soon ran down, in fact I would wager 40% of the power was wasted tuning in to a comprehensible station. So, when the battery needed charging there was much head scratching to see where the few coppers required could be spared to 'charge up!' In the meantime, the beast sat silent and mute on the sideboard. When the price for charging had been saved, one of us would be sent off carrying that glass cased monstrosity with the red and black terminals spouting out of the top, to the electric shop to be put on charge. Usually, there would be three or four other batteries sitting on the table top being charged from long red and black leads. These were to be collected later. Fetching the battery back, we would be mindful of the instructions from Mam and Ted,

'Don't spill any battery acid on you because if you do it'll burn holes in your jersey!'

I've thought many times since, 'stuff the jersey, what if it burns holes in me!?' The other direst and most potent warning came next......

'And watch he doesn't swing an old battery on you in exchange for our good one!'

A favourite trick in the district was for the kids to sneak around in the dark and disconnect the 'earth wire' from the outside, many a time the poor 'charging man' was accused of not putting a good charge in the battery before the real cause of the set not working was spotted.

It had to come, and one day it did – our wireless gave up the ghost and it wasn't the battery or the accumulator, because Our Ted said so! Naturally, Ronnie and I got the blame. Our protestations of 'it weren't us, Mam!' were to no avail. Never was a set so tapped, prodded and twiddled as much as our set was in an attempt to bring it back to life. All to no avail! Finally, it was put to one side to await better improvements in our family finances. In one way being without the thing brought about great improvement, for now we sat reading or doing the many times put together jigsaw puzzles that Mais was so addicted to. I swear we all felt better with not spending so much time standing around when it was switched on, shouting advice, or trying to make sense of the atmospheric crackles that issued forth. Out came the Hotspur and Wizard comics, much tattered and crummy, read and reread till our eyes must have nearly worn the print off the yellowing pages and I can still hear Mam's

'You'll ruin your eyes!'

It mattered not. We all loved reading.

Mam had a friend who had a husband....Our Arthur who, according to Mam's friend was the worlds most talented 'jack of all trades.' Not only that, but Arthur was prepared to look at our wireless set to see what was wrong! Unfortunately, we knew all of Mam's friends, and other friends knew that Arthur was the biggest bloody know all in the district but, beggars can't be choosers so,

'Come on in Arthur, and have a go!'

Oh yes, did I remember to tell you that Arthur worked in a shoe factory and didn't even own a wireless set of his own; never had in fact!

The appointed day arrived and so unfortunately, as it turned out, did our Arthur, with a kit composing of screw driver, pliers and a bloody great hammer!!!! What on earth did he need that for!?? After all, we kids were warned, and warned repeatedly, that a wireless was a delicate instrument and had to be treated with respect!!! With a look of deepest concentration which conveyed 'don't you dare interrupt me,' Arthur began to disassemble our treasured set. Valves were recklessly pulled out, wires disconnected, the pieces piled up, everything that could be removed, was removed. We hardly dared to breathe, then the verdict........

'It's not working!' declared Arthur.

Really? We could've told him that!!!!

Arthur paused momentarily before remarking,

'It's still not working!!'

For some reason Arthur wouldn't meet our eye at this last pronouncement and I'm pretty sure it was about then Mam seemed to be having a bit of trouble trying to stifle a sneeze! Anyway, she ran out into the yard to recover. Arthur stood erect and, still not meeting anyone's eye, began to put his plyers, screwdriver and hammer away. Finished, he moved towards the back door just as Mam, red of face from trying to stifle her sneeze (or was it a laugh) was entering. Head down, Arthur made his final pronouncement,

'I can't find anything wrong with it, Mary!'

I was just about to ask in my puzzlement whether he was going to put it back together again, when a hand was tightly clamped over my mouth. Still puzzled, I pushed the hand away and began again,

'Mam....?'

I then stopped dead for I could see her shoulders were shaking! Finally, the penny dropped and within seconds we were all rolling around, hysterical with mirth! We were still having hysterics as we began to shovel the bits and pieces of our well-worn and well-loved old wireless set into the dustbin, although I hung onto the Bakelite knobs to play with later. The sunshine of our laughter always helped drive away the black despair that even I, young as I was, felt so often and which kept us sane.

Yes, our lives could be sad, and what could be worse than the poverty we were already in? But all the pointers were there and perhaps it's as well I was too young to understand the significance of what to my elders, was very plain and clear to see. I didn't, though, and so 'Thank God' I was able to smile for just a little bit longer.

The Benefits Man:

We were sitting around the table eating our usual mid-day meal of boiled potatoes with a slice of corned beef mashed up in it. We'd been given our orders by Mam as she came racing in from work to serve out our meagre ration, already cooked (or boiled) by Maisie who'd been let out of school early to put the gas on.

Just watch your manners, we were instructed, and answer his questions! Whose questions? If he asks if you're hungry, just tell him the truth, Yes! (Too blooming true, we were always hungry!) Suddenly, HE was at the back door, and to this day I don't know who he was or where he came from, but this much I do know, he had come to investigate our rock bottom situation! Those of the family who are alive today, apart from me, don't remember the man coming.......but I do! I suspect he came to the back door to see if there were any signs of affluence, such as good clothing on the washing line, cycles in the yard or even coal in the coal house but, if that's what he expected to see then he was disappointed. The man began to ask Mam questions and as she answered she indicated by gesture for us to get on with our dinner. All the while his eyes travelled around our sparsely and poorly furnished living room. He wanted to know Mam's wages, and she whispered the amount to him.

'Was that in the shoes?'

Next, 'how much does your eldest boy earn?' again, a whispered reply (we younger kiddies, if we knew, might broadcast it around)

'Oh, he's an errand boy is he?'

Maisie at school, Ronnie at school, Norman.....

'Is he the youngest?'

ME......my chest stuck out, fame at last!

Rent? Insurance?

'Do you need to pay insurance, Missus?'

At this Mam dropped her voice but my sharp ears picked up her saying, 'it's for Mabel; Burial Club!'

'Mabel? Who's Mabel Missus?'

Mam whispered again....... 'Oh, I see Missus, let's leave Mabel for now then'

Everything was being put down in his little note book. Then came the big one! 'Husband?'

'He deserted us Mister, 3 years ago, he took everything!'

'What other expenses do you have then, Missus?'

'Mabel, Mister! She's in bed for most of the time. No Mister she hasn't the strength most days to come down the stairs, let alone go to work. No, she doesn't eat a lot now, I admit, but we try to tempt her appetite with a new laid egg once a week and she can take a drop of milk pudding, but for the drinking I can only afford to give her watered milk otherwise the younger boys would have to go without. Most weeks I manage to get her a jar of cod & malt. (my mouth was watering at mention of these goodies) Nobody would believe a girl could eat so little and still stay alive. I have to try and tempt her with tasty morsels; that's why I applied!'

For all the compassion the man showed, Mam might as well have spoken to a brick wall!

'Maintenance, Missus! He must pay you maintenance?'

'Mister, I took a court order out against him and they told him he would have to pay towards our support, but he still doesn't pay us anything although he says he does. He's the wickedest, rottenest liar God ever put breath into! Why, when he knew Mabel had consumption, this is before he left us, he turned her into the street then burned her bed!'

'Take him back to court then Missus, then he either pays up, or goes down!'

'That takes time and money and a solicitor's costs, Mister! I can't lose time from work, and I can't afford the money...don't you see Mister, that swine's got us all ways? If he went back to court and they sent him down he couldn't pay us maintenance anyway! What few coppers I have I need to buy food for us and Mabel otherwise the municipal would take the children off me and then I'd have nothing!'

The logic of what poor Mam was saying was unanswerable, and so our visitor was led to the door leading to the stairs. Even as he passed by we could see his eyes sweeping all around and, I suspect, even checking our plates to make sure every morsel had been consumed for, unconsumed food left on a plate would indicate the family had selective eating habits and therefore things couldn't possibly be all that bad!

Mabel's bedroom being at the top of the stairs was his first port of call. Inside, poor Mabel lay, whiter than the sheets on her bed. The dinner Mam had tried to make more palatable by adding half a hard-boiled egg lay untouched on a rickety chair beside her. If Mabel couldn't work up an appetite to eat the food then it had to be thrown away for her disease was now so virulent that any food that came in contact with her coughing was counted as contaminated. The overwhelming stink of the thick, Lysol disinfectant contained in the bottom of her lidded sputum mug, was not conducive to appetite. Hungry as we all were, even had the food not been contaminated by her breath, we wouldn't have been able to stomach the left over meal. Did the man mark how Mabel's cutlery and thick mug had identifying bands of cotton around their handles which, without saying a word, warned.....UNCLEAN!? Was he aware, even without seeing evidence of the mug's contents, of the great gouts of blood speckled phlegm mixed in with shadows of her putrid lungs, torn up from her poor frail body by those terrible wracking, debilitating coughs that ceaselessly, tore her apart.

Mabel knew what the man's visit was all about and, as she lay on her black painted, second hand bed, she was hopping mad. Her chest heaved as she fought to drag air into her almost by now, non-functioning lungs. This caused her to cough and choke, so much so that even our visitor began to look worried as she coughed that terrible cough which, even today, nearly sixty years later, still haunts me. If looks could have killed, that man would have dropped dead on the spot. We were poor, terribly poor, but even after everything fate, the world and that devil of a rotten Old Man could throw at us, we still had our pride, but if this man and the faceless wonders behind him from wherever he came had their way, we would lose even that.

The blood stained froth on dear Mabel's face could be wiped away, but the stain of this man's visit, never could. I, being the youngest, never guessed what everyone else in our poor household knew; we were on our knees and only the sheer guts and courage of Our Mam stood between us and the Workhouse. Every room in our poor house was scrutinised; cupboards were opened and rent & insurance books inspected, whilst copious notes were made. Even bank books were asked for. Bank books....can you believe it! Then, our visitor made some quick and rough calculations whilst Mam stood by, white faced, tight-lipped, and trembling with grief and shame. The moment got to me and I stood by, realising we'd reached yet another crisis point. Finally, the verdict.......we could have a few coppers aid each week but this was conditional upon Mam selling the one decent article in the house.....our beloved piano which we'd hung onto and cherished, through good times and bad. Lovingly polished from new, commented upon by family visitors. It stood there as immaculate that day, as the day Our Mam had bought it, and was until the day it was finally sold because there was no longer anyone left at home to play it. There wasn't a mark upon it. Our symbol of better times passed. This then was the deal......

'Sell the piano Missus, and what you get from it apportion out so much per week, as agreed to by us. When that money is all used up we will reconsider your case and might, just might, apportion you a few shillings per week!' Under iron control, Mam declined with thanks for, as she was to say years later, the piano was the only link to our former lovely home, and with that gone, we were beaten!

'No thank you Mister; I'd offer you a cup of tea but we haven't got any! You see, I used the tea money to buy Mabel that egg you saw she'd left on her plate. She couldn't eat it as you saw even though it was new laid, and we can't finish it up for her because it was with her whilst she was coughing that phlegm up......because consumption is so catching....so we'll have to throw it away, even though our bellies are empty.....but we don't begrudge it to Mabel!'

Even I could see that the man was shame faced as he muttered,

'Don't blame me Missus, I'm only doing my job!'

'Yes' said Mam, 'and so was my brother William and millions of his mates going off to the war; so many of them not coming back; dying for beggars like you who make the rules so that people like us have to go through all of this to try and put food in our kiddies bellies!'

Strangely enough, I could see she wasn't even angry at him.

By this time the others had gone either to work (Ted), or to school. Mam's going to be late for work, I thought! She'll get a 'lock out!' I have since realised she must have forewarned her Forewoman who was sympathetic to us and our plight for, with the man gone, poor Mam sat down at the table, still littered with our dinner pots and, putting her head in her hands, she sobbed as though her heart would break! Then, she stood up, and although those terrible wracking sobs still tore at her as though to rip her apart, she managed to gasp out those words which always seemed to make our dank, miserable, frustrating world a little brighter,

'Ah well, there are plenty a lot worse off than we are,' and she began to get herself ready for work.

Rummage sale and new coats:

Mam wanted to get me and Ronnie a better coat for the winter months that lay ahead and appealing to the Old Man was a waste of time! They needed to be warm coats because with our diet we'd feel the cold something chronic! Some of the children in our area (although not all) were at an equal state of poverty to us, although I have to say from outward appearances you would never have guessed it! Sadly, so many children in those times were in such a sorry state because the father would booze his parish money or pittance of a war pension away. The whole state of these children would deteriorate; they would be lousy, dirty, snotty nosed, ragged arsed etc., etc. Now it was October and the first winter frosts were with us. What we had, although clean and neat, were threadbare and so by practicing even stricter economies Mam managed to get a few coppers together. Then we did something we had never done before, and which afterwards we'd never do again. We went to a rummage sale. Oh, the shame of it all!

The rummage sale was held at the little Mission Hall at the bottom of our road. This was used for Magic Lantern shows, little concerts and, on Sundays, for the poorer children's Sunday school. (After all, it wouldn't do to mix our lot up with the more well to do parishioners!)

The Hall was also used by St Barnabas Church, which lay some half a mile away, as an overflow building for events which were not really suitable for the school hall at the side of the church itself: choir functions, Gilbert & Sullivan operas etc.

The Morton Road Mission Hall was my Sunday School and where, every Sunday afternoon, I, along with lots of other neighbourhood children, would walk around in a huge circle, holding hands and singing,

'Over the seas there are little brown children, mothers and fathers and babies too.'

As we did so we would drop our halfpenny into the collecting plate to be spent on the church overseas missions. Now remember this was a very poor area and most parents had little enough to feed their own children yet a mite would be found to put in that box, no question about it. Those halfpennies, freely given by our parents would, if it had been a bad week, drop to a farthing or worse, shame faced, nothing! But if it could be given, it was given. Today, when I hear people being accused of exploiting 'the blacks' (a term we all used in those days), I think back to our poverty stricken days when we who had nothing gave freely to those people overseas we didn't even know!

But why did so many parents insist that their children went to Sunday school? The order of the day was that families were large and houses small, which meant children had to share the parents' bed space.....so much for privacy!! It was quite the thing for parents to go to bed after the midday dinner on a Sunday, 'for the lay down' whilst the kids were at Sunday School! The old Mission Hall is still there, but no longer used for worship.

So, come Saturday afternoon and into the Mission Hall we went after paying the one penny admission fee! Even at that low price there were those who were so skint they used the push and shove tactic to get in without paying. The

Hall was large with bare floorboards and at the end, fixed high up on the wall, was a movable wooden screen behind which was a religious mural of Our Lord seated and surrounded by children of all colours and nationalities! I felt very much at home here even though it was being put to its present usage.

Out of the scrum around the 'rags and tat' the organisers had been landed with, Mam eventually emerged, hanging on like grim death to two coats which, even to my untutored eye must have come from a good home. Satisfied and having paid for the articles, home we went!

One coat was a navy blue gabardine mac with a belt....Wow! I had always wanted such a coat! The other coat was a thick Melton cloth material, quite bulky and from what I could see it was also in very good condition. Now, before I go any further let me explain that because at some time Our Ronnie had had pneumonia (and we were never allowed to forget it) he was considered something of a 'Dillon' of the family (after poor Mabel that is) and, as he was also, without any shadow of a doubt the favourite (I was bottom of the league being told constantly 'you're just like the old man') Ronnie was usually given the first crack at anything going. For some reason though, this time I was told I could have the first choice of coats! Now, young as I was, I was well aware that size didn't come into it for we were both the same size and build. So, would you believe that a seven year old would reason this way.......

'That gabardine mac with the belt is super, it's got pockets and isn't faded or worn anywhere....but the overcoat looks thick and warm! But hang on, Mam says Our Ronnie isn't very strong and he feels the cold a lot.....but if he isn't very strong why does he beat me in fighting?'

That did it. I went for the warmth of the overcoat!! Ron couldn't wait to get his mac on and, as he pulled the belt tight he looked smashing! Coming to just below his knees and promising protection from the icy blasts, for all the boys in those times wore short trousers. Ah well, I thought, his coat may look smashing but mine will be warmer! With this as consolation and trying not to feel too envious as to how well the by now parading Ronald looked, I put my coat on........only to find that the previous owner had suffered, or so it would seem from the evidence presented, from a permanently runny nose, and it would also seem, he never carried a hanky! There, for all the world to see, was the biggest, thickest, slickest SNOT smear, all the way down the right sleeve, 3 inches long by 2 inches wide! Oh well, these things happen, and so to hide the blighted sleeve I developed a walk when wearing the coat of carrying my arm twisted inwards to the back, this way hiding my own personal stigma. Of course it drew many a pitying glance from passers-by, and muffled comments of,

'Poor child must have been deformed from birth!'

And so that particular cup of happiness was full.....or was it!

1935 definitely wasn't to be my year for, do you remember that as a child I'd broken my collar bone? Well, I was then to find out that the weight of that lovely thick coat was such that within a few minutes of wearing it, a dull throbbing ache would develop which soon became an agonising pain where the collar bone had knitted together, and so I could only wear the coat for very short periods. Even today, 60 years on, I cannot wear a very heavy coat. I think it was about this time I began to suspect who the Dillon of the family, after Our Mabel, really was.......!

The Goldfish:

'Ragga bone; any old Ragga bone?'

That familiar cry of yesteryear, whose echoes can still be heard to this day, reverberated through our poor living room that early morning. How those men, and sometimes women, made a living even today still confounds me but that piercing cry, so much a part of those days, heralded the arrival of those whose bread & butter depended upon discarded rubbish which by rights should've gone into the dustbin, never to be resurrected. It was a health hazard sitting, as all the rubbish did, on the open cart. The Rag Man would take virtually anything that might raise a few coppers. God knows where he took the bottles, rags, stinking rabbit skins etc., etc., and rumour had it the Rag Men would also dispose of dead dogs & cats by selling them to people keeping pigs (and quite a lot of people did), to be boiled up in swill coppers along with tasty items like old cabbage leaves, rotten potatoes and discarded pieces of 'gone off' fish crawling with maggots, from the local chippy! Please don't mix 'Rag & Bone' people up with the itinerant tinkers around today who litter the countryside with their discarded junk. No! In the main these were ordinary people, the poorest of the poor, trying to earn a copper or two to buy a crust of bread, knowing that in the job market, they had no chance. Usually, they would start with a rusty, worn out perambulator, (pram) the body of which tilted at a crazy angle due to one or more of the springs collapsing. This put all the dead weight onto the wheels, and so within a very short time the wheels would buckle alarmingly, squealing in protest through lack of oil, threatening at every turn to fall off, and often doing just that, leaving the sweating, cursing Rag Man to hammer it back as best as he could with a brick end. For the irregular Rag Man, a small hand cart could be hired from the firm which hired carts out to the 'Moonlight Flitters' dodging the rent man! Sometimes, (but rarely) the Rag Man would make a go of it and graduate to a horse & cart but those with horses never spared the poor brutes. More often than not they were rejects no-one else wanted: old, broken winded, with sores, near lame, and made to pull loads of such a weight that at times it seemed those pulling the two wheeled cart would be lifted into the air. It was common to see these poor brutes, having fallen to the ground, being lashed and whipped by the driver, trying to get them back onto their feet before the police came and stopped the cruelty. Like most kiddies, Mais, Ron and I were great pet fanciers (that is until the novelty wore off) and be about right, you can't do much with minnows or tadpoles which we knew would end up down the lavatory anyway when Mam got fed up with the mess we made with the water.

'Ragga Bone, Ragga Bone, Gold fish for Ragga Bone!'

That did it, and so before the man could disappear up the street we dashed indoors, rushed to the bottom of the stairs and shouted up,

'Mabel, have we got any old rags, (That's a laugh, we were mostly wearing them!) We want to get a goldfish!?'

Mabel called back,

'I don't know!'

But then dragging herself to the top of the stairs and seeing our crestfallen faces said,

'Have a look in the kitchen; Mam said she was going to put some old bits of cloth out for dusters!'

Into the kitchen we sped with Mabel's, 'And bring them back if there aren't enough for a fish!' ringing in our ears.

It was better than we'd ever imagined for there on the old kitchen table was quite a pile of cloths which were scooped up by one whilst the others hunted around for a jam jar to put the fish in should we have enough bits! Out into the street we sped, all out of breath!

'Here Mister, please can we have a goldfish for these?'

The man took the small pile proffered, pawed over them whilst we waited with baited breath. No way was he going to push us off with one of those small celluloid whistles handed out to those unfortunates not able to provide the amount of rags for a fish! We had our orders from Mabel!!!!

With never a word said, the man pushed our items into a bag tied to the handlebars of the cart and scooped out one goldfish to be placed in our jam jar aquarium! We set off back home surrounded by a hoard of less fortunate who hadn't been able to do business with the man, all oohing & ahhhing and crooning,

'Let's see your goldfish then?'

Fame at last!

It was too good to last though. Mabel met us at our gate, quite clearly upset and hanging onto the fence, ashen faced and trembling. We didn't need to be told it wouldn't take much to send her over the brink thus bringing on one of her terrible coughing and haemorrhaging bouts.

'Have you moved any of my clothes?' she asked!

'No Mabel' we chorused, 'Do you want to see our goldfish?'

'I can't find my underclothes' she went on, 'I left them on the side of the kitchen sink; Mam was going to wash them out for me!'

'We haven't seen them Mabel, honest we haven't; we'd tell you if we had, but we haven't! All we did was take those old things off the kitchen table like you told us we could!'

It was at this point we realised..........now we knew why the Rag Man had so eagerly handed over the precious goldfish which in normal circumstances would've needed far more than our small pile of rags to claim!

I will explain........ Before the bad times really hit us with the desertion of the Old Man, Mabel had spent many weeks at a time in the sanatorium where she began to develop an interest in and talent for embroidery. She'd graduated to working on her pure silk camiknickers, which were purchased for her as gifts by various aunts and uncles. The undies when finally finished were beautiful; worked with various coloured silk threads into rose buds, lily of the valley, violets and pansies. Today they'd be worth a lot of money but to her then, they were beyond price as they were the flowers she'd known and loved in the garden of the house from where we'd been evicted. She loved flowers so much but was never to see or smell them again in our reduced circumstances. Just in case our worst fears were groundless we turned that kitchen upside down, looking and hoping, but they weren't there.

I can't speak for the other two but I was terrified, for I could see Mabel was getting more and more upset and I dreaded the onset of another haemorrhage caused by grief and anger, not to mention fear of what Our Mam would give us when she came home and discovered what we had done, however innocently! We just flew out of the house! Up and down the street we ran, goldfish in the jar and its contents hugged tight. God, if we dropped it now! I bet the poor creature was sea sick with the motion of our haste. Everyone we passed, received the same hurled question,

'Please Mister/ Missus, has a Rag and Bone Man come this way?'

Drawing a negative or don't know, from the bemused recipient of our questioning. And then finally,

'Yes! He's in the next street!'

And he was, we'd found him! Frantically, we pushed the jam jar and its contents at him with,

'Please mister, we made a mistake! You've got Our Mabel's best undies; they were only out for washing!'

He knew alright, for without even touching the trash in his cart, he reached into the sack tied to his handlebars and took out Mabel's pretties, already tied together into a neat bundle. They were never going to go to the rag sorters with the rest of the rubbish! Reluctantly, wistfully, we held out the jam jar with its precious contents in exchange for that little bundle of silk. He took the fish and the jar. Now, jam jars would fetch a halfpenny if handed in..... and the halfpenny purchased two little farthing sweets, but he just took the jar and fish and said nothing.

'Please mister......' began Our Ronnie!

'Yes?' snapped the Rag Man!'

'We gave you some other bits of cloth with those things!' No prizes for guessing who got a lousy little celluloid whistle, that didn't whistle anyway! Our luck was still holding; the bad luck that is........!

A New Year; New Challenges:

The winter as such had nearly passed. It's a shame the same couldn't be said for the bad phase we were going through! I can't remember what, if anything we had for Christmas that year. I know we must have had a few peanuts, an apple or an orange, and I feel sure I had a small white sugar mouse with a pink nose but I think that was it! How did that song go?

'He's the little boy that Santa Claus forgot!'

There were lots of little boys Santa Claus seemed to miss in those days!

Now it was February, and Ronnie and I were under Maisie's supervision, struggling along the main road in the direction of the local sanatorium. It was a nightmare of hail, freezing sleet and rain, all three of which were being driven with blinding force into our faces. The freezing grains of ice felt like bullets being driven into our brains and my forehead was so cold I couldn't feel it, even when I tried rubbing the circulation back with my red, freezing hand. The road inclined upwards but we couldn't be too sure even about that for if we opened our tightly closed eyes the force of the storm forced us to close them again! The sky was jet black what little we could squint up and see of it! The trams and buses didn't seem to run along this road and even if they did, we had no money to pay the fare. I couldn't stop shivering; my poor inadequate clothing gave no protection at all from the blast. My hair was soaking wet through and plastered to my forehead, and I was soaked through to the skin. My shoes had holes in and my socks squelched with each step I took. I'd been crying in my misery and even today I can hear Maisie saying, as she did on that terrible February morning,

'Keep going Our Norm!'

Whether it was shock of hearing our usually domineering Maisie being kind to me I know not, but I did keep going. It was either that or freeze to the pavement. We stumbled on and then,

'We're nearly there! I can see the 'Sanny' gate!'

We knew where we were. This was the hospital for consumptives where Our Mabel had spent so much of her time. I was 7½ years old!

Commander Maisie read out directions from the hospital signpost. We followed the arrows up the main path, turned and entered a swing door, and entered the hospital proper! Oh, the blessed relief; to get out of that storm and enter the warmth of the all-embracing X-ray department. I didn't even mind the smell of the place for once for I knew it wasn't my blistered feet that brought me here. We handed in our doctor's letter, the reason for our being there then, as ordered, we sat as close to the old caste iron radiator as we could get without actually scalding the skin from our flesh. As the steam rose in clouds from our dripping wet clothing, a very officious Sister came into the room and, eyeing us sternly asked,

'Are you children to be X-rayed?'

As young as I was I felt this to be a stupid question as we were the only ones in the room and after all, there were three of us! She then spoke to the lady/ nurse behind the desk and we stood up without being told to do so. This made Sister turn around and look at us more closely. We stared back respectfully, wondering whether she knew Our Mabel, her having been in the Sanny so many times.

There we stood, looking I suppose like three half drowned little mice, hair plastered tight to our heads and puddles forming around us as the melting snow and ice, mixing with the rain, poured down our legs, into our shoes and ran out of the holes in our footwear! We were shedding so much water I swear we could have paddled in it!

'Oh my goodness nurse!' said the Sister, 'These children are soaked to the skin! Get them out of these wet outer clothes at once and try to get them dry!' We got not one, but two lovely nurses to attend to us, tut tutting like nobody's business as we were taken into cubicles, near stripped and certainly I, the youngest, was wrapped in a lovely thick blanket before being deposited once again in front of the radiator to hasten the drying process! I could hear the nurses talking about us and our pitiful condition.

'How could any woman call herself a mother yet allow her children to come all this way unescorted in this weather, and without proper clothing!?'

I wanted so much to say it wasn't Mam's fault; that she hadn't got a halfpenny in her purse to spare! It was all our dad's fault as he'd left us with nothing! But I daren't for fear of being thought cheeky!

After a short wait we were called in, one after the other, and taken into a room filled with machinery; quite dark, airless and almost noiseless except for a low humming sound! In front of me was a large square plate which I was pressed against, my chin resting on the top of it, and I was told to take a deep breath then 'hold it!' I heard a 'click' and that was it! Thankfully, I pulled away from the icy cold plate. I don't know about the others, but the nurse who was ever near me all the time I was there, with films just taken, held them up to a light to make sure they were good enough for a doctor to read before being put into a large folder, paused at mine, looked again, drew a sharp intake of breath, went out of the room and came back with a mug of warm milk which she made me drink to the dregs. I needed little persuasion, I can tell you!

Dressed, warm and dry, in fear and trepidation, we went into the outside world expecting to find things as we'd left them but, trust our funny old weather, now it was as clear and bright almost as a summer's day. We set off home in high spirits.

When Mam came home from work she was worried to death about us. She'd seen that atrocious weather from the factory window yet could do nothing to help us. We needed her wages! Airily, Maisie put her mind at ease!

'It was alright Mam. We didn't even get wet! You feel our clothes if you don't believe us!'

Well, Mam didn't, so she did! Fortunately, the nurses had done a grand job in drying us out. It seemed to satisfy her so we, although only children, kept the secret to ourselves!

Hardly had a fortnight passed since our X-ray session. It was breakfast time of bread and dip before we set off to school. Mam was in the kitchen rushing around as usual, trying to do six things at once before dashing off to work. A good fire was burning in the hearth so when we left the house the living room stairs door could be left open to allow warmth to percolate upstairs to Mabel.

Mais was still in her nightie, staring into the fire. She looked odd to me, and all of a sudden she pitched forward. Had it not been for the big, heavy, old fashioned fireguard she would have fallen into the fire. Ted, who luckily hadn't left for work, picked her up and carried her upstairs back to bed. Mam had to go to work so, after seeing to Maisie's immediate needs, she told her to stay in bed and KEEP WARM! In the meantime, Ron and I were given our orders from big brother to,

'Come straight home at dinner time; put the potatoes on; don't start fighting or when I get in I'll give you both a bloody good hiding!'

Good old Ted! He knew more about child psychology and the control of an unruly child more than anyone before or since!

Poor Mabel, she was very worried and called asking whether she could do anything to help.

'It's alright, Mabel' said Mam, 'we can manage!'

I heard Mam whisper to Ted that Maisie was complaining that her throat hurt and she was hot and feverish. With our finely tuned budget being what it was, it was decided to 'wait & see' what happened. By evening Maisie had white spots at the back of her throat, so one of us was sent post haste to Mr Davidson the chemist for some Permanganate of Potash crystals so she could gargle. Maisie got no better, in fact not only did she get much worse but now a funny smell was noticed in the bedroom. A memory stirred in Mam's mind, of something being passed down from her old Granny, so the doctor was quickly sent for. He came at once as soon as the symptoms were recounted to him. This was in the days before the Hippocratic Oath was replaced with the Hypocrites Oath!

Ron and I were now standing against the old fence made from discarded railway sleepers across the road to our house, looking at our front door which was ajar. Further along the road, approximately 20 – 30 yards, an ambulance was parked, the back doors wide open and around it gathered a small crowd of neighbourhood children and adults. Ambulances and fire engines provided entertainment not to be missed!

A man came out of our front door carrying Maisie wrapped in a blanket followed by Mam carrying a small bundle. They walked past our small row of terraced houses, down the slope to the ambulance and into the back. With no time wasted the ambulance pulled away from the kerb and went hurtling away, alarm bells ringing. Our Mais was sick, very sick, with Diphtheria. Our little family closed ranks without being told! Hours later, Mam came back worn out. She'd had to walk all the way back from the 'Sanny' where Mais was now in strict isolation. Mam slumped in the big arm chair, all white and waxy, as near beat as ever I'd seen her. We got her a cup of tea;

'My God' she said, 'What else can go wrong?'

Without a word Ted passed her a hand delivered letter. It had come whilst she'd been at the 'Sanny' with Mais!

Dear Mrs Hastings, we regret to inform you that your son, Norman Hastings, recently X-rayed at this hospital, has been seen to have a lesion on his right lung and the sputum test taken at that time is positive for Pulmonary Tuberculosis. You should present Norman for admission to this hospital on Saturday. You will be required to pay for his keep whilst he's an in-patient etc., etc.

Groby Road Sanatorium:

I think at this point a lesser mortal than Our Mam would've given up! With no doubt about it, that dreadful trek up to the 'Sanny' a few weeks back had set Maisie up for the Diphtheria, and ME and my TB? Well I must have been infected long before then. Poor Mabel, her heavily infectious sputum and killing cough spraying the germs into the air, had made a mockery of the repeated warnings,

'Don't use Mabel's cutlery or her drinking mug'.

I must have been infected long before the warning cotton was tied around every item poor Mabel had used.

Let's be clear on one thing right now, THERE WAS NO MEDICAL CURE FOR CONSUMPTION. IF YOU RECOVERED IT WAS LOOKED UPON ALMOST AS A MIRACLE, and even then your lungs would be so scarred and pitted that a relapse was always on the cards. I have often wondered, was it just a coincidence that the largest cemetery in the county just happened to be sited next to the 'Sanny', or vice versa?! By this time cremation was getting very popular so, depending on wind direction, it doesn't take much imagination to guess what the feelings were of patients, considering they knew they were probably on a losing streak anyway.

After the Second World War this hospital for consumptives was full of ex-servicemen who'd contracted TB (Consumption) and there were dozens outside, waiting to be admitted. The number who survived could be counted on the fingers of one hand. I know, for I was to be one of the lucky ones, but that was in the future after I reached maturity.

The appointed Saturday arrived. I can't remember if I'd been told I was going to hospital; if I had, it didn't worry me unduly. I had my dinner in the normal way after being scrubbed and cleaned until I swear I shone! Clean clothes were put on me and always, when being prepared for anything special, Our Ted's bony finger was hooked under my chin and my head tilted back at an impossible angle whilst he put a parting in my hair. Never once whilst performing this simple service for me did he meet my enquiring gaze, nor use his favourite expression used at times such as this,

'Keep your bloody head still or I'll give you a bloody good hiding!'

That alone should've told me I was in bad trouble!

Then it was time to go. I clearly remember it being a truly lovely day. The sun had been shining and a gentle breeze was wafting the curtains of the living room. The window was open, I think because Mabel was downstairs with us and we had to watch those germs, although we never let on to her. The tenseness in the air had got through to me and I wanted to get off, otherwise I was going to start to cry. I had a new comic pushed down the side of my sock, a favourite place in those days of short trousers. On the floor was a small attaché case, although where that had come from, God only knows! I suppose it was borrowed. It contained only pyjamas and this puzzled me, for you see the penny hadn't dropped I was going to be admitted to the 'Sanny.'

I'd been thinking along the lines of,

'I'll be coming home in a few hours' and,

'Why have I got pyjamas?' After all, Ronnie and I slept with Ted, he in his vest and we in our shirts.

Mam came and stood looking down at me. I gazed back at her trying hard to smile. I didn't quite make it!

She sighed and said something along the lines of.... What with Mais in the 'Sanny' as well as you Norman, it'll make visiting that much easier! VISITING?!! I knew now; I was staying in the 'Sanny!

147

The living room door from the kitchen opened and my dear sister Mabel dragged herself in. She was hard put to be able to breathe and her eyes were red. She stumbled into the big chair under the window. Had she been crying? I wondered, why? Why do people shed tears often without good reason? (Much as I'm doing now)

Mam had her poor threadbare coat on now and was checking to see she had a copper or two in her purse. She didn't seem to want to move very far and her face was crumbling as though she too was holding back the tears. Mam picked up that little case and then said those words that even today brings me out fighting.

'Ah well, there's plenty worse off than us!'

I went over to Our Ted and lifted my face to be kissed, and was told very gruffly,

'Now, you just behave yourself!'

Then Our Ronnie kissed me. (Then he pretended to spit)

I looked around for Our Mais to kiss,........then I remembered where she was so looked at Mam enquiringly! You see we'd been told that we mustn't catch Our Mabel's breath, mustn't use her cutlery, drink out of her mug, and yet Mabel, slight frail little Mabel, was leaning forward so expectantly, that I didn't know for a split second what to do! She was looking at me as though it was to be the last time she'd see me, ever, and the way things were at that age, that wasn't outside the bounds of possibility either! Mabel spoke in that husky soft voice of hers, a voice in which I discerned a 'catch,' for she must have known that the odds were I'd caught the disease from her!

'Aren't you going to kiss me Norman?'

Well, there's not very much in life I've done I'm proud of, but what I did then makes me put my chest out. I pulled my hand out of Mam's hand, ran to my sister, threw my arms around her, and kissed her. I set the memory of that kiss among my dearest memories.

After a journey that took us first into town by tram, we then caught another which let us off at the terminus. 10 minutes' walk later we arrived at the 'Sanny'. Now the sun was shining perfectly as opposed to how it'd been just a short time before when we had the blizzard conditions.

The Sanatorium was the most imposing place, both from outside and inside, and as we passed along, guided by the signposts, we passed a great expanse of green lawn surrounded by various brick built wards. Mam pointed out to me the isolation building wherein Our Maisie was incarcerated. No-one but nursing staff were allowed in that ward. Visitors had to try to make themselves understood by shouting or miming through the windows. Many of the patients in there were very ill indeed, including Our Mais.

A lovely story emerged many years later:

Some 55 years after being in the Diphtheria Ward, Mais was in a Club talking to some friends when a woman in her late 50s sat at their table. Maisie got into conversation with this woman, and then clawed at the woman's blouse near the neck saying,

'I recognise you, you're baby Phyllis!'

The woman, obviously thinking she was in the company of a mad woman said,

'Well, my name is Phyllis but I'm certainly no baby!'

'It is you!' said Our Maisie, 'Here's the tracheotomy scar on your throat; you were in the 'Sanny' with me in 1935; you were only a baby and like me you had Diphtheria!'

'That's right; said Phyllis, 'but I don't remember anything about it, I was too young!'

'I know', said Maisie, 'but I saved your life!

Apparently, whilst the nurse was out of the ward baby Phyllis had started choking because in her delirium she'd dislodged the tracheotomy tube from her throat. Maisie saw what happened and started to scream for the nurse but nurse hadn't heard her. Maisie explained how she did no more than jump out of bed and push the tube back into the baby's throat! Maisie would have been about twelve or thirteen at the time. It says much for her common sense at that age.....although I must confess it would have been hilarious if it hadn't been baby Phyllis that Our Mais was mauling! She probably would've got locked up!

Some 60 years later, the ward I was taken to was still there at time of writing. Ward 10, although its usage had long since been altered to that of store room.

It was a long single storey block of small two bedroom cubicles, fronted by a long glass veranda. The ward was divided into two, with a Sister's office and nurses' minor treatment room in the middle. As to be expected, it was men on one side and women on the other. The cubicles were just large enough to contain two single iron, black painted, hospital beds against the opposite wall, a small bed locker cum wash stand, and at the foot of the bed a single wardrobe. So far as I was aware the cubicle itself was only used if the patient was very ill or dying, which at that time and in that place, amounted to much the same thing. For the rest, the beds were always outside on the 'open to the elements' veranda; winter or summer, rain, hail, or shine. Many times during those first few weeks, I would awaken in the early morning with the late frost freezing my face. In all truth, I don't remember feeling the cold and certainly, it did me no harm, although I bet all of those nasty little consumption germs I was carrying took an awful bashing. I can't begin to tell you how wonderful it is to wake up on an early spring morning, literally in the open air, with the dawn chorus ringing and singing, whilst the early morning breeze blows the scent of wallflowers and recently cut grass across the dew laden air.

If these conditions seem harsh and primitive, well let me tell you that some 12 years later I saw a Sanatorium in Norfolk where the patients lived in little wood huts scattered around a field, each containing one bed, nothing much else. There was no heating in winter or summer. The huts were mounted upon a turn table and the only concession made to the weather was that if things were very bad then the hut was turned around so the stable style door faced away from the icy blast.

At the back of Ward 10 was a corridor and leading off this were some toilets and bathroom. Any patient who died (and there were quite a few) were taken out this back way, washed, plugged and shrouded. During my time in the 'Sanny' I never witnessed any of these sad processions but nothing could mask the noise of the enamel buckets and swishing of water as some poor soul was prepared for his or her trip next door. Perhaps the most terrible aspects of the consumptive's final few hours was that so often the patient seemed to be picking up on the last day, almost right up to the end. The appetite lost for so long would return, they would find the strength to laugh and joke, and then the haemorrhaging would start from the chest and lungs via the mouth, and the eyes would start from the head, as the poor soul would begin that last terrible fight to get some air into the near non-existent lungs. Then perhaps a merciful needle.....not to prolong but to end....and after, the slushing water, the clanking bucket and the strong smell of the strongest disinfectant before cleaned & sealed, the last rites were performed, and the shrouded body was ready, first for the mortuary and then to be sealed in its wooden cell, in the earth for all eternity.

Over the centre of the administration block on Ward 10 was a slab engraved upon which were the words 'Hospital for Consumptives.' In those days it should have said 'ABANDON HOPE ALL YE WHO ENTER HERE!' Going under that engraving to be admitted upon my first day that early spring in 1935, I shivered. Nearly 50 years later whilst keeping death watch over Our Mam who was lying in a newer ward just below the by now disused Ward 10, I walked across and reread the words upon that old plaque, aware I was soon to lose her. I walked on and saw again the little cubicle I'd occupied as a child all those years earlier. I then walked further along to what in those days had been the women's side. In 1947 this ward had been turned over to an all-male ward and was the cubicle I'd occupied myself for a second term of consumption, along with so many young ex-servicemen. I thought of the thousands who'd known the ward and those cubicles before death gave them merciful release. Consumption had been beaten eventually but too late for them.

I remembered Johnny Pugh, Frankie Jordan and Carter, a man who, having had drastic surgery in 1947 had asked for, was given and now carried around, one of his own ribs! I remembered Juddie, Nurse Gilbert, Staff Carr and

Ted Birkin. Finally, I remembered Jackie Murgatroyd, my cell/ room-mate in 1947, who died like the brave lad he was. And so I stood in the gathering twilight and silently called the roll of honour, and wept for those dear friends, so long gone, and for she who I was about to lose in June 1983 – My Mam.

Sister and Nurse Gilbert were on duty that Saturday afternoon in 1935 and another nurse, Nurse Carr, who stabbed me in the wrist drawing off what seemed to be gallons of black looking blood. After this I was handed over to Nurse Gilbert whilst Mam and Sister went off into another room to effect the handing over of yours truly into Sister's care. It was at this point Mam paid off the first instalment of my keep. I knew belts would be tightened in the Hastings' household for the next few months.

Nurse Gilbert took me first into the ablutions block. She filled the largest bath I'd ever seen with hot soapy water and then, without even a by your leave, I was stripped and dipped and thoroughly scrubbed! I can still smell that rich, soapy, steamy, carbolic smelling hospital bathroom to this day even though most of my time in the bath was spent with me telling Nurse Gilbert Mam had already washed me down thoroughly only that morning! Cleaner than clean, I was then rubbed dry with a coarse hospital towel until blood was very nearly drawn, and then finished off with several big smacking kisses. I decided then that I was going to like Nurse Gilbert.

Years later Mam told me that besides having a large cavity in the top of my lung, they'd found neither lung was drawing properly and both were in a near state of collapse. (Trust me to go the whole hog!) Not to put too fine a point on it, a lot of expert chest doctors were shaking their heads and 'tut, tutting' over yours truly's chest X-rays! Frankly, had I known I wouldn't have been too bothered because:

a) I felt very well thank you very much and b) I was now madly in love with dear Nurse Gilbert.

Poor Mam, now mithered to death, she set off to visit Maisie in the Isolation Ward (Only looking through windows at patients permitted!) Now I had the time to weigh up Sister Moore more closely. First thing I noticed was that Sister had a big wart on her chin from whence several long hairs protruded. She had a stiffly starched grey cap on her iron grey hair and this was tied under her chin with a pretty lace bow. Her uniform was also grey and around her waist was a belt with an elaborate silver buckle. That wart was what attracted and fascinated me most, and my eyes went back to it even though Our Mam had told me so many times,

'It's rude to stare!'

I realised all had gone very quiet and, on raising my eyes my gaze met Sister's head on. I smiled shyly, nervously, the whole time holding her eyes with my own and then just for a split second I saw in her eyes the same something I'd seen in Wag's mother's eyes whenever she looked at him, no matter how naughty he'd been, and I knew everything would be all right; for deep down this was a very kind and caring lady who liked children and this was an all-male, mostly adult male, ward. Guess who was going to benefit? Those deeply penetrating eyes that could put the most difficult adult patients and visitors back into line, had given her away!

'Now, Norman' she began. 'I've explained to your mother that for us to stand any chance of getting you better, you will be absolute bed!'

This bothered me not one jot because I had no idea what 'absolute bed' meant! It meant of course that once I was in bed, I was to stay in bed, and not get out! Some hope!!

I was put to bed in a two bed cubicle next to the Sister and Nurses station. I felt very lonely and frightened. Mam had gone, so had Sister, and so I did what every small boy does in those circumstances.....I put my head under the sheets and had a good cry, emerging only after various sounds and then voices told me that others were now in the cubicle with me. This habit of diving under the bed clothes had developed from the rows and upsets I must've been party to as a very small child when the Old Man was in one of his mad rages. Red eyed from my weeping I now saw the other bed was about to be occupied by another youngster about a year younger than me. He was now introduced as Frankie Jordan!

'Say hello to the other little boy, Frankie dear!'

In answer, Frankie dear put out his tongue at me! Although Frankie's mum assured me she thought her treasure and I were going to be the very best of friends, well frankly, I had my doubts!

The dear boy's mum then departed holding a hankie to her face whilst Frankie went under the bedclothes to have a good cry, just like I'd done. We soon settled in however and with the mums out of the way in came Sister to read us the house rules. It was just like being back at home: Don't do this and don't do that......and then the biggy.....AND DON'T GET OUT OF BED! Sister then played what she saw as her trump card by producing a large tin whilst at the same time informing us,

'This is my sweets tin and if you disobey me the magic will go out of it and the tin will not fill up with a fresh lot of sweets after the first lot are eaten!'

I don't know about Frankie but I was more than prepared to go along with that load of rubbish about magic if it meant sweeties at the end of the day! Sister then departed. In a flash Frankie was out of his bed. (We were inside at that point and so not overlooked) He fished about in his locker and took out a box of wooden play bricks which I thought were rather babyish for a boy of his age. Caught red handed, for Sister, who was wise to the ways of young boys, had simply stood just outside our cubicle! So, we said 'goodbye' to our lockers. I have to confess here and now that I'm not complaining injustice that my locker went as well, for Sister had caught me also; not quite fully out of bed but lying feet still in bed, stomach on the flat seat of my locker, groping around to see if the previous tenant had left anything worth having that I might claim. In bed for three minutes and one strike down: 'One up to Sister!'

Frankie was still holding onto his box of square wooden bricks so I asked whether he didn't think they were rather babyish? In reply he threw one of them at me which, in retaliation, I threw back, hitting him on the forehead and drawing a smidgeon (pin prick) of blood! His howls would have woken the dead, which I would've preferred rather than what they did do ie bring Sister in post haste! I bet her backside hadn't touched her chair from the first episode! Three or so minutes since we'd been told 'absolute bed' and now we'd both had a monumental 'bollocking' from Sister! Not bad, eh!? I wouldn't have minded so much but behind Sister's back Frankie was laughing like a drain, and my Nurse Gilbert who'd just appeared at the door, was obviously on Sister's side!

'You just wait Frankie Jordan' I was thinking.

Revenge is sweet though and, as those who were now in charge of us disappeared out of the door, I could see I was going to get my revenge almost at once, for on the wall behind each of our beds was a red emergency button which we'd been warned by Sister not to tinker with; a plan began to form in my scheming, devious brain.

'Frankie?' I began 'Why don't we play a game of throwing one of your wooden bricks to each other and see if we can catch it!'

I then pointed out there was a gap of about 5 feet between our beds and this would make things more interesting in the catching. To my joy he fell for it! Little did he know........

Frankie tossed the brick to me; I tossed it back. He threw the brick at me etc., etc. Then I threw a short one and the brick rolled under Frankie's bed.

'You threw it, so you can get it!' said my little chum.

'Not likely' said rotten old me 'they're your bricks so you can get it out!' Stymied, Frankie could only glare at me. I had him and he knew it. First of all he leaned out of bed and, supporting himself with one arm on the floor, he leaned right over to an impossible angle trying to get his brick back. But no go; it was right up against the wall, as was his bed. Red in the face, he tried again and then gave up!

'Come on' he said 'you threw it, you ought to get it; fair's fair.'

Of course I refused! Beaten, he whispered,

'Can you hear if that Sister's coming?' I assured him all was quiet. He gingerly crept out of bed, the whole while casting anxious glances to see or hear if Sister was coming.

'It's all quiet' I hissed, and now committed, he dived right under the bed so all I could see was his bare little bum sticking up in the air as he groped about. You've guessed it; I had already pressed the red emergency bell push and, hardly had I had the time to take my finger off the button when Sister was in the room. She didn't make a sound nor did she hesitate for, seeing the bare soles of his feet and his even barer bottom, she took a 'gosh' almighty swipe at it. Frankie squealed and shot back from under the bed, so fast he cracked his head on the iron bed frame.

Sister was breathing blue fire!

'You naughty, naughty boy! What did I tell you about staying in your bed; and YOU..... don't touch that alarm button under any circumstances, it's for emerg........'

Here, she stopped short, puzzled. She looked first at the by now bawling Frankie Jordan, then she looked at my bell push, then squarely at me! I waited for the ceiling to fall in on me or for the lightning bolt to strike! Thinking hard, she again looked from one to the other of us and, meeting my, 'please miss, it wasn't me' gaze, I swear a look of admiration went over her face. This, she checked, before it turned into a grin and, turning on her heels, she left us to get on with it!

The revised score was now Frankie Jordan ONE; Norman Hastings ONE!

By tea time, having lost our lockers, Frankie's play bricks and then the hospital ear phones (we'd discovered we could unscrew them but sadly, not put them back together again as per Arthur and the wireless) our little room looked rather bare. Verdict? All in all, a very uneventful day!

I was settling in rather nicely; I was being X-rayed regularly which bothered me not at all but what I didn't like was the drawing off of my blood which was always taken from my wrist where the pulse lays. The thermometer was in my mouth rarely, if ever; they always put it under my arm or between my legs up in the groin. This I enjoyed not because of where it was but because Nurse Gilbert had to bend right over me to place it there and I was able to enjoy what little perfume she wore.

The X-ray was by way of 'Tone O gram'. This is where, whilst lying flat on a couch, the machine is passed back and forth over the body at all angles. I was told this measured the depth of cavity on my lung.

One day I was told a concert party was going to perform on the expanse of greenery near to Ward 10, and that I was going to be taken, bed and all, to see the show. That afternoon, my bed was pushed by a porter from the veranda (we were sleeping outside our room full time now) and deposited on the path. I was under one of those flowering cherry type trees just against a lovely little chapel with wide door type windows that could be opened whilst the consumptive patients were inside at service. For the same reason I was quite alone on the path. I was 'catching' and so in isolation, as it were. I was facing a huge expanse of grass, segregated from the other patients who were not infectious. It was a lovely spring day and I was all set to enjoy the free entertainment, however, I was so far back I couldn't hear a thing although I could see some pretty costumes far away. Ah well! I settled down in my bed and went fast asleep. I must have looked a sight when Nurse Gilbert and the porter came to fetch me, covered as I was with blossom from the tree; I was inches deep in the stuff!

What a very angry Nurse Gilbert said to the porter was something along the lines of,

'You could've stayed with him to make sure he could hear!'

It was around then Our Maisie recovered from Diphtheria and was sent home. It was also the Silver Jubilee year of Old King George V and Queen Mary. We children in hospital got a medal, a real 'wear it on your chest' medal! I soon lost mine (or did Mam sell it to help pay for my keep in that place?) If she did, she was welcome to it as she needed all the help she could get. Wag was brought in to see me on that special day and we had a photograph taken by Frankie's mum. The bed was trimmed up and Frankie had been put in it with me whilst Wag was sitting on the end of it. The photo was lost; I do regret that.

Although we were rarely inside our cubicle, an elderly lady who came very regularly to scrub it out decided once our visitors had gone that we kids needed cheering up and, pointing to an old chap walking in the gathering twilight, tried to kid us he was the KING! I knew at once that he wasn't, for he wasn't wearing a crown!!!!

Mam always came to see me at least once a week, either Saturday or Sunday. We lived two long tram rides away and she couldn't afford the fares for more than one visit. The Old Man always came on a Thursday afternoon but it was always Mam who opened her purse to pay Sister for my keep. I don't think he paid a penny for my keep ever, even in hospital. He would constantly ask question after question though; about the family he'd abandoned. 'Pumping' we called it!

I used to hate his big smacking kisses, full on the mouth. They were more the kisses of a lover than a father and always, his bristly chin and cheeks rubbing and sticking in. It was like being kissed by a warm, sucking pin cushion.

On one particular afternoon the Old Man had hardly sat down before he said, 'Did you know your uncle Jack is dead?' (straight from the hip – no messing!) Uncle Jack (26) was Mam's youngest brother. On the day in question, a Saturday, he'd been playing cricket for his firm (Smith Faire, St Saviours Road, Leicester) and he'd done more than his fair share of the bowling even though he'd suffered from heart palpitations for years. That evening along with his young lady, they'd gone to the old city cinema in the Market Place. During the performance he'd slumped against his young lady who'd called for help, and he was carried out. Jack's sister (my aunt Annie) believed people were under the impression he'd fainted, as they kept pushing his head between his legs. Whatever, he was pronounced dead at the Leicester Royal Infirmary. (LRI)

I know that on having had this news broken to me so gently by 'dear papa', I showed little or no reaction, being so young, too young really to take it in at the time. That night as usual Nurse Gilbert carried me into the bathroom where she'd already run a lovely warm bath. Some of the soap must have gone into my eye and it began to run, setting off a chain reaction, for I began to blub in earnest. Nurse Gilbert was quite upset and wrapped me in a towel and sat me on her knee; giving me a cuddle and 'there, thereing' as hard as she could. Finally I piped down. Poor Nurse Gilbert, she must have wondered whether it was something she'd done!

'Norman, whatever is the matter?' she asked.

I could only blurt out,

'Please Nurse Gilbert, I think my Uncle Jack is dead!

'Ooooh, you are a funny boy' she said, 'don't you know?'

'Well, my dad says he is' was my reply 'but my Mam says he's such a bloody liar you can't believe a word he says!'

As far as I can remember, I was still on no treatment, unless you counted the regular pushing up of the pyjama sleeve and the drawing of blood from the wrist. In fact, I was so blasé about the needle I rarely lifted my eyes from my comic whilst the procedure was being carried out. However, one day I was wheeled away in my bed, past the Sister's room, to the women's side of the ward and into a room...... still in my bed. From here I was lifted onto a couch and told to lie on my side. What set me off was the size of the needle the doctor had in his hand and guess who was going to get that!! They had to hold me down for I think it went in my side at waist level, and certainly it went in deep! My screams and shouts nearly set the lady patients off rioting; the things they were shouting at that poor doctor. Afterwards Sister Moore called me 'a baby' and even Nurse Gilbert sniffed hard when she passed my bed, ignoring me completely. Years later, dear lovely Sister Moore and my beloved Nurse Gilbert, I confess it didn't hurt and I was a baby! Please can I have that day's sweetie now? PS I love you both, and Sister Carr!

After two months, three weeks and four days, I was as near to perfect health as I could be. Mam was told I could go home but I still had that lesion on the top of my lung and would have for the rest of my life. I saw that lesion for the first time on X-rays when I was 64 years old. This was after triple bypass surgery. Not to worry though, the sputum was clear!

Years later I realised that, although poor Mabel had probably passed on the TB infection, she had also given me, as it were, a sort of protection, for over those first 7 years of my life I had absorbed quite a few of her germs. When the grand slam did come I had a certain immunity which had built up and now allowed me to fight this beastly disease. All I have to show for it now, apart from a thick medical dossier and many, many memories, is a scarred lung that bothered me not one iota through all the changing scenes of my life.

Getting me ready for discharge wasn't too difficult. On the Thursday, Sister came along to my bed and placed my clothes upon it.

'Get dressed' she said, 'and sit on the edge of your bed just to get the feel of things!'

After I was dressed I sat swinging my legs whilst being watched by Frankie. 'Right' said Sister, 'You're to walk slowly down the ward. Don't run, just take your time!'

Off I set, being greeted by the adult male patients who up until then had just been figures in the distance. I wonder now how many of those poor souls, coughing and spitting up their lungs more and more every day, managed to get out? Not many I should imagine! After half an hour I was returned to my bed. Friday was a repeat of Thursday, and then the great day finally arrived.....SATURDAY – GOING HOME DAY! On the last morning, dear old Nurse Gilbert gave me my last bath. She was very quiet. At around 2pm the Old Man arrived........and would you believe it, he was on his old motor bike! Sister was flaming mad!

'Can you believe it?' I heard her saying to Nurse Gilbert, 'Three months absolute bed and he arrives on a motor cycle to take the child home!'

It should be noted she used the term 'child', and not the patient or Norman! Already, like Nurse Gilbert, she was distancing herself from me. One of the last presents the Old Man gave me was a sword with a bright red handle guard, painted on which was a skull. I can clearly remember the Old Man saying, as he lifted me on the pillion of that infernal smelly machine,

'For Christ's sake, don't get that bloody sword caught in the back wheel or we'll both come off!'

I didn't, but it was a close thing! With my pyjamas tied around my neck and the sword thrust through my belt, we set off. I don't think I even had time to say 'goodbye' to my fellow bed mate, Frankie Jordan! I hope he made it; I will probably never know! I was going home! My eyes were full of tears, not from emotion, but from the wind that tore at me as we sped to my home. I hung on like grim death. The Old Man didn't take me right into Morton Road, instead he dropped me just past the old Shaftsbury picture house (cinema) giving me on parting one of those big, smacking, sucking kisses; all bristly and horrid! I ran as fast as my wobbly legs would carry me down the road, around the corner and up the entry, bursting in. They were all there, just as though I had never been away; faces beaming and shining with joy! Dear Mabel was smiling the most. Oh Mabel, I would give everything I own just to see your face again; so full of happiness at seeing your little brother return home. Bless you! I was back to poor food, poor housing, poor clothing but that's how I wanted it. I WAS HOME!

Following my discharge from 'the sanny' I was very shaky and come Monday morning at around 9:30am I was in the living room. All the family (bar Mabel) were out: Mam & Ted at work; Ron & Maisie at school. I could hear Mabel moving around upstairs, getting ready to come down for a wash in the kitchen sink. A bathroom? You must be joking! It was only me downstairs.

A loud knock came at the back door and I answered it to find a man in uniform standing there. I recognised the uniform even though neither he nor any member of his authority had ever had cause to call upon us before. It was the dreaded 'Boardman' – the representative of the Education Department who set every kid in the neighbourhood running for dear life, even though they may have a perfectly genuine reason for being out of school!

'Are you Norman Hastings?' he asked.

I stared up at him. He was a tall man wearing a dark suit, small peaked cap and cycle clips.

'Please sir, yes sir, I'm Norman Hastings' I answered, trying hard to turn on that smile of mine which could turn Nurse Gilbert's knees to water!

'Humph' he said, 'and why are you not at school little boy, that is what your headmistress would like to know!?'

All of a sudden I wanted to pee because in my family circle the headmistress came somewhere between God the Father and the Holy Ghost!

'Please sir, I only came out of the sanatorium on Saturday and Sister Moore said Our Mam had to take me to the clinic on Regents Road to see the chest doctor before I come back to school. Sister Moore said so!'

(You probably notice I used the Sister's name twice in the hope of frightening him off – it didn't!)

'I know all about that' he said, 'but the headmistress wants you back as soon as possible having missed so much school already.'

Let me say here and now that the man was not nasty or unkind in any way he spoke to me; it was just I was a young boy facing authority for the first time. School authority, that is, and just couldn't cope, so I did the next best thing and resorted to tears. At that moment, Our Mabel dragged herself into the kitchen and seeing me sobbing went 'up in the air!' Panting for breath, she demanded to know if he had nothing better to do than chase a sickly child!? She then enlarged on the theme,

'Can't you see he's as weak as a kitten?'

Honestly, she was weaker than me but she was ready to take this bloke on in mortal combat! I have to add here that on the day before (Sunday) I'd been tearing up and down the street with Wag and Bernard, another friend!

'I only wanted to know when he'll be back in school?' said the man, but by now Our Mabel was really in a 'paddy' and reaching for the brush! Give the bloke his due he could move, because he was off down our entry like a bullet from a gun. Please don't take this as a criticism of the old Boardman, for many battered and abused children counted the Boardman as their defender and only friend. From personal experience I know that when the children were down, the old Boardman never backed down! Years later, when a Boardman myself, I remember talking to my Chief Officer; I asked him, after he'd confided to me that our old home was on, or part of his district around 1935, 'Were you ever given/ do you remember, a monumental 'bollocking' by a little consumptive lass in Morton Road for chasing up her little brother who'd only two days before been discharged from the Groby Road sanatorium?'

The Chief went very red in the face, swung on his heels, and marched off. We never spoke of it again!

I soon got back into the old routine, and honestly, I never thought back to what had passed. For the first few days I stayed at home awaiting my appointment at Regent Road. This was the chest clinic for consumptives where periodically they would be examined by Dr Laurie, a gaunt, pale, skull like sort of man, after an X-ray had first been taken. I think the other big shot there was a Dr Thompson who I cannot remember. The overriding impression I have of Regent Road was a large upstairs room, all white paint, windows open even in the coldest weather, and me shivering with the cold of the breeze and icy stethoscope being pressed to my chest. Breathe in; breathe out, then rap, rap, rap of the doctor's bony fingers as he sounded my chest. His verdict on that first visit after the hospital was,

'Mrs Hastings, your son should go to an open air type school as he will always be susceptible to chest problems.'

Did I go to such as school? Did I hell! Firstly, I would've needed tram fares, and two, well I just didn't know what 'two' was but some three years later when he was singing on the clubs, Our Ronnie went to Western Park Open Air School. How Mam wangled that, don't ask me!

Onward Christian Soldiers:

Our pal, Wag, was a Roman Catholic which meant very little to us except for his stories of how the teaching nuns in his school could swing a really vicious, stinging strap when some brash youngster (Wag) failed to toe the line. As I remember, the nuns had a house on the Mere Road close to Dale Street. Wag served as an altar boy. Religion was never discussed but if all Catholic mums and dads were as kind and caring as his lovely Mam & Dad, then I was all for the Catholic faith! (Although when the mood was on her, Wag's Mam had a tongue like a wasp sting!)

Periodically, the local Sacred Heart Catholic Church held a procession which was well worth seeing, in fact people came from near and far to witness it. It was one of the highlights of the social, as well as church calendar and the streets would be thronged along the processional route. In the lead was a massive cross, as it should be. Next came 'The Sally' (Salvation Army) band belting out hymns with their usual gusto, with banners flying and instruments gleaming as though made of gold and silver. On they marched – God's own: the men wearing their peaked caps whilst the women wore those quaint old fashioned bonnets, at the back of which could be seen their hair, plaited and wound round and around like Catherine wheels. As they marched a few waved as they tapped their tambourine, beribboned and manipulated, whilst keeping time to the music as though tied to a master keyboard, and THEN, right at the very back of the band, the one we were all looking out for, the big drum carrier & beater. Red of face, he brought up the rear of the band, the last but certainly not the least, often as he tired, leaning back at a seemingly impossible angle as he sought to counter balance the drum. Did Our Sweet Saviour, one asked oneself, carry such a burden on his way to martyrdom? Of course, this was long before the days of light plastics, and so should the march be a long one, one other person would pace beside him. He was ready to bear a little of the burden when the beat began to fall off due to that exhaustive weight, for they, or most of them, were on the same poor diets as the rest of us.

Our Mam used to tell a story about a character named 'Ducky' Simms. (In those days a 'ducky' was usually a large stone or brick end for throwing) It seemed that our hero Ducky stood watching an open air Sally Army meeting in Humberstone Gate, Leicester when he got 'carried away' with the SALVATION FEELING! When the meeting ended and they marched off to the Citadel, Ducky marched with them. In the Citadel, those who felt they wanted to repent all their sins were invited to come to the front. Ducky led the few. To everyone's surprise, our hero was there again the next week, and the week after, always at the forefront of those who felt they had been saved until, the Salvationist in charge called Ducky to the penitent's stool and asked him,

'Mr Simms, do you feel true penitence?'

'Yes' shouted Ducky.

'And has this repentance made you happy?" was the next question.

'Happy, of course I'm happy, in fact I'm so bloody happy I feel like kicking a hole in the big drum!'

After the band came the church dignitaries and sideman, each with their wand of office, then the priests in black or crimson cassocks with pure white surplices trimmed with the most intricate lace, then the choir and altar boys, Wag amongst them. Suddenly, Mrs Bishop's little devil looks like an angel as he swung his incense burner. I always tried to get a smell of that incense but never could. Sprinkled within that throng of procession would be the statues and effigies I loved to see. Each would be carried on four shoulder shafts and carried on the shoulders of four very strong men. They had to be strong for those statues were very heavy and they had a long journey ahead. Grave faced they passed by, but proud, for it was counted to be a great honour to carry those effigies of the

Holy ones; Here, the Holy Mother, head downcast adoringly at her blessed son 'Our Lord'. She was dressed in a sky blue cloak under which was a pure white shift. The child, often depicted as naked, gazed up adoringly at his clear eyed mother, one chubby hand outstretched to touch her dear face. The hand as yet unblemished or marked with those terrible nail wounds, his brow still clear of the scratches and tear marks of that final indignity; His crown of thorns. Caught up a moment or two later with the raw emotion of what was now passing, a low moaning sob came from all sides, Catholic and non-Catholic, as we now saw the terrible sight of Christ, carried aloft, nailed to the cross by grotesque nails in hands & feet, the great wound in His side, blood streaming down His poor tortured face from the holes in His head and forehead, made by the crown of thorns crushed down upon His innocent head until it seemed His skull had been pierced. Now we could see a near miracle as the ladies who lined the processional route, rich & poor, Catholic and many non-Catholics, believers and doubters, hesitatingly dropped a knee in a curtsey, whilst the men bowed their heads submissively. Finally, as though to reassure, (and isn't that what Christianity is about) stands Christ the risen Lord, proud and yet so humble, strong & yet so vulnerable. Stood on that rough wooden platform, held so proudly aloft for all men to see if only they would look, to seek, standing in a heap of flowers, so lovingly arranged. Spread throughout the procession were the children, lovingly and proudly dressed, all in white by parents, many of whom going short to provide for this special day. In stark contrast, the nuns accompanying them in their black habits with the stiffly starched pure white cowls framing their faces, all of whom seemed to have peaches and cream complexions. Most of the little ones carried a posy; their dresses were white, sandals were white and white ribbons or flowers adorned their hair. How did the families of these children, so many to my certain knowledge very poor, as poor in fact as the proverbial church mice, manage to get the money together? Perhaps it was the parable of the loaves and fishes in another form?! The boys too were dressed in white; white shirt, white trousers, white sandals. Now we were coming to the end of the procession, so far back that the sound of the band could not be heard, with the men and women walking in silence. The men, red faced and sweating in the warmth of the day, dressed in thick serviceable serge and stiff celluloid easy to sponge collars which sawed into their necks, the wearers no doubt hoping that the end would soon be in sight so they could quench their monumental thirst in the pub. No doubt the 'Father' (priest) would join them, for many of the Fathers liked a drink. With the men came the ladies of the church, sometimes with them, sometimes marching apart. Today when I hear the expression 'the church militant' used, I think of the 'Sally Army' and those Catholic ladies in procession. Many choked with emotion as though at this time they really were going, as others' centuries before had gone, to see their adored one nailed to the cross. Equally, I am sure that had they been at that wicked place of execution, they would soon have put a stop to the murder of an innocent man. Choked with emotion then, the ladies walked, some hand in hand, dressed in black and veiled, the proud and the meek, old grudges forgotten, and then, seemingly spontaneously, breaking into that glorious hymn to Mary the Mother of God........'Ave, Ave, Ave Maria! Had I been in Satan's shoes and had I seen those devoted women advancing upon me as they advanced that day giving witness to their faith, then I think I would have turned and run back to Hades!

Ronnie and I called at Wag's house late upon the afternoon of this great procession and were not at all surprised to be received with the greatest suspicion by his Mam, understandably so for she had spent the best part of the day polishing his face & hands and getting him ready for the procession. It was Sunday afternoon, and Ronnie and I had just returned from the Morton Road Mission Hall Sunday School. We looked pretty presentable so what was the harm in letting those tidy, clean little boys, who now stood before her, in to see 'Our Wag' in all his glory! I think Wag's mother must have temporarily forgotten that 'boys will be boys', either that or she had, without realising it, lost her reason! Wag came at his mother's call and stood beside her in all his processional glory! He looked great! His normally rosy cheeks shone like two apples and his clear, grey eyes fixed on Ronnie and me in turn, daring us to laugh, whilst on his brow was a bead of sweat which Wag was never without. White was definitely his colour; white shirt open at the neck, short white trousers, white knee length socks (as usual with Wag, one was heading down towards his ankle) and, to finish it all off, white sandals. We stood in awed silence surveying the glory that was our 'bestest pal', Wag! His Mam, with her face pouring with perspiration (it must have taken some exertion to get her Wag as clean as that) wiped her face on her apron, impressed with our reaction to the new look 'Wag Bishop'.

'I'm just going to get you a clean hankie, Charlie' she said.

This was a first, calling him by his given name.

'Now, don't you dare move off that step!' She added, thereby proving she HAD temporarily lost her mind!

Next door to Wag's parents' house was Ballard, the Coal Merchant's Yard, where a lorry and various old worn out buses were stored. Running free were lots of hens. They were quite safe as the yard was bounded by high brick walls on two sides, high entrance gates at the front and on the last side, Wag's side, a low brick wall with wooden fencing fastened to the top. It would've been difficult to look over that wall but for the fact that running up alongside it were wooden steps leading up to the loft over Mr Bishop's horse's stable. (Tommy)

Now, as the cock crowed to Peter signalling his denial of Christ, a hen over the wall cackled, which was to lead to Wag's near martyrdom as we shall see. The three of us chimed in chorus,

'That hen's just laid an egg!'

Lay, those hens certainly did, for often we boys would climb halfway up the steps and through the broken windows of the bus just to see the eggs. With an awful feeling of impending doom I followed Wag and Our Ron as they tip toed down the yard and crept up the loft ladder. Please, please Mrs Bishop, I was desperately thinking, come downstairs and see what these two are up to before it's too late! Sadly, my prayers were not answered and so, like a lamb to the slaughter, I joined the pair of them crouching half way up the stairs to the loft. Wag as always, the born leader, was giving us a running commentary....

'I bet it was laid by the one that came out the old bus,' he said,

And then without a by your leave or what do you think chums, he straddled the fence, dropped into the coal yard and, running crouched down to the door of the wrecked bus, he vanished inside.

'You won't half cop it, Wag Bishop' I was whimpering, only to be told by Ron to, 'shut up Our Norm or his Mam'll hear you!'

A moment or two later, which to me seemed like hours, and then to my relief, Wag emerged from the bus. All Ronnie was interested in was,

'Have you got the egg, Wag?'

Nothing came back by way of reply except Wag holding aloft ONE EGG – and he still looked clean! He came to the wall and gazed up at us.

'Give us your hand' he said to Ron, who at once leaned over to such an impossible angle that I was sure he'd go over 'arse over tip'.

'I can't reach you' whispered Wag.

Hardly had the words left his mouth when from the house we heard,

'Charlie, Charlie, where are you? I warn you, if you've dirtied your clothes I promise I'll skin you alive!!'

PANIC STATIONS............Wag took a leap for the top of the fence again but he couldn't hold on with only one hand. (The other was holding the egg!) Again,

'Wag, come here this minute!'

Now, with Wag running back and forth the hens began to panic; dozens of the things squawking loud enough to wake the dead. His Mam wasn't deaf or dead but I had the feeling that if she saw her pride and joy in that coal yard Wag soon would be! That decided him. Going right back he put the egg in the breast pocket of his shirt then took a flying leap up to the top of the wall. Hurrah! He made it, although his body slammed with such force against the wooden partition I quite expected it to collapse. It held. Over he came, joining us as we sprinted up the yard to arrive just in time as his Mam arrived at the back door.

'If you've messed up your clothes Our Charlie, I will kill you, I swea......'

She stopped short. There we stood like three innocent angels, reproach in our eyes! How could she think that in five minutes flat we.......her eyes softened, the kill glare faded....until at that exact moment Wag looked down as he wondered at the sticky feeling at his breast, and saw to his horror, as did she, soaking through that lovely immaculate pristine white shirt, the yellow yolk, closely followed by the white of the egg which had been crushed against the fence boards! It gets worse for the yellow had a nasty greenish tinge to it, and the smell! Be merciful dear reader and allow me to draw a curtain over what happened next!

The Summer of 1935 and the wretched poor:

Summer 1935 seemed to consist of long, scorchingly hot days. Our throats and those of our pals, as we roamed without fear through the lovely countryside, were constantly parched for a long cool drink of water. As the days drew to a close and the early evenings came in, the storm clouds would gather, drawn along by a coolness and great black clouds I've rarely seen since. The feeble breeze would be gone and a great sultry heaviness descended upon the streets. Doors, front and back, would be flung wide open in order to draw some air through, and you could smell the thunder. Accompanying those great heavy clouds could be seen the first flickering's of lightening, and as the storm came ever closer, the streets would begin to clear.

'You'd better run off home Mr/ Mrs or you'll get soaked' was the cry directed at passers-by. Then the elements would take over. A cold wind would get up, followed by the sky darkening as though night had come, then the first heavy splats of rain which, beating down upon an unprotected head, felt like small chips of ice. It was so dark, only relieved by the great shafts of lightening which accompanied deafening rolls of thunder. I cannot remember any storm since that carried so great a turbulence. Mabel would cower under the stairs, terrified, whilst those caught outside ran with coats, and even paper carrier bags, over their heads. They were saturated in no time, for who amongst us had money to buy a proper raincoat or umbrella! Oh, the blessed relief! Afterwards, the streets were washed clean as excess water still rushed into the drains and gullies, and the air smelt clean for the first time in months. Best of all though was the incoming night, for it was then Mabel was able to breathe easier and we all slept sounder, not disturbed by that terrible cough or the clank of her sputum mug as the filth off her chest was expelled. How many nights of broken sleep did our poor Mam have as she was roused to go into that back bedroom, stinking of Lysol and sickness? Often I would hear Mam creep past our open bedroom door and hear the low murmur of her voice as she held her dear daughter's head as she fought to get her breath. Next morning Mam would be heavy eyed for lack of sleep. Poor Mam; she had to get us our meagre portion of bread & dip, wash herself and eat what little food she'd apportioned herself before dashing off to the factory. How on earth did she keep going, especially when Ted complained,

'I pay my board and I want more than bread and dip for my breakfast! (bread dipped in a frying pan of melted lard) I WANT BACON!' On hearing this, I'd look down at my one round of bread and dip and feel guilty.

Talking years later with a cousin whose family was equally large and financially insecure as ours, she'd asked whether I remembered the fresh fruit we young ones had as a yearly treat at Christmas; whether I'd ever asked a child eating an apple whether I could have their core; if I remembered children, affluent enough to have an orange, being followed by other kids and asked, 'save us some orange peel kid' and, if lucky, whether I could remember how oily and bitter that peel tasted?"

'Yes' I'd replied, 'and we were never too proud to beg a child who'd just fished a round of bread and margarine wrapped in newspaper out of his pocket in the school playground, to 'tear us a piece off pal'...... and didn't it taste grand if he did?'

Then, the final confession of my cousin, 'if I was in the street and saw a sweet that someone had spit out, I would pick it up and eat it!'.......Shamefaced I replied, 'yes, so did I.' Was it any wonder so many children had diseases, so many in fact that the City Health Department in Grey Friars would pin up a list of infectious disease notifications outside the office.

The 'Sally Army' van would often come into those hell holes of streets during the hot summer of 1935. It was like a scene from Dickens. The women, old before their time, and many young mothers too, sat in the wide open front doorways on old boxes, stools and chairs that had long since lost their back. Nothing, if it had the slightest use, was ever discarded. Looking into the open doorways, passers-by would see how some of these homes were better described as hovels, but don't stare too long lest you be called 'a nosey bleeder' and told to 'piss off'. There they would sit, summer and winter alike, with just an old shawl around their shoulders. Often they would be wearing a cast off old cap that once belonged to their lord and master, and around the waist an old 'pinny' made from old hessian sack. To complete the ensemble one or two would be sucking on a man's unlit pipe. Thus attired, they would sit, the only movement being the head as they gazed up and down the street before the evening chill drove them inside, or when they leaned forward to 'gob' or spit onto the already filthy pavement. Sometimes they would shift a snotty nosed brat on their knee to make way for the lord and master coming through; the man of the house, if you could call him a man. With his hair slicked down with water from the communal tap, muffler tightly knotted around his throat in lieu of a tie, coat and trousers green with age and mould that grew so profusely on the filthy damp walls of those houses. Wardrobe, what the bleeding hell was a wardrobe? The master would push past, not addressing a word to his grey faced spouse, desperate for food to feed her kids. Shame faced he was, for he was on his way to spend the few coppers they had down at 'The Great Northern' or 'Uppy' pubs. (Uppingham Road) Coppers that would have put a little, just a little food, into his family's belly would now be spent on beer and the forced false humour of mates in a similar situation. Money all spent and thirst unsatisfied, he was no longer a king among men in the pub, and with pockets empty, he would shuffle or stagger home through the chill of the night, flexing his muscles as he went for, not able to bear the reproachful recriminations of his spouse already at her wits end, he would get in first by punching his fist into her defenceless and undernourished body. The streets would then come alive with the screams of children as they ran into the street, often naked, for who had pyjamas to wear, screaming 'please, please help Our Mammy; daddy's killing her!'

The weekly 'Tally men' and debt collectors had a ball, for when a woman was in arrears with the rent and knew she and her children could be thrown into the streets or taken into the Workhouse then, with her husband at work and the children at school, she had only one item left to barter; her body. Our Mam always paid on the nose for whatever we had, and if we couldn't afford it, we went without!

7: Mabel:

School had finished for the day. Although it was understood we had to go straight home to make poor Mabel a cup of tea, and I was usually the first one home, I'd been distracted and started playing with my friends. Suddenly remembering Mabel's needs came before anything or anyone else, I raced in through the back door some ten minutes later than I should, but was still the first in. The drill was to make a mug of tea for Mabel using her mug and no other. I was ever mindful of the strict instructions drummed into us all,

'Don't drink out of Mabel's mug; it's the one with the red cotton wrapped around the handle!'

In the same vein we always knew which was Mabel's knife, fork and spoon as they also had red cotton wrapped around the handles. Mabel was very weak by now and Mam spent hours trying to get her to eat more, for in those days appetite was equated with getting better. Now at dinner time today, weak as she was, Mabel had asked,

'Mam, that rabbit gravy is lovely; is there any left I can have?'

Of course the gravy would have quickly been cleaned up but today, what Mabel didn't know, was Our Mam hadn't cleaned her own plate, so the little extra gravy Mabel received come from Mam's plate. As Mabel had been too weak and fragile to come downstairs for the last week or so she had missed Mam's sleight of hand but Mam was thrilled to bits and went back to work to tell the girls all about Mabel's returned appetite. Years later Mam told me,

'I hadn't realised they were regarding me with pity in their eyes. They'd known something I hadn't; that often with TB when the end was getting near the sufferer would appear to perk right up!'

And so, on that dreadful day I boiled the water for Mabel's tea and reached for her mug where it stood, isolated along with her other eating utensils.

'I'm coming up now Mabel' I called as I started up the stairs.

At the top facing me was her bedroom door. Mabel had been alone for hours whilst we were all out, forced to listen to the screams of pigs and clattering of cattle hooves as they were despatched in the slaughter house at the bottom of the garden.

Mabel was so terribly angry with me that day and I was frightened as she was fighting for breath,

'Oh you naughty boy, where have you been? You know how thirsty I get. I haven't had a drink of tea since dinner time!'

She said a lot more in a similar vein. Dear Mabel, who was always so kind to me, who always had time for me although rarely, if ever, was I allowed to stay for more than a few minutes in her room in case I caught her breath. Now I realise she must have been having those terrible coughing bouts whilst we were out and the blood staining on her sheets and pillow must have warned her that her time was close. In fact, that must be it, for several times in those last few days, as Our Mam recounted years later when she could bring herself to talk about it, Mabel, whilst holding her loved and often consulted little blue bible, would say to her,

'I don't want to leave you Mam, but I want you to know I'm not afraid to die.' Poor, poor Mam; as she wiped the blood from her so adored and adoring loved one's lips, she would say,

'Now don't you be so silly, Our Mabel, you aren't going to leave us!'

Mam's words were either very carefully thought out or prophetic for, although I can't speak for others, I know Mabel has never ever left me, and I know she never ever left her adoring Mam.

The flesh, as I stood before her that day, laying as she was in her old black painted single bed, had fallen from her face, and her frame was so frail I felt that here I was, an eight year old boy who could, with no effort at all, pick her up – she a 21 year old woman. I was very frightened, not in the physical sense, for I cannot ever remember Mabel even lifting her hand to me, although at times she must have been sorely tried. No, I was terrified that with me in the house alone with her, she might begin to haemorrhage from her lungs. The warning signs could clearly be seen. Her eyes, those lovely big grey eyes, were beginning to stick out of their sockets and her frail chest was heaving as she began to fight for breath, trying to draw life giving air into her dying body. She knew, my God she knew, but she was fighting a last battle so that I, her little brother, would not be crucified with her. Terrified, I deserted her in her hour of greatest need, running down the stairs, and blacking out the here and now, shutting everything off; the house, the table that needed to be set for tea, everything! 'Thank God.'

Just then, Maisie and Ronnie came home.

'Have you taken Our Mabel her tea?'

I could only point to the stairs. Maisie went up, took one look and, dashing out of the house, ran to fetch Mrs Perkins, my playmate's Mam. On seeing the state Mabel was in Mrs Perkins told Maisie to run as fast as she could and get a message to Mam to come home. Mrs Perkins was another gem of a Catholic soul and she stayed with Mabel.

Mam, probably still on top of the world because Mabel had got her appetite back, stopped on the way home to buy a new bottle of peppermint concentrate which she honestly believed would help her beloved child breathe better. We had that bottle for years after and it really kept very well, but it was never opened. When Mam saw the terrible state Mabel was in Ted was ordered to go and get the doctor, and to tell him Mabel was desperately ill!

With everything going on, no-one had time for Ron and me. At 7pm the pair of us, along with Wag and Bernard (Mrs Perkins' son), were in the street when Wag drew our attention to Maisie and Nina Warren from the corner shop walking up and down the street. Maisie was crying and Nina was all red eyed but we had no idea what was the matter. Remembering all the times Our Maisie had shouted at me (I'm going to tell Our Mam of you Our Norm) I didn't feel at all sympathetic, so simply said,

'I bet Our Mam's hit her.'

Even though I was feeling very uneasy at the amount of activity around our house, I decided it must be alright as the doctor, having answered Mam's 'SOS' with some speed, had been gone for some time! He must have made Our Mabel better again, I decided. Oh, the simple innocence of a child!

Bernard went into his house and a moment later came out again to say he had to go in. This seemed a bit strange as it was still early, and he looked at us so strangely?! Still more time passed, and it started to get chilly. Finally, Wag had had enough and decided he was going home too.

Ronnie and I decided that as no-one had called out to us, and family and friends were still passing in and out of our entry, we would accompany Wag to his back door, passing as we did his lovely sister, Our Kath, who we kids were very fond of. It was strange when, to our cheerful greeting, she made no reply, passing us with her face averted. She was all red eyed too – stranger and stranger. We pondered this, and even Wag was shaken, for Kath was so lovely.

We headed up to Wag's back door with Wag leading. By now he was beginning to look a bit bothered and I think being older Wag had put things together better than we had. We turned to go home and began to say 'See you in the morning....' but stopped as his Mam appeared at the door looking distressed with Wag's dad hovering in the background.

She tried to speak, but the words didn't seem to come. She tried again, 'Charlie, go into the house.'

With Wag inside and me and Ron nearly in shock as she'd called him 'CHARLIE' (she never called Wag 'Charlie' in our hearing) she bent her head down towards us.

I'm glad it came from her rather than anyone else. No long preamble, no trying to break it to us gently, there was no need, for all the sadness was in her voice as she said,

'I have to ask you, in fact to tell you, that Mabel is dead.'

That was all she could trust herself to say. To this day I cannot explain my reaction, but I burst out laughing! A look of shock and horror went across her face.

'Norman, it's no laughing matter' she began, and then she stopped. I think she realised my reaction was a nervous reflex over which I had no control, for already I was becoming to come apart inside.

Quiet now, Ronnie and I went and stood in the street across the road from our house. We stood in silence, watching people go in, some coming out crying. It was getting colder; the evening shadows were drawing in. Neither of us had a coat and so we huddled together for warmth, too frightened to go in. In the collective grief of those inside, we two were forgotten. Our Mabel was dearly loved. Now it was really getting dark; we could barely see across the road even though the lamplighter, bouncing along the road with his long pole over his shoulder, had lit the street lamp and gone on his way long since. Finally, the front door opened and we could see the yellow gas light from the living room reflected through. Our Ted stood there, looking up and down the street, obviously looking for us. We waved our hands, too frightened to break the silence that lay over the street. He indicated with his head to 'come in' and, without waiting, went back inside and shut the door. It seemed the street was holding its breath as we tip toed across the road, and then tip toed down the entry. I know that I was shivering, and I'm sure Ronnie was too. Through the yard and nervously pushing open the back door as though afraid someone would be behind it ready to jump out on us, we went into the living room. Sitting around the three walls of the living room were relatives, friends and neighbours; some red eyed, some still crying, who, as we went in, turned in our direction and stopped doing what they were saying and doing, putting on brave faces for our benefit. My eyes swivelled to the left, to that big old arm chair under the window that nowadays would have been straight down the tip, but it was in its all-embracing warmth Our Mabel found what little comfort that could be provided.

Mam was sitting in that big old arm chair, white faced and anguished, shoulders still heaving with sobs she was trying to control for our benefit. She tried to say something normal but couldn't. She forced a wan smile to her face, looking straight at me. I stopped dead in my tracks, tried to smile back at her but couldn't, then, with terrible wracking sobs I threw myself into her arms, joining my tears with hers, both of us clasped tightly together, sobbing as though our two hearts would break.

I do know that in one thing, if nothing else, we both loved Mabel equally. I was not to cry like that again until nearly 50 years later when I looked into an open coffin and saw Mam lying there; so white, so waxy, so still.

We two boys were now so exhausted by events of that terrible day we both went to bed without any protest, although I certainly hadn't had any food since dinner time. Our Ted led us upstairs, the only illumination given by the flickering candle Ted held. Mabel, we knew, still lay in the room at the top of the stairs, its door tightly closed, for in those days it was unheard of for the dead to be taken away immediately. Past that door we went, knowing that in there Mabel would be laid out and bathed, ready to be brought down in the morning for Mr Stanion to measure, probably being piggy backed as the stairs were too steep for a coffin.

My over active imagination was already working overtime, and I grasped Ronnie's hand tightly as I tried to block out, without success, what lay in there. Our Mais and her ghost stories again! My state of blind terror lay just below the surface and at just eight years of age I could not reason that Mabel, who would never ever hurt me in life, most certainly would not hurt me in death. Death was the bury hole, and ghosts and haunted houses; death was now Mabel and so all of those things.

I was in an impossible irrational situation that my disturbed childhood had put me into; a situation no child could be expected to cope with. I was without, and had been without for as long as I could remember, the one prop that every child needs and has a right to; a father. This was a fight I couldn't win.

Ted stopped with us as we threw our clothes off and scrambled into bed. He said no words of comfort, in fact he said nothing at all; as far as we could see he hadn't shed any tears either. As he went to blow out the candle we both screamed,

'No Ted, please don't blow it out – we're frightened!'

'Mabel is dead' he said, 'she can't hurt you!'

Why did he say that? Why didn't he say 'she won't hurt you.' A small point but we mark it. He left the candle alight.

Ronnie was in bed closest to the wall, I was next. Normally with Ted next in bed, I would have been in the middle, but he wasn't in bed so I was closest to the door! If Our Mabel came back to life and came into the room it would be me who would see her first!! Every creak in that old house had us both bolt upright; any whisper of a draught and we both stopped breathing......listening, and ready to dive under the bedclothes which was a sacred spot for me when frightened! But nothing could shut out the drum beat of my heart from deafening me, and so we lay huddled together, clutching each other for comfort. Two terrified little boys, visualising that closed door next to our bedroom door at the stair head, waiting to hear that terrible wracking cough, the clank of her sputum mug lid and smell the thick disinfectant as the lid was lifted and then closed. Or, to hear the sound of her trying to clear the thick phlegm from her chest and the final little sigh of resignation she always gave before sinking back onto her pillow.

'It's not that I'm afraid to die Our Mam; it's just that I don't want to leave you!'

Don't let anyone try to tell you that silence is golden or restful; NO WAY! Silence is ominous, frightening, waiting to pounce; silence is sheer terror, whispers in the dark. Silence is what drives a child's mind over the edge until......A demon from hell is in our house! Its terrible sobbing cries echo and re-echo up the stairs. Ron screams; I scream, but my screams are muffled by the bed clothes over my head. It was the most terrible unearthly cry I have ever heard, then or since. Pray God I never hear another like it. Now Ronnie was sat up in bed screaming and shouting, and my cries, more muted, joined his. Terror! Sheer abject bloody terror,

'It's Mabel, she's come back to life' I'm screaming!

Now footsteps pounded up the stairs and into the bedroom rushed Ted,

'It's alright, it's alright!'.........

But no, it wasn't bloody alright; Ronnie was still screaming and I was like a piece of jelly shaking so hard!

Ted explained that terrible sound. It seemed when it was clear Mabel would not survive the night, Uncle Wal was sent into town to the Old Man's favourite pubs, leaving messages for him to get round to 1 Morton Road asap. Eventually getting the message he'd come post haste only to arrive when it was all over. In his own twisted way I think he loved Mabel, after all, she was his first born. Those awful sounds that had driven Ronnie and me to the brink of insanity were the terrible sobs of a man just told his child was dead. I also think, and will to my dying day, that in his secret heart he always wanted reconciliation with Mam, but on his own terms. Now he realised there was no chance. He was a soul in torment for the rest of his life. It was just as well he didn't know then, nor was he ever to know, (I hope) that just before the last haemorrhage, Mabel had said that he (the Old Man) was responsible for her being like this, and if she died, she'd come back and haunt him!

With all my heart I hope, no, I know that she forgave him, and they now share peace along with all those other members of my family who went before.

Until we finally drifted back to sleep, an adult sat with us but it was obvious our nerves were shot and we couldn't stay at home whilst Mabel lay in the house unburied. In those days the dead were kept at home in the front room. All the curtains were drawn and kept tightly drawn day & night. Caring neighbours would have their front room curtains downstairs drawn too so passers-by knew which house had death in it. A six inch board painted black or covered in black felt was screwed down vertically in the middle of the front room window. Passers-by, seeing that board, would often, if men, doff their hats. Better off families would pay for straw to be spread on the road so as to muffle the sound of the horse's hooves, for there were still more horses than cars on the street. The open coffin then lay in the front room on a trestle supplied by the undertaker, and so in the shaded quiet, family and friends could come and view the deceased. No fire, even in the coldest weather, was the order of the day, and they lay in the bosom of the family until the grave received them.

Mrs Hollies, a pal of Our Mam from way back, after hearing how badly Ronnie and I had taken that first day, volunteered to sleep us both on her kitchen floor until it was all over even though she had four children of her own. She received no objections from us two. For myself, I never wanted to see the house again! What a relief to be out of our house of death, although I soon found out a hard brick floor was not the most comfortable place to sleep! Sometime during the first day away I bit my lip. During the night I had the feeling my lip was still bleeding and that in the morning I would have bled to death. The imagination of a child can be advantage; in my case it was a curse!

Thus we came to Mabel's funeral. Since she had died neither Ronnie or I had been home. Now it was a Saturday and the last grim ritual had to be gone through. Our kind hostess, Mrs Hollies, told us on that dreadful morning we were to go home to 'see your Mabel' for the last time in her coffin. We were scrubbed and polished, all clean & tidy, and sent off. The last words to us from that lovely lady were,

'Now don't be frightened boys, for there's nothing to be frightened of!'

The day was lovely; the sun was shining and a cool breeze caressed our cheeks as we tip toed up the entry. At the back door Our Mam met us, looking bright and cheerful. God alone knows what it cost her to put on such a brave face for remember, it was only three months before that her beloved youngest brother had died, and the grave so recently closed up was now to be reopened to receive another treasure.

'I wanted you to see Mabel for the last time in her coffin' said Mam, 'then you'll feel better knowing she's at rest and not suffering anymore!'

Even I could see the effort this cost her to say that. I can clearly remember how the closed living room curtains were gently moving in the breeze and as we went into the darkened front room I saw for the first time the glint of the brass handles and brass name plate on the coffin. The coffin of highly polished light pine was standing on black trestles. THE COFFIN LID WAS CLOSED! As if in answer to my thoughts Mam said,

'We had to send for Mr Stanion the undertaker to come and screw the lid down because with this stormy weather and the heat Mabel was beginning to smell.'

We stood in silence looking at the coffin which seemed to be more for a child than a 21 year old woman. For our visit, Mam must have worked hard to ensure the room and its contents did not frighten us. The curtains were drawn of course but the shaded room seemed so right, as the venetian blinds that had come with the house were pulled right up and, so that possibly we might not smell any lingering odours from the time up to the coffin being closed, a slight pine disinfectant was evident. Again, as the window was slightly ajar, the curtains were gently moving & fluttering. It was as though the gentle spirit that had once resided in the now empty shell, which was all that was left of my dear sister's earthly body, was hesitatingly reluctant to make that last farewell before slipping away to her maker.

Mabel Lillian Hastings, born 1914; died 1935 (21 years) R.I.P

We returned to our hostess after an hour for a meal and then, being too young to follow the coffin with the mourning party, were escorted by Mrs Hollies to St Barnabas Church, each step (or so it seemed) accompanied by the tolling of the funeral bell which gave the age (and so I am told) the sex of the deceased.

The curate was Mr Strudwick, he who was not above borrowing an invalid carriage to push Mabel to church when she was up to it, so she could draw closer to that God she loved and trusted without questioning her unhappy lot. The Old Man was not to be seen but we saw Mam, heavily veiled and in deep mourning black, being supported on Ted's arm, and other relatives following close behind the coffin.

I seem to remember the words in the service including 'never more shall sun shine upon her' and was very indignant inside! 'That must be wrong', I thought, 'what about heaven! The sun always shines up there, doesn't it!?'

The service ended and the small sad procession again passed us to leave the church. On emerging we saw the coffin being put into the hearse. Out in the brilliant sunshine of the early afternoon the first person I saw, after momentarily being dazzled, was Wag's sister, Kath. Kath, like all the Bishops, was a Catholic, and I have the idea that Catholics were not supposed to go to any but a Catholic Church, (I may be wrong) but that lovely girl had come into the Church and prayed with us for Mabel's soul. Kath looked down at me and smiled so sweetly, so sympathetically, that my heart broke and I sobbed so hard that concerned friends came and held me, telling me to be brave. How could I be brave though? I wanted my sister back!

I was told years later how, even in her death agony, that brave, stout hearted sister of mine refused to give up the fight willingly, and it was our family doctor who had looked after us for several years, that had turned to Our Mam and said,

'I think Mabel has had enough Mrs Hastings, don't you?'

Mam could only nod her head in agreement.

The doctor told Mam to go and kiss Mabel goodbye; he would then give Mabel an injection. In a few moments it would all be over.

The doctor had filled a syringe and placed it into position. To Mam's nod he then injected. Mabel went slowly and peacefully into her deep and final sleep; free from pain and the cares of the world. Thank you Doctor Mac.

What was in that needle? You may form your own conclusions.

The funeral had to be paid for of course. In those days there was no one, Government or otherwise, to pick up the bill unless the nearest and dearest were willing for the departed to be buried 'on the Parish' in a Pauper's grave. So, like Our Mam, those who could possibly manage, paid out a little each week into insurance to offset in whole or in part, the funeral costs. The elderly dreaded the thought of being 'put under' by the Parish and said so; Internment in an orange box type coffin in an unmarked grave with strangers! Horrendous tales were told of these 'on the cheap' coffins falling apart as the bearers tried to lift them. Some tales had more than a hint of humour to them. I remember being told how one of these pauper graves was so deep so as to cram as many as possible into it, that when it filled up with water in a sudden rain storm, the coffin had to be weighed down with stones, otherwise it kept bobbing to the surface like a submarine!

The Old Man had to stick his nose in of course, just to try and cause trouble. First he went to Mr Stanion the undertaker.

'You won't get paid for that funeral you know' he said, 'my old woman hasn't got any money!'

To his credit, Mr Stanion showed him to the door, telling him as he went, 'your wife has shown me up to date insurance papers and they are as good as money in the bank, and furthermore, you should be bloody well ashamed of yourself for trying to cause trouble and embarrassment to your wife whilst she's trying to get through these terrible days!'

The very next day the insurance man, who'd been calling round weekly to collect the insurance payments on Mabel's life, came to see Our Mam. What he had to say was almost unbelievable, but true. Whilst in the insurance office the previous day he'd heard our family name mentioned, causing him to listen intently. What he heard was the Old Man trying to claim the insurance money on his daughter, Mabel, to be paid there and then, as she'd died the week before and he needed the money to bury her! To his credit the insurance man intervened, for he knew the Old Man could be violent.

'You have no right to that money, Sir. I've been collecting weekly payments, always from your wife, and I intend to see that she gets the money to pay for that young girl's funeral.'

Foiled again, the Old Man slunk off!

Why did he do such rotten things? To this day I maintain, and to my dying day I will think, that he wanted his family back. In desperation he was going to use that money as a lever. With that money in his hands and the funeral debt unable to be cleared, Our Mam would've had to take him back or face the debtor's label, possibly prison. But, he was foiled again. As he had sowed, so he reaped; now his harvest was coming home!

And now that final part of the ritual to do with death by reason of an infectious disease, had to be gone through, and be in no doubt, in those, the final few hours, were when the most contagion abounded; it was rampant. The local Health (Sanitary) came in. Mabel's bed, blankets, pillows, sheets and even curtains, were taken away to be 'stoved.' (Fumigated or burnt) Mam had already put the cotton marked eating utensils in the dustbin. The men who came in wore masks. Everything in the death room had to be declared and taken although Mam had hidden Mabel's little blue bible. (I have it now)

The next stage in the cleansing was that the windows in the bedroom were tightly locked or screwed shut and then sealed against any air coming in or going out, with brown sticky paper. The man in charge, before leaving the room, released something into the air and then quickly coming out, he sealed all around the door with great wide strips of the same sticky paper, making it airtight. We were told the room would remain sealed for several days whilst the deadly fumes killed off any germs or spores still in there. We kids were warned to keep right away and not try to go into that room or we'd be dead!

A few nights later, although I must confess I did not hear it, in the middle of the night a most terrific din came from that room. Afterwards, Mam put it down to the paper seals breaking loose as the temperature began to increase. If I had heard it I would've been under the bedclothes in a flash!

When the room was finally declared to be safe, and after the Sanitary man had gone, we went in. It was so empty without Mabel's great big grey eyes smiling at us. We never used that room again whilst we lived at 1 Morton Road. Even Our Ted, who was now 20 and still moaning that in the night 'that bugger's playing football with my legs again in his sleep' and had always wanted a room of his own, would not go in there.

Dannet Street and living with Aunt Lucy:

I could not understand what happened next, or why? Our Maisie and Ronnie weren't at home, so there was only me and Our Ted sleeping in the bed. The cold weather had arrived and I was missing cuddling up to Ronnie until Ted came to bed to warm me on the other side. Something must have happened, but what? The last month or so had become a blank, like I was sleepwalking; now it was like a dream. It was early evening and Mam was getting me as warmly dressed as she could, which wasn't very warm as I only had one warm coat and that was threadbare. Even though the coat was relatively light it made no difference; my old collar bone ache was gnawing away. It was raining outside; I could hear it on the window and with no coal and no fire, the gas light was a ghastly yellow.

'Now, we're going into town!' said Mam.

That was good because I liked riding on the trams, and if there weren't many passengers I could slide my bum up and down the long highly polished seat that ran the length of the passenger car. Better still, we might go and sit in that funny little front or back compartment! (But perhaps not; it gets cold in there as you're cut off from the warmth by a sliding door and I'm cold already!) But why was Mam taking the good socks off my feet and putting on some heavily darned ones instead? She knew darned socks made my heels blister, and then I'd get septic feet! I could hear her muttering to herself...... 'Let that rotten bugger keep you for a bit; I've kept you long enough.'

Kneeling in front of me her eyes, level with mine, were tired and misty. I tentatively reached out and touched her face. She tried to smile but tears started in her eyes. I remember thinking 'I bet she's thinking of our Mabel again, that always makes her cry.' But now, what was she saying?

'It's alright Norman. He'll have to buy you some new socks; I can't, they've put us on short time again, and with having to pay extra for the funeral, it's cost me everything I had. Why did I think that insurance paid for everything?!'

She was talking about my father as 'Dad', although she always referred to him as the 'Old Man. The word 'Dad' frightened me and I didn't know why. I hated those big smacking kisses and he breathed into my mouth as he did so...... and everyone knew you didn't breathe onto or into the mouth of other people or you'd get consumption like Mabel did, and I didn't want to go into the bury hole in a bury box like Our Mabel! Besides the bristles on the Old Man's chin and around his mouth stuck into my face and hurt! Why was Our Mam talking about 'Dad' – he lived somewhere else, and anyway, where were Ronnie and Maisie?

It all became too much and I could feel myself closing down, shutting it out! Now Ted was saying 'Ta rar Norman!' He didn't kiss me even though he sounded as though he was going away, but it was me being got ready. He didn't kiss me but that wasn't all that strange for he never did kiss his little brothers or sister.

We were on a tram and I began to take an interest, for it was swaying and clanking along. I began to worry....what if it came off the rails and we got killed? It was still raining outside for I could see the spots running down the window. I was cold but they never put heaters on trams. I sometimes saw the driver put straw in his wide open cab to stand on, but what I wanted to know was how the conductor managed to clip his machine on the narrow slot on his chest without missing? We now changed trams. All around us people were scurrying to get out of the rain. The street lamps made things look much worse; they were a sickly yellow, like our gas mantle when it needed another penny in the gas meter. I snuggled up to Mam as I was so very tired. I could feel her coat was soaking wet through and it made me shiver, feeling even colder than I did before, but it looked even colder outside of the tram.

We got off and I watched as it went clanking away, flashing blue sparks from the top of its pole. I wished we were still on it. Mam didn't look at me as we stood still, pondering. I could see the beads of rain in her hair and on her coat. Her face was grey, a ghastly grey, and she shivered with the ague. Our threadbare coats were no protection against the night. I don't know why but I wanted to throw my head back and scream at the sky, 'it's not fair, God, it's not fair! Why?'

Mam now leaned over me.

'I'm going on an errand. Now, be a good boy and don't move from here!'

I blinked the rain from my eyes (was it rain) and in that split second she was gone!

Time passed and I was still standing there. The wet chill of the night was all around and the rain was running through my hair and down my face in rivulets, dripping off my nose. Something had happened, but what?!

The brightly lit windows of the nearby shop beckoned to me, 'come in and shelter; get warm' but Our Mam said 'don't move' and so I don't. Passers-by pushed me out of the way, and a nearby pub was busy with its early evening trade, the door opening & shutting, giving out gusts of warm beer smelling air. I was tempted to go in and join the small group of children sheltering in the pub porch but dare not. I was a stranger to them and they might hit me. Where am I? 'Stand still' she said. I stand still!

It seemed like hours passed but then I heard a familiar voice,

'Come on Our Norm, you're to come with me!'

It was Maisie. I'd wondered where she and Our Ron had been for the past few weeks and now I was to find out. One at a time, Maisie first and then Ronnie, had been 'dumped' on the Old Man, or rather on his long suffering sister, Aunt Lucy, who I hardly knew. He always fetched up with her after he finished with various, what Our Mam called 'his fancy women.'

Poor Aunt Lucy; She was a saint to fit us in with her own family. She lived in Dannet Street, off the King Richards Road. Her husband, four sons and a daughter, now three more besides and the Old Man, but Maisie had to be boarded out as you will see.

In later years Our Mam, who had little good to say about the Hastings family, could always find a good word for Lucy. Unfortunately, the Old Man was such an accomplished liar in slandering Our Mam, the feeling wasn't mutual.

Ronnie, me and the Old Man had a three quarter bed in the back room. Maisie was boarded out with a nurse but I can't remember her name. Childless themselves the nurse and her husband had set ideas on how a child should be raised. For example, every morning Maisie was sent out to sit on the lavatory then, every few minutes until she passed a motion, nurse would shout out, 'have you been yet, Maisie?' It didn't matter if sitting there made Maisie late for school, she had to remain there until mission accomplished and inspected. No room for doubt entertained. Maisie said years later, 'I bet I was the only kid in the district that could shite to order!'

Again, our sleeping arrangements saw me sleeping in the middle of the bed, 'crammed in.' Beer in those days was pretty potent stuff and what with his love of stews & plenty of onions, well oh dear, oh dear, the smell at times was dreadful when he came to bed with flatulence. Ronnie has since said that his memory of those dreadful days was waking up in the night and, in the faint illumination given by the moon, seeing the Old Man standing at the side of the bed sobbing as though his heart would break. Perhaps it had finally got through to him how many lives he'd wrecked, and yet so far he'd gotten off lightly.

In the mornings we would waken to find the Old Man had gone to work so Ronnie and I, eyes gummed up from a restless night's sleep, would go downstairs to find the tiny kitchen fully overcrowded with our cousins. We would wait our turn to wash at the sink in a bowl of cold water. Bathrooms, what were they? Aunt Lucy would use a plain bar of soap for washing out our ears with a screwed up flannel. That same bar of soap, as in most households, would also be used for scrubbing floors. This explained why it so often felt gritty.

Before being allowed to eat our breakfast, usually a round of bread and dripping, each of us would be handed a spoonful of the contents a jar kept in a cupboard next to the window. That yellowish grey stuff was goose grease which we swallowed as quickly as we could, although to be fair it had little or no taste. According to Aunt Lucy that stuff was excellent for greasing the chest, and I suspect lubricating the bowels! If that nurse had only known, things would have been so much easier for Maisie!!

Years later as an Education Welfare Officer (Boardman), I was looking through some very old 'Leavers' books in the Education Offices and quite by chance alighted upon Aunt Lucy's name: Lucy Hastings, her home address, age on leaving school etc. Against all of this was written 'a sickly child.' Perhaps her mother, my Grandma Hastings, started the tradition of goose grease? Whatever, Lucy lived to a good age.

I was very quickly taken by Aunt Lucy and enrolled at King Richards Road Infant/ Junior School and, because of my date of birth was put in the last year of the Infants. The Headmistress had, of course, to be told the whole rotten family history; the version told by the Old Man to his sister. I tried to remain aloof, pretending it was someone else they were talking about, then Auntie gave me a kiss and I was taken to the class I was to join. I tried to settle and then realised I wanted to pee. I was too shy a new boy to want to ask to leave the room but lucky for me, just before the dam burst, a teacher saw me crossing and uncrossing my legs.

'Do you want to leave the room?' I was asked.

I nodded, teeth clenched, as the first warm trickle seeped down my leg. She must have seen how desperate my plight was for it was,

'Off with you; quickly now!'

I was out of there at a rate of knots then realised I hadn't the faintest idea where the toilets were. I daren't go back and ask for I feared I would disgrace myself in front of the whole class. Fortunately, an older boy came around the corner and, guessing my desperate plight he grabbed me by the arm and ran me through a door, across the yard and into the toilets. How did he know of my plight? Easy, for if you see a small boy trying to walk with his legs crossed and pinching the end of his willy......!

Our Mam would come to see us when she could, always in the evening, but it was winter and the nights were dark. She would stand at the bottom of the entry to Aunt Lucy's house and call us by name: 'Ronnie, Norman!' If we hadn't heard her then she would take off her shoe and hit the house wall, then we heard! At once, we would leap up to go to her but if the Old Man was in he would say,

'Sit down, let the bleeder wait!'

We had to obey but would sit crossing and uncrossing our legs, impatient to go to her – Our Mam. Often it would be Aunt Lucy who broke the impasse.... 'Now then Our Ted, let them go to their mother; they want to see her!'

I'm sure Aunt Lucy and her husband, Ernie, were a bit cagey of the Old Man, brother or not, but being a Mam herself she knew what we were going through. Bless you Aunt Lucy!

Mam must have been frozen to the very marrow. I think back to that time and it feels only minutes ago her nose, so cold, pressed against our cheek as she hugged us. How cold she must have been, all because he wouldn't let us go straight out to her. I think it must have been because of these days I developed the fear and absolute distrust I had for him.

'Fear', years later when I began to trace the Hastings roots in Canada, I wrote to his brother, Fred Hastings, and confessed that, although the Old Man (his brother) had been dead and gone for so many years, that I was still frightened of his memory. What an awful confession for a man of nearly 60 years to make about his father!

Before kissing us goodbye, Mam would usually find us a halfpenny or penny to buy a few sweets from the little shop. It was in the front room of an ordinary house just below Aunt Lucy's. I always used to buy two for a halfpenny, jelly like baby dummy sweets. What would present day head shrinks make of my choice of sweets? Sometimes she had no money to spare but this was usually the exception; it mattered not, it was enough she was there, battling on until such time that the shoe firm 'Smith Faire' went back onto full time and she could claim us back.

The Old Man was a great trencherman, his favourite saying being 'get plenty of packing inside of you!' This philosophy he followed to the letter. Aunt Lucy had the money out of him to feed us as we'd been on short rations at home for a long time and he was earning. In fact he had always earned good money, of which a goodly portion he spent on food for himself as I witnessed many times later on. He would go to the local market and buy a whole rabbit. Then he would buy turnips, carrots, swedes etc. All of these would go into a big pan which was placed on the hob or the fire to cook slowly whilst he was in the pub, telling all and sundry what a marvellous dad he was. Oh yes, I forgot to mention the two or three onions! Large ones! After the pubs had closed he would come home to Lucy's and polish the lot off then come to bed where he would be breaking wind for the rest of the night. POOR ME, for it was me who was sleeping next to him!

Finally, and I cannot remember the details, we were on our way home! Mam was on full time again, although probably Aunt Lucy had put her foot down, after all, every inch of floor space had been occupied in her house for far too long. If so, perhaps the Old Man had to back down and offer some money to Our Mam for our keep? Perhaps, I doubt it! Even now I can see our home coming very clearly. Ronnie, Maisie and me bursting into our living room – we were home, joy, joy, joy! Mam was with us and Our Ted was at home in the living room. He was, or rather, had just scrubbed the floor linoleum so all the chairs (that's a laugh) our two chairs, were stacked on the table, and the scrubbed floor, still damp, was covered in newspaper to keep it clean longer. I'm not sure, and I can't swear to it, but I think his collective greeting to his younger sister and two little brothers was.... 'keep your bloody dirty feet off the floor, I've just this minute scrubbed it' and then he finished with those words of encouragement that our dear eldest brother always used to make a point, 'or I'll give you a bloody good hiding!' We heaved a sigh of collective relief. That confirmed it, we were HOME!

8: Back to Morton Road & how to catch a Newt

Wag, Ronnie and I set off on a lovely early spring/ summer day to go to the Scraptoft golf links, one of our favourite spots for an afternoon newting. The links lay a good four miles from our homes but a round trip of this magnitude held no terrors for us in those days of restricted transport. Anyway, transport cost money, which we did not have. The final decider was that no trams or buses ran there anyway. It was the first time we'd made this trek with Wag and, as was customary, we'd been warned, as had Wag, by our elders, 'don't you dare get into any mischief!'

Such warnings were common place and could quite easily be given by a parent to other people's children without fear of retribution, and rightly so. Today of course a mum or dad would probably say 'don't you talk to my kids like that!'

Thus, with a round of bread (once again I ask myself, why was a square of bread called 'a round?') wrapped in newspaper, which gave it a smashing flavour, tucked inside our jerseys so as to leave our hands free to carry the bottle of kali water (a sticky concoction made with kali powder) we set off. Kali powder was purchased for a halfpenny and was usually eaten by dipping a saliva moistened finger into the bag then licking the resultant sticky digit. Several of us could take turns in dipping into a bag of kali and it was easy to identify kali dippers by their yellow tongues. Today we'd scrounged a bottle in which we'd poured tap water then poured in the powder before finishing off with vigorous shaking, making lovely yellow kali water. We carried this in turn, passing it on with the warning, 'don't drop it; there's a penny on the bottle!'

To help us on our way we silently ran after any carrier's horse & cart that passed by, and then jumping & hitching our bums on the tail gate of the cart. We had to watch out the driver didn't see us though because he wouldn't hesitate to use his whip on us if he knew we were aboard. Many carriers had a boy at the back of the cart who clung onto a thick hanging down rope with a huge knot at the end, mainly to make sure none of the cargo was stolen as well as being a warning of approaching scamps like us. Wag was perspiring freely already. His fair hair, damp with sweat, was plastered to his head, and he kept blinking as the sweat ran into his eyes due to the salt he was losing from his body. Now we were at a critical stage of our journey for before us lay the long street that stretched arrow straight through the new part of the council estate, Tailby Avenue! It was alleged this was the home to gangs who (rumour had it) would beat up any kids from other districts. The road looked to be clear and so we ran as hard as we could up the concrete road, passing piles of builders' rubble outside some of those houses waiting to be completed; rubble which we imagined would provide an abundance of ammunition to throw at those unwanted outsider kids! US!

They must have been hiding, lying in wait for us, because seemingly from all sides, kids popped up and we were bombarded with all sorts of missiles! Thankfully, none of these were 'duckies,' our name for brick ends or other large stones that could easily split a head open if they connected. I suppose this explains the term, 'DUCK', from the shortened 'ducky.' (or you'll need stitches!)

We were almost clear but one particular virago of a girl about my age did not give up the chase, and it was clear I was selected to be the object of her abuse. We were out of breath and panting like broken winded cart horses but I had to keep running, hotly pursued by HER, still hurling clods of earth and other rubbish. I was definitely the object of her hate for she addressed me in words that brook no denial,

'Hey you, that sloppy kid in those shitty brown shorts! I hate you, I do, and my little sister could fight you, she could! You're frit, you are, FRIT, and you're rotten and I'm going to come to your school and tell your teacher on you, I am!'

Ron and Wag looked at me with admiration,

'I think she likes you,' said Ron!

'I think she loves you,' said Wag!

I looked or tried to look suitably modest as I'd could see a grain of truth in what they were saying, for in those days, admiration between children was often expressed by shouting abuse at each other. I wonder now if this stems from the fact that in those days so many men knocked the living shit out of their wives when drunk and yet, in the next breath became all sentimental and 'lovey dovey.'

It was Wag who put a stop to this seemingly impossible budding romance by selecting two large missiles that lay close to hand. One was a clod of earth and the other a large pulpy (by reason of it being rotten) potato. First he threw the clod of earth; a clear miss!

'Yah, you can't throw for toff.....'

That was as far as she got, for the next missile, dispatched even as she dodged the first, got a bull's eye, right slap, bang, wallop, into her open mouth! She let out one scream and then, spitting out piece after piece of the stinking spud gabbled,

'I'm gonna fetch the coppers, I am! You wait till you come back, you'll see!'

We flew off, making plans for a wide detour on the way back!

Now we'd reached Garden City. (Is it still there or has it gone, like so many of my boyhood memories?) This was a very select area, each with its own lovingly cared for and tended front & rear garden. It was only about 20 minutes since we'd left our homes, or so it seemed, but that was time enough for us to have consumed our sticky, sickly yellow kali water ration. Wag had drunk the most. He had a perfect right to for it was he who'd found the money for the kali and it was his bottle. I swear that even his sweat was turning a sickly yellow colour but, like all little boys on a hot summer's day, we were parched with thirst. We called a halt to decide what to do.

'Let's knock on a door and ask for a drink of water' suggested Wag, our leader, 'and if they give us one we can always ask them to fill the bottle!'

It was the 'if they give us one' that put me on 'Troop Alert' for in my family if Ted or Maisie said, 'I'll give you one' it meant they were going to hit me! Ronnie thought this an excellent idea but I didn't, especially as both sets of eyes swivelled in my direction.

'What are you looking at me for?' I whined.

'Cause you're the littlest!' (I wasn't, Our Ronnie was, but they were in no mood for an argument) 'and you're the youngest and they might let you have some, whereas they might tell us to clear off!'

'I aint going; they might hit me!' (I always looked on the black side!)

'Right; said Wag, 'We'll all go; they can't hit us all!'

Really, my fears were infectious!

Now, as we stood debating the issue, we were aware that all around us lace curtains were twitching as the locals observed us and stood by to 'repel boarders.' We chose a house at random, then cautiously crept up the path to the front door. Ron reached up to the bell push whilst I kept well back, ready to lead the retreat if it became necessary. The speed the ring was answered told me that our approach had been observed and expected. Framed in the front door stood a sweet faced, elderly lady, and just behind her was an equally friendly looking gentleman. Just looking at them told us we'd struck gold!

'Please missus, could you give us a drink of water, only we've come a long way (about six streets) and we're very thirsty.'

Without a word spoken, but with a big smile at her husband, that dear sweet soul went inside and returned with a big jug of homemade lemonade.

'Careful now my dears; don't gulp it all down or you'll give yourselves stomach cramps!'

Her warnings fell on deaf ears for each one of us drank long and deep. I can still taste and feel that cool nectar sliding down my throat. We handed back the now empty jug, profuse in our thanks, preparing to depart but she gestured to us to hand her our empty bottle, and whilst we wiped away the last drops of the drink from our chins, she went back into the house having rinsed out the scummy dregs of our sandwiches, and refilled it with more of our by now favourite drink. All of this time her hubby had not said a word, he just beamed at us. I think in retrospect, that in us he was living his own thirsty boyhood. We knew our manners and we thanked them very much, besides we might want to call in again someday. So, strengthened and renewed, we set off again, only turning to wave to those lovely folk as we reached the corner.

This part of Garden City was lovely, more country than town. On our right were houses whilst to our left was the open countryside, bounded by rough shaggy hedges, over which were fields that seemed to stretch on forever. Every house had a garden which was a riot of colour from masses of flowers that spilled and over-spilled onto the paths and footpaths. It was a perfect background to the bees and other insects murmuring & muttering in the background, gathering the rich harvest of pollen which turned them the predominantly colour, yellow. In those days, flowers were grown for their colour and perfume, not for the size of the blooms. Even the cardboard pictures of flowers were heavily impregnated with scent. I remember Phul Nana...Californian Poppy and Lily of the Valley, but these garden flowers had a perfume that could not be duplicated.

Fruit trees? Every garden seemed to have fruit trees but it was too early for the apples, pears and plums that would eventually need to be harvested, and what harvests they were in those days, before the chemical insecticides killed off those self-same insects whose happy noises accompanied us now. That part of our heritage has been lost for all time. Oh, to think of it now fills my heart with tears.

In those days to see fruit trees immediately spelled 'scrumping' for, make no mistake about it, Ronnie and I rarely saw fresh fruit. At Christmas though we'd find a few nuts, an apple or orange (what has happened to those gorgeous blood oranges?), a white sugar mouse and perhaps a sixpenny toy. Of course, Wag's family being much better off and having contacts through Wag senior to market folk, probably saw fresh fruit every day. Now, without a by your leave, Ron was through a gate heading towards one of those trees. It mattered not that the fruit was small and hard and would be bitter, Ron had to have some. Of course, today the kids would probably nick the tree as well. We saw him reach the base of a tree and begin to climb whilst at the same time beckoning us to join him. No way, not me!! Ronnie climbed up into the tree itself and was soon lost to sight in the dense foliage. The only indication of him being there was the small fruit, and as I had guessed it, it was sour, that seemingly materialised out of thin air, landing at our feet. Bulging now in the oddest places due to the fruit he'd stuffed all about his person, Wag began to back up to me, the unofficial 'cavey' watcher. The door of the house opened and the man who lived there appeared. In one second flat, with me well out in front and Wag a close second disgorging apples at every step and the man a close third, we hastened away. Wag sensibly pulled his jersey out of his trousers and shed the balance of the fruit. Fortunately, the chap could not run as fast as we could and soon gave up, waving a fist after us before going back, making sure he trod on every apple that we (or rather Wag) had shed. I burst into tears.

'I bet Our Ronnie's been caught and he'll have to go to court and be sent to prison!'

I was such a 'worrit!'

Wag told me to 'shut up' and rightly so, but I would not be pacified. Our poor Mam had enough on her plate without a court appearance. But, surprise, surprise, down the street, hands in pockets full of fruit, grinning all over his face, came Ron. The man had not realised the villain of the piece was still up his tree, and so waiting until the coast was clear, down he came and, filling his pockets as he did so, he calmly strolled out. Naturally, I demanded a share, and I got one. I suspect to shut me up.

Norman (right) was such a 'worrit' (Ronnie left)

To get to the golf links we had to pass along a rough lane deeply pitted with carthorse wheel tracks. Passing through several gates, all of which we carefully closed after us, our eyes were never still as we observed the wonders of nature which my brother had a knack of seeing and identifying before I did. He was a born naturalist. I remember that if he wanted a few wild violets to cheer Our Mabel up, he always knew just where to find them. On one memorable occasion Ron had returned home with several young leverets or baby hares which he'd spotted although we others had nearly walked over them. Not a small copse or spinney went unobserved and as we passed by we'd sing ditties which we thought in our innocence were rather rude, such as,

'Inkey, Pinkey Chinaman kept a little shop, all he sold was peppermint rock. Peed in a bottle and called it pop, Inkey Pinkey Chinaman'.

Sing that today and the trouble makers in the race relations industry would have you in court, and yet this was a popular ditty especially for girls skipping with a skipping rope. Simple things like these gave us pleasure.

In most of the fields were horseshoe shaped ponds that for centuries had served to water the field stock of cows and horses etc. Each in turn was visited and many times our shoes were sucked off our feet by stinking, clinging mud, as we looked in vain for frog spawn even though we knew we were months too late. We knew that as we'd harvested a mass of the slimy stuff months before, and what we'd gathered in jam jars were fed on watercress filched from the skip in Wag's yard. When the tails had developed, turning them into small frogs, the whole mess had been poured down the lavvy by our long suffering respective parents to cries of, 'Oooh, you aint half cruel, Our Mam!'

Any movement seen by us in those still, stagnant waters was identified as stickleback, robin or roach, even though the truth of the matter was that these barren pockets of cattle drinking water found it difficult to sustain even a few water beetles or larvae.

Now, after many detours, we reached our goal; the golf links with newt pond on the corner of what is now Keyham Lane and Hamilton Lane. (Don't bother to look for it now though as it's been cemented over!) There, in the quiet of the sunny afternoon, disturbed only by the flash of dragonfly wings, on a small island reached by passing over a narrow rough plank on the golfers teeing off green, or rather just to the side of it, was the newt pond.

The waters of the little pond were green with all manner of algae which concealed all sorts of aquatic creatures but most important...here lived the newts; some crested! Did we call these the Tiger newts? I wonder how many kids today have seen a newt, let alone observed one in its natural environment. But there was a ritual to go through first before we began newting in earnest. Kneeling down and bending over at an impossible angle we would poke sticks into the water, pushing the weed aside as we searched for any golf balls that might have been miss hit! It must have been a sight, those bums sticking in the air all around the perimeter and clumps of fished out weed flying through the air to cries of,

'Watch out, that bloody stuff's just hit me in the chops!' (face)

Any balls retrieved here, or anywhere else on or in the rough, would be sold to the Pro in his club house for whatever it was worth condition wise. This day we were unlucky; we usually were, and so we got down to the serious business of catching newts. If you've never been newting now is your chance to learn the gentle art.

Each of us now took a last swig of our lemonade. The sandwiches had been devoured some time ago and so the lemonade was rather cloudy with crumbs, but that bothered us not at all. We dived into our pockets and pulled out a length of ordinary sewing thread, on the end of which we now tied a very thin worm which Wag produced from a tin. These had been dug out of Tommy the horse's manure. Next, we allowed the wriggling line to drop just below the surface of the water. My goodness, those newts had voracious appetites, for hardly had the worm been dipped to just below the water when a newt would rise slowly under it and suck the bait down its throat. When sufficient of the worm had vanished down our little chum's gullet we would slowly pull the cotton in with the catch still on the end of it, reluctant to release what was obviously a very tasty meal had we but let well alone. With the newt held gently in our hand we would slowly pull on the cotton and out of the poor frustrated creatures mouth emerged the whole worm, still alive and kicking. The bait was then returned to the water for another catch. Those newts never seemed to learn, and for us the best part was that. One worm could last all afternoon. The long lazy afternoon drew on and we lost all sense of time. Occasionally, we had to get out of the way of the golfers who wanted to use the tee, and some would ask us, 'how many have you caught?' before pausing to admire the lovely creatures. I do believe some of the golfers would have loved to have a go at the gentle sport themselves. Of course, we also got the nasty one who told us to 'clear off, you're not supposed to be here' but as soon as they'd gone, back we came. When I think of that sacred place now being concreted over, the word 'vandalised' comes to mind.

And now it was time to go home. We rolled up the cotton and threw the contents of Wag's bait tin into the pond along with our catch. No way would we dream of taking these creatures home. This was their home and so back in they went to enjoy the bounty we'd just provided.

We'd been told of an old dead tree just slightly off our route home and as it was said a nest of young owls was in a dead branch hole, we decided to confirm or deny the story. It was denied. No young owls. We were on the track that led to Barkby, heading back. On our left was a low hedge and over it the long fairway. We heard a soft 'plop'. At once, three heads craned over the hedge and there, glistening white in the late afternoon sunshine, was a golf ball, just rolling to a stop. We didn't need to be told the golfer who'd struck it was in the vicinity because we heard the cry 'Fore!' Three heads swivelled to the left. In the near distance three golfers, one of whom who'd just clouted the ball and was bending down to pick up his bag of clubs as the second golfer prepared to 'tee off.' As though in a dream I heard Wag say, 'I'm going to have that ball!'

I looked at him as though he were mad whilst Ron giggled nervously.

'I mean it' said Wag, and before we could stop him he'd burst through the hedge and was streaking over the green, pausing only to scoop the ball up before haring back to us. Give Wag his due, he was fast, in fact I swear on that memorable afternoon he could've run a deer down but, even so, Ronnie and I were faster. Heads down we sped up that lane like greyhounds from the slips for we knew what the term 'collective responsibility' meant, and we were collective with Wag. This meant it would be no use saying, 'please sir, it was him that stole your ball!' Oh dear no, it would be good hidings all round before we were handed over to the police. For a few vital moments, possibly because the sun was in their eyes, those golfers had no idea what was going on in front of them but the penny had to drop, and so the afternoon peace was shattered with, 'come here you little bastards' and 'just wait till we get hold of you, you'll wish you'd never been born!'

In full flight, a good few yards in front of Our Ron who could really move, I glanced back and there was the cause of our immediate problems catching up with us fast. We turned off at right angles onto Keyham Lane, heading back towards Garden City and I nearly wet myself for coming the other way, and then passing us, were several men on bikes and I realised that once the golfers who were in hot pursuit and the cyclists met up, that would be our lot. They were sure to join the chase if only for the fun of it and whilst we could out run adult male golfers, it would be no contest against cyclists.

'It's your fault Wag' I whined, 'you just wait till your Mam finds out you've pinched that man's golf ball!'

Wag very sensibly told me to 'shut up' and 'save your breath for running; we aint caught yet!'

Running until we thought our lungs would burst, sucking in air as best we could, wracking our brains what to do? Where to go? By now we'd reached that rough rutted lane we'd so recently traversed, where trees, shrubs and bushes grew in the small copses and spinneys at the side. I was in a terrible state. Who was it again that'd been in the Sanny not so long back with TB!? The hunt was still out of sight although we could hear the faint cries and tinkling bells of our pursuers on bikes. It was only the badly rutted cart track that was holding them back for fear of bursting the tyres. We were done for, exhausted, we'd had it.....then panting Wag said,

'Quick, in here' indicating a small but sparse copse, in the middle of which was a dense blackberry thicket surrounded by stinging nettles. Did we hesitate? DID WE HELL! We dived in and burrowed into the middle of the blackberry bush. We were stung with nettles and the thorns went in deep, but so did we, deeper and deeper.

'Down' said our leader, and we needed no second telling. We grovelled face down into the dank soil, our hearts going like trip hammers. I felt our pursuers would certainly hear us gasping as we tried to get air into our straining lungs. I think what saved us though was that in those days summer wear for boys was khaki shorts with a jersey, and our jerseys were green. Perfect camouflage! The grand procession streamed past our hiding place, never giving us a second glance. I swear I could have touched them had I stretched out my arm....... (if my arm had been 10 feet long!) Just that one dense bush and the slight depression saved us, for that was the only cover.

The cyclists led the chasers, heads down pushing hard at the pedals, striving to keep balance as the rutted lane threw them about. Next came a small band of boys around our age (where the hell did they come from?) and, bringing up the tail of the chase, the golfers, waving clubs and shouting out loud what they would do to those bloody kids when they caught them. What they had in mind wasn't nice!

With the chase in full cry, right down the lane and out of sight, we crept out of our refuge, heads down, using the hedges as a means of getting clear. They really did give excellent cover!

By making a massive detour we got clean away, for not a soul did we see. They must have still been in hot pursuit half way back to Leicester. We arrived home very late indeed for no way were we going to try to cut corners and run slap bang into those wronged golfers. By the time we'd eaten our tea it was too late to play out and so we weren't going to see the cause of the problem until the next day when we went to Wag's house to call for him. Now, what we had in mind was a game; probably standing at opposite ends of the street and throwing the ball as hard as we could to the floor just to see how high it would bounce. That was the idea but, going towards his house there he was, Wag, perched on top of the irons running alongside the raised pavement. We stared aghast, for Wag, getting bored with waiting for us, had cut the outer casing from the ball and was now stripping out the yards of elastic contained inside which gave it its bounce. As we arrived he was surrounded by yards of the stuff from the ball's innards and was just in the process of scratching open the little bag of gunge that was at the very heart of the golf ball. I could've wept!

Mam's Illness:

With poor Mabel's death, a terrible, and at times insurmountable, burden had been lifted from Our Mam's shoulders. Those extra little luxuries of eggs, cod liver oil & malt etc plus the other invalid foods purchased to try to tempt Mabel's jaded appetite and hidden on the back shelves of the cupboard just in case the hardship people had come around; they who might have offered some financial aid to alleviate some of the crippling burden Mabel's needs had put on Mam's meagre purse. Now Mam could afford to buy the cheaper (and to us more useful) basic essentials that would help fill our bellies. The only item left over to gather dust was that bottle of peppermint cordial which Mam had stopped off to buy on that last terrible day. There it stood gathering dust for years, the last financial sacrifice that was made. Nobody could bear to drink it.

Now those last terrible months had taken their toll, and Mam was taken seriously ill. Not for her the comfort of a hospital bed. No indeed, she chose to stay at home, refusing to go away lest the Municipal took us kids into Care. I can so clearly remember the terrible smell of blood that she passed with or in lieu of a bowel motion. Ulcerative or was it mucus colitis? Once again the house reeked of Lysol disinfectant. It seemed to be in every room. Lysol, the disinfectant used in Our Mabel's sputum mug, and which was now staining the bottom of Mam's chamber pot; the pot that she tried to shield from our young eyes, pushed right under the bed, or carried out, covered in newspaper, to be emptied down the pan of the 'lavvy', leaving blood stains in the pan even after flushing. But nothing could mask the almost animal moans that came from behind the closed bedroom door or outside toilet door as, fist clenched, she tried to rub the pain away. Weak and worn out she was, finally forced to take to her bed. Dear God, what despair she must have felt? What other agonies were awaiting just around the corner to be heaped upon her and her brood? But in one of her darkest hours Mam was to make a friend who remained a friend for the rest of their lives. It came about in this way:

It was a warm sunny afternoon. Ted was at work and we younger children were at school. Mam was alone, upstairs in bed. The door wasn't locked in fact the door was slightly ajar to let a draught of air through. This was quite safe as we had nothing worth pinching! Mam was in a light doze when a woman's voice called up the stairs.

'Don't be frightened my gel; are you up there?'

Mam shouted back, 'Yes, who is it?!'

Back came the reply, 'Is it alright if I come up?'

Obviously, in her weakened condition Mam was in no position to say other than what she did say,

'Yes, come up!'

Heavy steps were to be heard on the stairs then, around the bedroom door, wheezing from her exertions, came the fresh open face of a big, and I mean BIG, woman. Mam's sense of humour burst through as she said,

'For goodness sake girl, I don't know who you are but sit down before you fall down!'

The visitor did, and at the same time mopped her brow with a spotlessly clean, lace trimmed, handkerchief! Mam later confided that that's what told her she was alright, that lovely hanky!

'My name's Sally Brown' began the visitor, 'I live just around the corner on the next street. I've been told you've had more than your fair share of troubles; that your husband deserted you and that you've just lost your daughter. Now you're ill. Well I'm not surprised. It's a wonder you haven't gone under yourself with one thing and another!'

It was then Mam used those words with which she was to greet every disaster,

'Well, there's plenty worse off than me!'

'That may be so,' said her visitor, 'but you've children in the house and children get their clothes dirty.....so, where do you keep your dirty washing?.....and I want fresh sheets for that bed!'

'We put them under the sink downstairs, but you mustn't..........'

But she found she was talking to thin air!

Later, before she'd left our house, Sally had put the old coal fired copper on, washed everything that needed washing, changed Mam's bed linen and night clothes, put them on the line to dry, and don't forget that in those days before washing machines every item was washed in bar soap first then pounded with the washing Dolly (an instrument of torture if ever there was one) before being pegged out. In between she got Mam a cup of tea, chased me and Our Ronnie around doing errands and finally left with, 'and I'll be back in the morning to iron the washing!'

Sally had Mam smiling more times in a few minutes than she had in months, and so a friendship was struck that was to last until that good, kind Sally Brown died. God Bless her, she had more Christian charity in her little finger than most of us have in our whole body. I have never seen her like since, nor do I expect to see it again, this side of the grave anyway. If that dear kind lovely woman, gone these many years since, as I'm writing this, is reading it over my shoulder, then may I say I have and will try to keep your love and compassion alive so that others may know what a queen among women you were.

Probably being the youngest, I suppose I was the most vulnerable of all us children. My nerves were shot to hell. For example, I daren't go upstairs on my own, even in broad daylight, if I were the only one in the house, which I so often was. I developed a chronic twitch which was at once diagnosed as St Vitus Dance. The corner shop didn't stock the magic elixir called 'Parishes Food', a sovereign remedy for those who suffered from nerve trouble, and so a bottle was purchased from Mr Davidson, the Chemist on the corner of Overton Road/ Uppingham Road. Even to look into his window with those enormous shaped jars of coloured water, made one feel better even though, as we know now, all it was, was coloured water. That Parishes Food was powerful stuff indeed though due, I was told, to the high iron content it contained. I was soon on the mend, with a strong after taste in my mouth for days following the last dose.

If one of the family were upstairs, I would creep quietly up and stand outside that back bedroom door of terrible memories, willing myself to open it and step inside. I would step down that one step and stand on the bare wooden floorboards, looking at that old iron, black painted bedstead on which my elder sister had suffered for so long. Standing very quietly, I would shut out all the intrusive noise, and a great peace would descend upon me; alone and yet not alone, afraid, unfeeling....I know not.

My First Black Man:

It was about this time I was to see my first black man. It's hard to believe, I know, but until the black American servicemen came to England during World War II, these were a people we only sang about at Sunday School and knew from the children's story 'Little Black Sambo.' We knew songs such as 'Poor Old Joe' and 'Massa's in de cold Ground.' Uncle Tom's Cabin' was also a reading 'MUST.' Back then to that first black man seen in Morton Road: He came capering down the street and we kids ran home to tell the family.

To our untutored eye he was indeed jet black! He seemed to be wearing a large white bed sheet and wore sandals on his feet, the likes of which we had never seen before. We kids, with eyes popping, followed closely behind with repeated warnings of, 'don't get too close to him' in our ears. To us he might well have come from Mars. His behaviour was most strange. His eyes rolled and he muttered to himself although we kids had not provoked him in any way, just merely followed. He turned and made to chase us away. The best was yet to come though, for giving us best in the racing stakes, he turned and went into Mr Warren's corner shop and came out holding several wax candles which he promptly began to eat! In a parody of a request always made when some fortunate child had an apple or an orange (do you remember, 'save us the core' or 'give us a bite') one of the wags amongst us called out,

'Save us the wick, Mate!'

I think all this was a publicity stunt for something or other, perhaps a circus, but who the hell had money to waste upon a circus in our little community? Whatever, that little episode provided a talking point amongst us for weeks afterwards.

Memories of school days:

Whilst in primary school, I did rather well, all things considered. I was well up in the three Rs and was given a book prize to prove it! However, I had no idea who chose the book and, try as I might, I could not get into it until I was around twelve years of age. I often wonder what happened to it. I know now that in every school a child has a record folder locked away in the Head's Office which gives details of the child's home circumstances, so it was obvious I'd come from a broken home - although 'smashed' would probably better describe it.

I believe two teachers shielded me from the trauma of those early years:

My infant Headmistress was a very tall, beautifully groomed lady who, to my young & immature eyes seemed very old indeed as she sat at her desk on a raised dais in the school hall under a picture of 'The Boyhood of Raleigh' or was it a picture of a child dressed in blue velvet blowing bubbles? Certainly, it was one or the other. Her desk shone with layers of polish rubbed in by successive caretakers over the years, and on it, in pride of place, was the school's brass bell which shone like gold. It was every child's ambition just to be allowed to go into the yard and ring that bell, so calling the children into lines 'ready to go in.'

One item of school equipment I used to gaze at longingly was a May Pole that stood in the hall with its coloured ribbons wound round and around as they descended downwards. Unfortunately, I only saw this in use once, probably because it was so huge and heavy. Had it toppled over a child could've been seriously injured, (or would it be that the poor caretaker having to drag it to centre floor might have ruptured himself), but that one occasion we danced around it was so memorable because, having danced 'in & out' to the teacher's shouted instructions, intertwining & interweaving, the finished coloured interwoven result looked good enough to eat!

I also remember the excitement that pervaded the whole school when we were told, 'children, as you have been so good, you are all going to be taken into the hall and the school radio will be switched on'. We will then hear the launching of the huge new liner The Queen Mary!'

Well, that promise was kept up to us all filing into the school hall, but when the monster of a wireless was switched on, probably due to ignorance, bad reception or both, all we got was static! Very disappointed, we all filed out again! Ah well!

One day the Headmistress sent for me via her monitor.

'Please Miss Dunn, can you send Norman Hastings to Miss Wicken?'

Now, usually when summoned it meant a child had been up to something and was to be given a telling off or, terror of terrors, was to be punished. At this, Miss Dunn, who'd received me back from the 'Sanny' and must have known something of my disturbed past, queried whether the monitor had got the right name.

'Do you mean Norman Staples?' Miss Dunn asked.

'No, Miss Dunn' came the reply, 'Miss Wicken said Norman Hastings, and she wants him at once!'

Grumbling under her breath, my champion said,

'Well, I'm sure you've made a mistake and it's Norman Staples Miss Wicken wants however, you'd better go along, Norman, and we'll see if I'm right!'

My heart was going like a trip hammer as I approached the Holy of Holys, Miss Wicken's desk. She was sitting there just as she usually did, head down writing. Why did I want to pee so badly all at once?

She looked up and, seeing me so wide eyed and apprehensive, smiled sweetly. She beckoned me to come forward and I stood at the side of her, no longer worried. That soon changed!

'Don't be worried, Norman' she began, 'only for some reason your father wishes to speak to you!'

Startled, I looked around, and he was there, standing just inside the other entrance to the hall. I was petrified. School had always been the one safe place I could rely on to shelter me from the hell that at times was our home. Now that illusion of safety was gone. I felt betrayed.

Miss Wicken must have seen I was terrified and, leaning forward she said, 'Don't be frightened Norman, I'm here and if you feel it's all too much just put your hand up and I'll put a stop to whatever it is about your father that so worries you, for I do know about the upsets in your home life.'

Trembling, I approached my family's nemesis. What did he want that could cause him to fetch me from my classroom? He looked as fierce to me then as he always did. With no preamble, he took hold of my arm and demanded to know,

'Did the Old Woman (Our Mam) go out with her fancy man last night?'

That did it, for that was all he'd dragged me from my lessons to ask. My hand shot up! Miss Wicken shot across the hall and ordered him out whilst I, sobbing as though my heart would break, was escorted by her back to my classroom and to Miss Dunn who directed a glare at her Principal for allowing me to get so upset.

From that day on I never did any good at school although tested several times as I was, I could always score high marks, but as for the rest? Well, I'd just shut off! By letting him into that one safe place, the one place I felt would always hide me, I felt I'd been betrayed.

Remember, this was only a Primary School! I don't know about today but in those days, as I remember, every class seemed to have a 'bad' boy or girl, and even in the case I'm about to recount, a class 'fall' guy or girl. Let anything go wrong and let the teacher ask 'who did that' and the cry would go up naming one particular child even though the named child would more often than not be innocent. Which brings me to, or back to, Miss Dunn!

I could never love this teacher of mine although she was always so very kind to me. The social barrier was too great. Young as I was, I knew I was a 'poor' child from a 'poor home'. Not a bad home or a dirty home but a home where we were living from hand to mouth; nothing to fall back on. She, Miss Dunn, was posh. On the minus side though, she had very bad feet which, being quite a large lady, did not help. I never ever gave her any problems and so was obviously counted as one of the class 'good boys'.

Now, the class 'fall guy' was a girl I'll call Mavis Greenwood. Let a desk lid be slammed down and to Miss Dunn's cry of, 'who is that noisy child?' the call would go up 'Mavis Greenwood, Miss!'

Again, if a child laughed out loud or made a noise, in answer to the enquiry, 'who made that loud noise?' back would come 'Mavis Greenwood, Miss!' Until that one day, and I can see it all as clearly as I saw it 64 years ago......

Miss Dunn was walking between the rows of desks when all of a sudden she stopped dead in her tracks. Her nose wrinkled, and I knew why, as I'd heard quite clearly a muted 'trump' or 'fart' which was identified by most of the class if the hastily suppressed giggles were anything to go by. Miss Dunn took out a piece of lace which was her hanky, for she never blew her nose, she just dabbed it. Holding this to her nose, for the most awful smell had begun to assail all our nostrils, she demanded to know,

'Which of you children is responsible for that awful smell?'

As though led by a conductor's baton, the whole of the class chanted, 'Mavis Greenwood, Miss!'

'Go to the front of the class at once, Mavis Greenwood, you naughty, smelly.......'

Here Miss Dunn stopped then,

'Oh you naughty, naughty children, Mavis Greenwood has been at home in bed with a severe chill for the last three days!'

And so, whilst dear Miss Dunn was limping back to her desk at the front of the class on those poor aching feet of hers, the children were looking around for the next 'fall guy' to replace Mavis. I kept my head well down!

New Clothes (and torn trousers):

From somewhere Our Mam had managed to find a little extra money to what was normally available to us. It could've been earned by us as a family doing some 'thonging' - home work from the shoe factory which we would all do in the evening for a few pence a pair, anyway, Mam took me and Our Ronnie on the tram into town, swaying, clanking and clattering along with our noses glued to the window. Seeing the steel tram rails sunk into the road bed I would often think heaven help any poor cyclist who got his or her front wheel trapped in the rail groove, for off they would come for sure. The overhead pole that carried the current to the tram's driving system had been known to become detached and to cater for this eventuality each tram carried a long flexible pole to lift the pole back into place to make the connection. These trams swayed alarmingly especially on the down slopes and on this day I sat holding tightly to my seat just in case the flanged wheel biting into the rail groove became detached and the car left the rails completely. I was such an old worry guts!

At the town centre we were taken into Marks & Spencers which in those days was only slightly more upmarket than Woolworths and stopped at a rack holding boys blazers. These we tried on until a near perfect fit was achieved. These blazers came complete with a badge on the breast pocket; the intention was to make the wearer look like they attended a posh school. The family joke afterwards was that Ronnie attended the Berlin Academy of Dance, and Norman was a Winchester 'Old Boy'. Next we were both fitted with thick, worsted grey, long trousers. Even at that first fitting they itched like the dickens! This was only to be expected as all boys, some even up to the day they left school at fourteen years, always wore short trousers. We two must have been some of the youngest ever to wear 'long uns.' I was about 8 and Ronnie 10 years old. In retrospect, I think being supplied with these articles of clothing was a throw-back to the time Our Mam lived in Canada, as shorts would've been impossible in those severe Canadian winters; perhaps it was also her way of telling the world 'we're not beaten yet!'

Wearing our new gear for the first time in the depressed area where we lived, we caused quite a sensation. Of course it was wearing apparel for Sundays and Church only and our progress along those mean streets was accompanied by 'Oooohs' and 'Ahhhs' from various elderly 'chair at the front door' ladies, who commented 'don't them little boys look lovely.' The best comment we had though was 'are they dwarves?'

Norman left & Ronnie right

229

A final treat to celebrate the new gear was set for the weekend. We were dressed in our finery and Ted's bony fingers held our heads back at an impossible angle as he combed in turn, a parting in our hair, leaving us both as we discovered when the ordeal was over, as though we had red hot tram lines running through our scalps. Ted could really 'scrawp' a mean comb! Then, and only then, did we accompany Mam for our treat; A short bus ride to Swithland Woods. (Silly me, I'd been telling anyone willing to listen we were going to Switzerland for the afternoon!) And so we arrived, scratching away at our legs which, sitting on the leather seats of the bus, had caused the trousers to itch all the more. We were determined to enjoy the free amenities even though we were wishing we'd been able to come in our cool khaki summer shorts.

There were two very high slides or chutes which daredevil Ronnie promptly climbed via a steel ladder. At Mam's urging I dared to follow, not wishing to draw the charge so often levelled at me of 'Our Norman's got no confidence!' At the top of the ladder the ground seemed to be a hell of a long way down as I peered over Ronnie's shoulder, and I was a mind to climb back down but then, horror rose up, for behind me were other sliders. Ronnie positioned himself at the peak of the slide, slid forward and then down. I sat and, letting go of the sides began my descent, noting as I did so that Ronnie was by now at the very bottom standing in a curious half twisted position with Mam just behind him looking at his backside. Approximately half way down and at speed, I heard them both shout something to me whilst just at that very moment I felt a slight tug at the seat of my trousers and an unmistakable ripping sound. I too had found that piece of metal sticking out from the metal of the chute. Would you believe it, both Ronnie and I had identical 2 inch tears in the seat of those trousers. Mam's bad luck still held. Pinned together with safety pins, we left for home; how disappointing. Poor Mam and poor us; brothers with darned arses!

It was about this time Our Ronnie got the nickname that was to accompany him through those early years: Titch Hastings! He never grew as tall as me in spite of being two years older. I was always the taller of the two but he was always the leader, and make no mistake about it! All the family doted on him and I realise now that in an attempt to get some of the attention I sometimes over reacted. This, coupled with the fact I was the one who most looked like the Old Man, never exactly made me flavour of the month, however, I never ever resented his popularity within the family. He was my brother and we'd shared so many difficult times together that in my eyes he could do no wrong, except........when knowing my fear of loose cattle in a field he would blithely scramble over the field gate and walk off, ignoring my yelps of 'wait for me, Our Ronnie!!'

Chest clinic review:

It was time for me to attend the chest clinic in Regents Road for a review of my condition since being discharged from 'the Sanny.' The chest physician was a Dr Laurie, a tall thin man whose skull like face made him look as though he was in the terminal stages of consumption himself! I mean no disrespect in putting it this way for he was always kindness itself to me........but if only he'd warmed his hands before sounding my chest! Dr Laurie put it to Our Mam that I would benefit from being allowed to attend an open air school for sickly children but sadly the family finances did not run to the expected expense of tram fares, school meals etc and so I was left to 'get on with it' even though I was nothing but skin and bone. Two years later, when it was discovered Ronnie had a good singing voice (good enough to earn money on the clubs) he was enrolled at an open air school where free school milk was provided and children were allowed to have a sleep after dinner. This enabled him to catch up on sleep lost during the weekend nights of clubbing. So much for justice!

Mam, isn't it the truth that I was expendable, and I'm not being disloyal when I say that. After all, who was it who was always pushed to the back of the queue when there were any goodies going; but who was it also who, in spite of all of this, stood by you right to the bitter end!!?? But, I'm overstepping mine, and Our Mam's story.

My first male teacher:

My first male teacher was in his mid 20s, and I was led to believe he'd been in hospital. This I could believe because he was a horrible colour. Our first upset came some three months after I'd left 'the Sanny!' Each child in the class was handed a large buff folder and we were instructed to write our name in large black capitals on the front. Unfortunately, due to my hospitalisation, I'd missed that particular lesson and so I was guessing as I laboriously did my best. Several others made mistakes and collectively he yelled at us all.

'Do it again, underneath the first attempt!'

One or two in the next lot got it right and so dropped out, but not me. The agony of it seemed to go on and on until only I was left. I was in a blind panic and fast running out of space. My envelope and I both looked a right mess, and yet still this apology for a teacher was shouting and raving at me. I was in a blind funk, terrified and thinking that at any minute I was going to pee myself. Afterwards I found out it all came down to the letter 'G'. I was doing the small 'g' and not the capital. At the eleventh hour someone in the class came to my rescue. God Bless whoever it was because he/she piped up with,

'Please Sir, Norman Hastings has been in the Sanatorium for three months. He was never shown how to do capital letters!'

When my former teacher got to see the folder she questioned me closely. When I told her the details she muttered 'that man has no right to be a teacher.' Sadly, I was stuck with him. To be fair though our next encounter was indeed all my own fault. The register was being called and we answered to our number. I was twenty three. We began...One, two, three etc. but as we went along each boy was shouting his number louder than the boy before. I fell for it and when we got to twenty three I too shouted my number. I think the bugger was waiting for someone to make an example of, and he chose me.

'Go to the Headmaster and report yourself' he bawled.

I stood and left the classroom, quaking in sheer bloody terror because in most people's opinion that particular Headmaster (and only recently I met a former pupil who referred to the Head as 'evil), was a bully who seemed to enjoy nothing better than beating the living daylights out of any child unlucky to be sent down to him. I can see the swine now, striding through the classrooms or corridors with his glasses pushed to the top of his head, shouting and bawling at us cowering children, all of us under 11 years of age, the cane which he used without mercy, in his hand. Time and time again we saw the evidence of his brutality in the red wheals and bruises on our chums' hands. Time and time again parents, without jobs, money or hope, would come to the school to complain and he took joy in talking down to them, threatening them with the police. It was only when fathers, goaded beyond reason by the way their son or daughter had been abused, offered him violence in return, that he showed his cowardly colours, for then he would shout for his deputy head, a former ex-soldier and six feet tall, to come and protect him. This then was the walking horror to which I was being sacrificed. I crept along the passageway leading to the hall from whence I could hear his voice. It was very clear that as usual he was in a vile, filthy temper. I peeped around the hall door. He was standing on the stage, hands on his hips. I gave it best a few moments, then retraced my steps. Outside my classroom door I paused and listened. It was like the grave in there. As quiet, I imagined, as a prison would be as they waited for some poor soul to be hanged by the neck. I went back in. Every eye of every child, and including my nemesis, looked at my hands and then my eyes, for those who'd been brutalised always came back with their hands stinging, tucked into their arm pits, crying. The teacher said nothing, he just looked at me. I think in the meantime he might have had time to remember that this boy's dad had a record of violence - as per his school record card. You know it's a funny thing but although the Old Man would knock us kids about, let anybody else try and he'd come along, fists flying, and this poor bloke, if my doting daddy did show up, would not have had a deputy head to protect him. The Headmaster could hide; the teacher could not. I told him a deliberate lie,

'Please Sir, the Headmaster said he was too busy to bother with me. I'm to go back if you feel it necessary.'

The teacher made no comment, nor did he send me back. I think he knew I'd told a 'porkie.' I'd gotten away by the skin of my teeth. Never ever was I caned at school.

Social problems – poverty and drink:

This, as I've tried to convey, was a tough district, noted for tough family groups. In fact, I would dare to wager that had there been such things as social workers in those days, even they would've gone around in two's.

Husbands were out of work, six or seven children per household and families living on the dole; Parish relief and only the Workhouse and a Parish Burial in some unmarked plot at the end. Yet these men could be seen on Armistice Day. Men who'd been through the Hell of the Western Front but now stood revealed as men promised a better and happier life only to be denied any of what had been promised. No wonder they so often acted as men with no conscience. Disheartened, broken, no hopers. These fathers so often poured what little money there was into the Publican's pocket whilst his wife and kids went hungry. Drunk, the men would stagger home, often singing and full of good cheer, a mood that could, and often did, vanish in a moment. Then the women would scream and the windows came flying out, followed by the chair that'd done the damage. The 'Black Maria' police van would hurtle up the street and, as the policemen disappeared inside the house the wife could be heard screaming,

'Don't try to hit the copper! If you do you know they'll paste you black and blue when they get you inside!'

I'm reminded of the true story of the prisoner in the dock claiming how the police had given him a 'good hiding.' The Magistrate looked hard at him before looking at the prosecuting officer's 'black eye' then said, 'You know Mr Jones, you really must learn that if you play rough, you're going to get hurt!'

Indeed, Mr Jones should not have needed reminding, for every 'hard case' in the town knew that the surest way to get the hiding of his life would be if he dared to hit a policeman. God help you if you did, for when they got you to the 'Nick'.......

Other poor children:

This particular family I'm now thinking of were very, and I mean VERY, VERY POOR. One of the numerous boys in this family was easily spotted when out, for every hair was sheared off so close to his scalp that, had it been cropped any shorter, the Barber would've been skin grafting. All that was left to the child, for he was still only around twelve years of age, was a fringe on the front. We all knew that this type of cut was given to boys who were usually 'lousy' on a regular basis. His looks did nothing for him. Left well alone he was no problem to other children in the bullying stakes, never the less, he had a countenance that shouted, 'Brutalised Child Watch Out.' He, like so many other near starving children would pick up from the gutter and devour any discarded food he found and was not ashamed to be seen devouring it. I cannot think of him as being 'dirty,' for his mother, I'm sure, did try to keep him as clean as she possibly could, but sadly his close set 'piggy eyes' and his ghastly grey face, set him apart. For all I knew he may have been a gentle boy. Like so many other boys who lived in those terribly deprived days, he wore great hob nailed, steel shod boots. These were likely supplied by the Parish or the Education Department. His boots were so dilapidated they were held together by bits of string and fervent prayers not to get any rain, otherwise the cardboard inner liners, put in there to keep some of the pavement filth off the bare feet, would disintegrate. This then was he. A product of Government and Local & Central indifference. May God forgive them; I cannot. That a child of near twelve years should show such obvious signs of deprivation, and as we will soon see, near madness, and society remain indifferent, is shameful.

His classroom that day was warm and close, and the subject (taught by a young student teacher) was boring in the extreme. Imagine, if you can, the bare brick walls painted in one of the standard colours, brown or green, unrelieved by any sort of decoration. The floor was bare wooden floorboards, splintered and rough from the hob nails and studs in the boys' boots, supplied courtesy of whichever charity or institution. All of the boys, for this school was an 'all boys' school, sat at single planked desks held together with cast iron brackets at the sides which hurt like hell if you accidentally caught your foot or leg against them, and those hard wooden, unpadded seats, soon found the weak spots in the skinny shanked, unpadded bums that occupied them. It was too warm, hot and sultry, and the uncirculated air in the classroom was foul with the smell that some 30 plus overheated and unwashed, lice infested bodies were releasing into the atmosphere. In his inexperience, the young teacher had called the class to attention and in an attempt to keep them awake had ordered the boys to 'sit up straight and put your hands on your head.' This is sheer torture after 10 minutes or so on a normal day, but today!! Murderous! The next order was to 'take deep breaths' with himself setting an example, but all this achieved was several bouts of coughing. Now, any teacher with any sense would've seen that these kids were hot and bored, unable to concentrate, and so would've ordered them to all lay their folded arms on the desk and lay their heads down. Even 10 minutes would've helped, but no. The more the kids sitting straight up dozed off, the more the teacher bawled at them. In a momentary quiet lull to the proceedings there came a loud rasping 'fart' which jerked the class awake as they dissolved into hysterical giggles. The teacher did not leave well enough alone. He screamed, ranted and raved, and then chose his scapegoat; the boy I've described.

The teacher's insults were wide ranging as he worked himself into a rage although how much of it was feigned I do not know, going from the general to the specific, and finishing off by calling the boy a 'filthy pig!' That did it. Eyes blazing the boy stood up,

'It weren't me who farted, and I aint no filthy pig either!'

Without further ado he bent down and, as the teacher continued to shout at him, the boy removed one of his hob nailed boots and let fly. If the teacher hadn't ducked down quickly the rest of the class swear to this day that the flying boot would have taken his head from his shoulders. As it was, the blackboard was split from top to bottom. The end of that episode was predictable and for the boy, very very painful. That shit of a Headmaster had a field day!

Mablethorpe:

We'd been promised a treat and today was the great day. We were going on a trip to Mablethorpe - Mam, Ronnie and me. The Omens were not good though, for it was a grey overcast day with a miserable drizzle of rain wetting us as we made our way to the local garage. This wasn't the scenario we saw in our picture books or comics, usually entitled 'A Day at the Seaside' which showed little girls with long golden ringlets, wearing blue velvet dresses which would be the same colour as the huge floppy bow in their hair, accompanied always by a coy, simpering little brother with chubby cheeks and fat, dimpled legs. The sort of kid who, had he dared show his peaches & cream complexioned face in our neck of the woods, would've had his life made a misery. Thus, the whole family of them, who had already been labelled by us as 'toffs' would be climbing into the family Rolls Royce (mummy always safely in the back seat waving, one feels, to the poor people or servants) whilst daddy strapped a huge picnic hamper to the luggage grid, already piled high with buckets and spades and often 'Fido' the family dog. For us reality was a rickety old Red bus whilst we carried a flask, bread & jam sandwiches, and Ronnie's bathing costume & towel in paper carrier bags. Ron was determined to swim in the sea but I wasn't; people drowned! We didn't see much of the scenery as by now it was raining quite hard, and due to the closely confined passengers the bus windows were streaming with condensation. Anyway, we soon got hoarse pointing out cows in the fields forty or fifty times, so Ronnie and I took it in turns reading the week old comic we'd acquired. Our Mam, ever the sociable being, was soon deep in conversation with the adults around her. It never failed to amaze me how quickly women got to know each other's business. Several times I heard the words 'my Old Man'...... 'The lousy bleeder'....which gave us a clue as to who Mam was talking about. After what seemed like hours, we arrived; it was still pouring down. I know many would've preferred to sit it out on the bus but this wasn't permitted, so out we all got. We staggered down to the front then wished we hadn't, for the wind off the sea was sending huge, monstrous waves pounding and thrashing onto the beach, and keeping our eyes open was near impossible!   How we escaped being thrown into the air I have no idea but the canvas stalls on the beach weren't so lucky. We turned back in full retreat and, would you believe it, all the way back to the shelter of the shops and arcades, Ronnie was moaning,

'But Mam, I wanted to swim; can't I go for a swim? Hey Mam??"

Her reply was unprintable.

Lady in the club:

Financially, we were now slightly better off, but all of us knew we were still living on a knife's edge. The Old Man was still not paying a single penny maintenance for his children if he could dodge it, although his nocturnal visits when he would stand in the street shouting insults at the top of his voice, were still something of an event to be dreaded. Reports filtered back as to what he was getting up to and one in particular stuck in our minds over the years. On one occasion a woman went up to Mam in the club and said,

'Is it right you're Ted Hastings' wife?'

'Yes' said Mam, 'and who might you be?'

The woman then said,

'I was short of money and your husband said that if I let him have sex with me, he'd pay me.' She went on, 'I let him have me and when he was finished he gave me tuppence. You know, your husband calls you every name he can think of but now I've met you, I think you're nice.'

I won't say any more on this incident.

There wasn't a Welfare State net spread beneath unfortunates such as our little family group, as there is today, just waiting and eager to help those in need. How wonderful it would have been if Mam could have stormed into the

DHSS offices and demanded 'I want this; I want that; I'm entitled to this, that and the other!' Chance would've been a fine thing.

Lost sixpence:

It was Saturday afternoon about 2:30. Ronnie and I had been sent to the Co Op store (was it off Prestwold Road?) for the week's groceries. We'd handed the list over to the man behind the counter then stood looking and sniffing at the aromas which filled the shop interior. The smell I loved the most came from sides of bacon hanging from 'S' hooks. The shop assistant would lift the side down and place it on a machine with a big round cutting knife along the front end. After asking 'what cut/ thickness would madam like?' the machine would be set in motion, either by hand cranking or electricity. The table would go backwards and forwards with the bacon going into the blade as slice after slice was peeled off. Not for us though. Our finances didn't run to that quality of bacon. I think ours came from the market late on a Saturday night when pieces could be purchased at a great saving, but items such as sugar and tea were easily purchased loose for which thick blue paper bags were used. After pouring the loose sugar/ tea in with the aid of a scoop, I loved to see the man close the bag so carefully and tightly. You know, I can never remember the contents escaping on our way home. Having laid our meagre purchases together upon the counter, the shop assistant, who'd been writing the prices against each item as he put them down, now started to add them up. In those days he was working in farthings, half pennies, pennies and silver, but he just rattled the figures out loud and, having arrived at a total he would slice a piece of sheet metal between a book of divided chits and enter how much was to be paid over to him. (Mam's dividend number was 36913) Everything would then be put into a small round container that screwed into its mate on an overhead wire. This done, he pulled on a handle (not unlike a lavatory chain handle) which sent the container whizzing off somewhere. At its destination a cashier would check his figures and a moment or two later the container with the change would come back. Mission accomplished. On the way home along Prestwold Road, we boys were checking empty fag cartons for fag cards and kicking tins, generally larking about. We had sixpence (a tanner) change which Ronnie was holding, him being the eldest. But then tragedy! Ronnie flung out his arm and I saw something silver fly through the air.

'Norm, I've lost it, I've lost Mam's change; the tanner!' he wailed.

But he hadn't, not quite, for my eyes had registered the small silver coin's flight path before it disappeared into a heap; a large mound of builder's lime on the site where some houses were going up. Young as we were we knew we didn't stand a celluloid cat in hells chance of finding that lost coin! We'd been warned that lime could burn you something awful, plus if we did start to dig around we'd be trespassing..... which meant the police! We ran home to tell Mam but she didn't tell us off; she didn't need to. The look on her face said it all. That sixpence was all she had left until next pay day which would be the following Friday, and this was Saturday. First thing on Monday morning, after gulping down our bit of breakfast, Ronnie and I put into operation the plan we'd formulated and intended to carry out even if it meant being late for school and dealing with any sanctions that might be imposed for lateness, as this, we'd been told time and time again, showed a sloppy attitude towards life! The pair of us dashed along to the building site and found the place where we both knew our family financial reserve had vanished. Getting ready to mix a batch of the stuff that holds bricks together we found an old chap; a labourer complete with cloth cap and moleskin trousers. Alongside him was another worker who wore a soft peaked cap, which strangely seemed to have a very flat top to it. We soon saw why for this second man, after stacking a number of bricks (about twelve) onto a board, gave a whistle to the old chap who helped him to lift the board, bricks and all, and place it on the top of the flat of the chap's cap. Without touching the board or the bricks, he then walked over to a ladder leading up to the near roof of the unfinished house, where he deposited the bricks, all ready for the bricklayer to cement them in.....We were fascinated for a few minutes, and then remembering why we were there, we called to the old labourer – he with the moleskin trousers tied with string just below the knees. With an old clay pipe jutting from the corner of his mouth, he was already shovelling together the ingredients of a mix which, besides sand and cement, incorporated lime from the heap in which we'd seen Our Mam's tanner vanish.

'Please Mister........' we began.

The old chap took his pipe from his mouth and, resting on his shovel, his faded, tired & watery eyes passed from one to the other of us as we disjointedly gabbled the disaster that had befallen us on the previous Saturday afternoon.

'In there, Mister!' we repeated over and over again, whilst pointing at the pile of lime. Finally, our voices faded into silence. The old gentleman asked us first for our names and then where we lived.

'Where does your dad work?' was his next question.

'Please Sir, our dad cleared off and left us.'

Really, the old chap was so easy to talk to that Ron and I forgot the often repeated maxim of Our Mam that 'you keep your troubles to yourself because others have troubles enough of their own without listening to yours!'

With no prompting from him, apart from the odd interjection, we gave a potted version of the lives and times of our family, ending with Mabel's death. I have often thought since of the picture we two small boys must have presented; both dressed in khaki shorts, patched and darned, a well-worn but clean jersey, well-scrubbed faces & hands; very respectful. We always knew our manners because Mam insisted on that. Finally, we looked around to find other labourers and their 'Brickies' had silently joined us, contributing nothing, just listening. Our old gent blew his nose loudly and then spoke,

'Just leave it with me lads. If I find your money I'll bring it round to you tonight when I finish work.'

I still don't know how but his words comforted us, and so we thanked him very much and hared off to school.

At 5:30 the same day, there came a knock at our back door and upon opening it Mam found the 'Brickies Labourer.'

'I think your little boys lost this, Missus' was all he said as he placed a sixpence into her hand. To this day, I still wonder whether he actually found our lost 'tanner' or whether he put his hand into his own pocket to make up the deficit in our family finances. Whatever, we wouldn't go short of food for one day that week. Old Gentleman, for that you truly were. Thank you again, and God Bless you, for our need truly was greater than thine.

9: More memories, hygiene and health

I was always to be a lonely, insecure child, feeling isolated and unwanted, even more so as things began to improve for us. I can see why now. In the space of five years Mam had lost everything she held dear: first her own mother, her husband had deserted her taking with him her beautiful home, then with Mabel upstairs dying and Maisie very ill with Diphtheria, days later I was diagnosed a Consumptive. Then her brother (John) aged 26 collapsing and dying in a cinema and within 3 months the grave having to be reopened to receive Mabel's poor, wasted body. Is it any wonder that within a short time her own health suffered? These then were her tragedies. Mine was that I resembled my father too much in looks. In fairness to her, when years later I looked objectively at the whole picture, I began to understand but, her indifference to me during the most important and formative years of my life, a period when I was most vulnerable, nearly broke me. More I will not say, except,

WHAT I AM MY PEERS MADE ME; WHAT I HAVE I EARNED FOR MYSELF

The Old Man was still active and he went into our corner shop,

'Don't let my old woman have anything on tick; she won't pay you!' he said.

The shop keeper, had he but known he was taking his life into his hands replied,

'Your wife doesn't have anything on tick (credit) from me because she's never asked for it. She always insists on paying cash for everything. However, if she ever did want credit I would give it to her gladly, to the limit in fact. Now Mr Hastings, SOD OFF OUT OF MY SHOP!'

The Bath Lady:

With so many children coming from terraced houses with no bathroom or bathing facility, a bare brick bathroom was incorporated within the school building and a 'bath lady' employed to make sure it was used to full effect. I was on the Monday morning rota and it was then, along with another child, I would enter the high ceilinged and steamy room to be greeted with,

'Big bath or small bath?'

Once this decision was settled, usually without acrimony although of course we both wanted the big bath, we were very quickly stripped, immersed and thoroughly scrubbed down.

The 'bath lady' was a dear, very kind, very thorough, and tactful lady, who didn't give the slightest hint that part of her job must have been to inspect each naked little body for marks of bruising etc. I thank God that never ever did I show marks of flea or bug bites, as so many must have done. No, my marks were internal. I wonder if my bath had to be paid for? I can't ever remember being asked for money on a Monday.

Like so many who'd come down in the world, Mam had a ritual of washing us that was rigidly adhered to. Twice each week in the early evening, Ron and I would, in turn, be stripped to the buff and sat on a towel placed on the table. I suspect this was to stop us getting splinters in our bum from the rough table. We were then thoroughly washed from head to toe.

In between these table scrubbings we were expected to keep ourselves clean; not easy when you stop to consider that before going to school we were expected to sort out our own clothes and do our share of the household chores, such as clearing the table of breakfast or dinner pots, washing up and resetting the table ready for the next meal.

The Nit Nurse:

Perhaps the most dreaded part of the school routine for most kids was the visit from the school 'nit nurse'. Oh, the indignity of being held in a vice like grip, head squashed against a crisply starched bosom, unable to move, whilst the dear lady in question went carefully through one's hair looking for evidence of fleas or eggs of the same. Those kids found to be lousy were sent home to be cleaned, and woe betide any parent who didn't start the cleaning process tout suit! Those of whom it was said (by us of course) 'they aint got fleas, the fleas have got them,' went to a special cleaning, delousing clinic and returned smelling heavily of the various lotions, whilst some, oh the shame, came back shorn of all their hair apart from a ridiculous little fringe at the front, thus telling the world, 'I come from a dirty home.'

To Mam's credit, no one ever from our family were found to have fleas for the simple reason that nearly every week, with our hair still wet from being washed, each of us in turn would kneel before Mam as she sat on a low chair with a sheet of newspaper on her lap. With the aid of a 'nit comb' (fine tooth) she would scrawp through our hair trying to make any fleas that we may have picked up, fall onto the paper where they could clearly be seen. They were then quickly dispatched with a satisfying 'crack' by a thumb nail. We did pick up fleas from other children in the class, and thinking about it, we only needed to scratch our head for the comb and newspaper to come out. In turn, each of us would be done to cries of 'there's one' and 'you're scratching too hard with the comb Mam.' Indeed, afterwards, our scalps felt as though they'd been bisected with red hot tram or train lines.

The Foot Nurse:

Next in line of the Local Authority Horrors was the 'foot nurse.' This dear lady would visit the schools quite out of the blue, to inspect children's feet for cleanliness etc. Now, bear in mind that so many of us had shoes that not only let in the wet but also the dust and dirt from the pavements, and often, all that stood between our feet and the floor would be a piece of cardboard or, if available, a piece of foot shaped linoleum pushed into the shoe. The lifespan of these emergency repairs was not a long one so the frequency of replacing them soon ran us out of materials. In the meantime, our feet got dirtier and dirtier. The first intimation that the dear lady was on the premises would be the arrival of a monitor to call out the class a few at a time. We would be taken into a side waiting room and invited to take off our shoes and socks, all ready for our inquisitor to make her inspection. Remembering now the horrors that this unveiling revealed, makes me realise that however much the Education Committee paid her, it most certainly wasn't enough for what was now revealed! Probably due to the practice of passing down shoes from child to child, many feet revealed all sorts of deformities, from curled over toes from being crammed into shoes that were too small or too tight, as well as verruca's, corns and sores etc., all covered in layers of dirt to varying degrees. Those of us who saw the chance would, once we knew the foot nurse was around, shoot up our arms and, catching the teacher's eye ask, 'Please Sir/ Miss, may I leave the room?' whilst at the same time screwing up one's face in an expression of agony to show how desperate the need for the toilet was.

Once inside the toilet, socks were whipped off and used as a flannel after being well moistened with spit. Anything, but anything to avoid having to take a letter home that declared, 'your child has dirty feet!'

Our battle of wits was never ending, and ways of dodging glares and accusations of being dirty taxed our ingenuity to the limits. I even saw one child, still at his desk in the classroom waiting to be called and, knowing he was to be first alphabetically, when the teacher wasn't looking, eased his shoe and sock off under the desk and, with the teacher still with his back to the classroom writing on the blackboard, our little chum spit on the cuff of a very torn and dilapidated shirt and scrubbed the worst of the muck from his feet. He then rolled his sleeve back up! His efforts awarded him a 'good' from nurse when his feet were inspected a few moments later!

Sore Thighs:

Another plague to strike all boys was sore inner thighs caused by a combination of factors. One was the coarse material used in short trousers. Another was most little boys were always in such a hurry and pulled up a leg of their shorts to 'pee'. Unfortunately, that restricted us giving our 'willies' a good shake to get rid of all the droplets, which of course trickled down our legs. The coarse shorts material then rubbed against the skin and combined with the ammonia in our dribbles, great areas of the inner thigh were rubbed raw. Gosh, it was painful. I swear half the boys walked around as though they were saddle sore.

10: St Barnabas Church Choir

Ronnie joined the local St Barnabas Church Choir. I wasn't very interested but to keep the peace when I was told 'you can go as well', I went. It wasn't an old church but I suppose it dated back to the early 1800s. Like so many town churches it was bounded on two sides by a privet hedge which was used to carry on a choirboy initiation ceremony called 'Bushing.' This meant that after serving one's time as a probationer the newly enrolled boy was carried and tossed into the privet hedge. Ronnie, being a newer entrant than me, was to be 'Bushed' first. One, two, three, LET GO! Now, the throwers were big lads who misjudged things completely, and instead of landing on top of the said hedge, poor Ronnie sailed straight over it and was brought up short by a stone buttress. When he emerged, blood was pouring from a head wound. We hurried off home and when we arrived, Our Mam went mad! The one good thing about that business was that when informed Titch Hastings and his brother had gone home for medical treatment, Bill Worth the Choir Master, demanded to know the whys & wherefores of the business. The Choir Master later called in personally to apologise and from then on 'Bushing' became a thing of the past! I was the first to escape the ritual.

Choir initiation that Norman escaped

IN 1937 when the **Hastings** brothers **Norman** and **Ronald** joined the choir at Leicester's St Barnabas Church - as probationers they could expect to be put through an initiation known as 'Bushing'.

This was a practice dreamed up by the regular choir members which required newcomers to their ranks to be thrown into the hedge surrounding the church.

"Unfortunately my brother - always called Tich Hastings because although two years older than me he was two inches smaller and much lighter - instead of being brushed winged into the hedge sailed over it and split his head open on the church border," explains Norman Hastings.

This led to Mr **Bill Worth**, the choirmaster, banning 'Bushing'. "Thank goodness, as I would have been next on the list." confides Mr Hastings.

"At Christmas the choir sang carols at various venues in the area including the Towers Hospital.

"I still remember the mouth-watering smell of freshly baked bread wafting down the highly polished corridors," he continues.

He also recalls the choir sitting on stage singing their hearts out in the hospital's main hall when a patient began mounting his feet on the floor.

"Seconds later male nurses were ushering the man out who was kicking and screaming - leaving us to carry on singing despite being utterly petrified," he adds.

NORMAN (left) and Ronald Hastings in their choir robes in 1937

Choir practice was twice a week and church services on a Sunday, usually morning & evening. I believe we were paid once a year, although it was more a gratuity than wage, for in my first year I believe I was paid sixpence which I duly turned over to Mam. A paid job that often came our way was singing in other churches for Weddings. I think we were paid one shilling. I only ever sang at one funeral and that was because the gentleman concerned had been a choir member.

Singing in that choir gave me a love of music and a talent for reading a tune or melody straight from a hymn book or Psalter, even though I couldn't, and still can't, read a note of music. I could sing the words and follow the music of Te Deum or Magnificat without prior rehearsal or knowledge of either and, although we did practice I realise now we would sing Steiner's 'Crucifixion' without prior rehearsal. We really were that good.

Our organist cum choirmaster was a fanatic. Not only did we have to sing and breathe properly whilst doing so but most importantly every word had to be clearly heard and understood by the congregation. Today, I listen to some of what are professed to be the elite of choirs and find myself echoing his words,

'I can't hear a word you're singing; you might be singing Rag & Bone for all I know!'

Choir practice was held in the school room at the side of the Church of England church, and the large school playground in front of the school room was used as a football field to pass the time until we were called in. The football was actually a tennis ball, always referred to as 'the pill', and all of us boys joined in, playing for whichever side suited us. I think so many good footballers were produced in those days because it took real skill to dribble and control a ball as small as that 'pill;' That was about the only ball most youngsters had to kick around.

The Head Boy Chorister was coming to the end of his time. Although he still had a good voice and could hit notes that most of us could only dream of, he was of that age when a boy's voice would break. I can remember so very clearly that time when he was singing a solo. The church was hushed; the dust motes drifting oh so slowly and lazily through the sun's late evening beams, streaming through the stained glass of the church windows. His voice was soaring, swooping and spreading throughout the church as we and the congregation listened entranced then, reaching for a note which we all knew was well within his range, his pure, clear voice was gone, to be replaced with a horrible rasping sound. To his credit he didn't falter, but that was it. He never again sang solo. He gave it his best and then he left the choir.

Close friendships existed within the framework of the Men and Boys Choir. Many boys referred to a particular man or other as 'My Pal.' These were purely friendships; there were no homosexual connotations. It was just a man and a boy would take to each other and exchange winks and smiles, but that was all.

One of the leading lights among the older boys, which would make him perhaps 14 years, was 'Ginner'. (No prizes for guessing the colour of his hair) Ginner was a very smart and refreshingly friendly boy who always wore his grammar school uniform as though it were 'best.' He was to all our minds a 'boys' boy.' The sort of lad we would've liked to be, but Ginner was to my mind, a one off!

Although it must have been pretty obvious that we two brothers came from one of the poorer homes whilst he obviously came from one that was better off, Ginner was never a snob. I'm sorry to say one or two of the others were though. No, he was always ready to wink at us and snap his fingers under our noses and, as we used to say, 'kid us along.' We admired him; Ginner was great! We did, however, share one thing in common – consumption. I was led to believe it also ran in his family.

Perhaps his most noticeable trait was he always said what was on his mind. For example, one of the choir boys had a sister who was Ginner's age and who was noticeably sweet on him. Now, one of the ways she had to gain his attention was to wait until we were kicking 'the pill' around and then when Ginner had the ball she would swoop and snatch it from his feet. This forced Ginner to grapple with her to get it back. Finally, even his patience snapped, and with her still holding tightly to the ball, he forced her gently back so she was trapped between his body and the stake hold fence, and with the ball tight between them he leaned over her and whispered in her ear. She went crimson, dropped the ball and ran like hell. Ginner, his face split by a huge grin, bent, retrieved the ball and ambled back to the game.

"Watch ya say to her Ginner? Did you tell her you'd tell her dad on Sunday?"

Ginner threw his head back and laughed, then snapped his fingers under my nose.

'No kid, I just told her that if she didn't stop snatching 'the pill' I would have to take my trousers down to her!'

I knew he was being rude, but had no idea what he meant, so just laughed.

Another memory of that lad was this:

It was Friday night choir practice and I was on my way along a street I regularly used when I saw a woman I'd never seen before come out of her house with a pram which she parked on her front. It was summer and after bending over the pram for a moment or two, she went inside leaving the front door ajar. Coming abreast of the pram I glanced in. Oh, that poor mother; I didn't know then but I know now her child was suffering from water on the brain. That poor little mite; its head was enormous, taking up nearly the whole width of the pram, and what made it look more grotesque was the child was wearing a huge woollen hat with a pompom on the top. Poor little mite; poor father; poor mother. To say I was shaken to the core would be an understatement, and I was still in a state of shock when I arrived at the church for choir practice. I stood against the schoolyard railings pondering the unfairness that was life as I just couldn't get that poor mite's image out of my mind. Football was in progress as usual. The yard was full of heaving, panting, red-faced, breathless boys. A scrummage developed in front of me as I stood aloof from it all and as it broke apart there stood Ginner, dear old Ginner all out of breath and having a great time. He stood beaming at me but for the life of me I could not raise a smile back. His beam failed,

'Now then young un, what's the matter with you today? Ay? Cat got your tongue?'

I blurted out what I'd seen, and the other boys crowded around and exclaimed with shock and horror as I described what I'd seen. Ginner stood listening, taking it all in without making any comment. My imagination was running riot and I'm sure had I said the child's head would need to be transported in a separate pram to the one with its body, they would've believed me. Ginner pondered long and hard not saying a word, not making a comment until I dried up and then, true to form, with a few words he erased all my shock and horror with,

'And if you don't stop playing with yourself young un, then when you get married and give your wife babies, they will all be born with big heads!'

Everywhere went dead quiet, and then a roar of laughter went up from all sides. He then snapped his fingers and re-joined the game! I wager I wasn't the only choir boy who was to remember his words!

Years later, and at the end of the 1939-1945 war, I had another bout of consumption which saw me confined to hospital. Mr Strudwick, the former curate who'd officiated at Mabel's funeral, came to visit me. By now he was based in Loughborough so Heaven knows how much he inconvenienced himself by doing that. 'Struddy' as he was more popularly known, was a man who had a following as the packed to capacity churches showed, and was both charming and sincere. Reminiscing about old times I asked him about Ginner who I knew had gained a commission in the Royal Navy.

His face darkened and, as though questioning God himself, he said,

'Why did he have to die? There was no need; he was safe but he went back!'

This was the first I knew about Ginner's death. He said no more than that....he had no need to, he'd said it all. I realised that to him Ginner was someone special, in the same way he was special to all of those who knew him. 'He went back, there was no need to'.....that just about sounds right for Ginner and I will lay odds he went back with a smile on his face and a snap of his fingers. What a waste but isn't all war a terrible waste?!

On special occasions (Harvest Festival, Christmas, Easter etc) the church would be packed, requiring chairs to be borrowed from the nearby school and set down in the aisle to cater for the overload. For me, the best part of being in church was to sit quietly in the beautifully carved choir stalls, with the rays of the evening sun streaming in on me, bathing me in the multitude of rich colours cast from the stained glass windows that depicted Our Lord and his Saints; the light reflecting off the great brass Lectern Eagle so gloriously that I thought for sure in my childish ignorance that it must be made of solid gold. I would then feel a great calm descend upon me and the strains and stresses of my life would go from me.

From that day to this, I have been able to testify to my faith. Pray God it will serve me to the end.

The Vicar and Trustees of that church must have been very, very enlightened people for the times; One Christmas, I think it was 1936, the choir boys only, plus the choirmaster accompanist, were invited to sing carols in a Social Men's Club on Coleman Road, which we did. The Club Chairman for once did not have to call for 'Order' as he did so many times during ordinary concerts, for those men in that 'men only' club, stood in absolute silence as our voices carried the message of Christmas through the smoky, beery hall.

The choir engagements I dreaded were the Christmas and Harvest services at the local mental hospital (The Towers) which in those days was commonly known as the 'Lunatic Asylum' probably because it was hard to think of them as hospitals. Treatment was so sparse in those days and nowhere near what's provided today. I have no doubt at all that the ordinary public attitude towards Asylums was pretty much the same as what the attitude to Bedlam was in the early Victorian times, when inmates were considered figures of fun. Remembering some of the 'looney' stories that went the rounds, I'm sure many, even in the so called enlightened days of the 1930s, would've paid admission to go and poke fun at the inmates the same way they'd now pay to go to the zoo. Lumped together would be the feeble minded, deranged and other defectives. Only the truly dangerous were segregated in locked rooms and wards, under restraint by virtue of keys and straightjackets, and guarded by the fittest and strongest of attendants.

My overwhelming impression of the place was of long, clean, highly polished corridors smelling of urine and freshly baked bread, stale clothing and cooking odours.

The choir would pass along the same corridors used by the inmates, although I have to confess we thought of them as 'looneys'. We met them coming in the opposite direction, passing us, and as they did so, pressing themselves against the wall as though they feared we might do them harm; a group of inmates, young, middle-aged and old, both male and female, wearing the oddest collection of clothes imaginable.

This was Institutionalisation, as taught in the Social Studies classes of today.

What caught the eye first of all was the assortment of head gear worn by the women. Bonnets and hats of all shapes, styles and description, covered in masses of artificial flowers, faded and battered beyond repair. To go with these monstrosities, the ladies worse shapeless 'mother hubbard' type dresses, beltless and unbuttoned, not one of which could even loosely be described as fitting. To complete the ensemble, stockings, if any, were thick Lisle type, sagging and drooping around the ankles. Slippers were the order of the day for all the inmates; Boots were hard, especially for anyone on the receiving end of a kick. The men were similarly shoddily attired, wearing baggy trousers, and collarless shirts, torn and unbuttoned. Most likely these poor souls were deserted by kin and family. They were just waiting for it all to end.

I was petrified at such close contact with the inmates, but not one made any sort of threatening gesture towards our group. On the contrary, many of the women turned drooling mouths in our direction and screwed their faces up in what I now realise were intended to be smiles. It had obviously got through to those damaged brains that we were children in a place where children were rarely, if ever, seen. And so they moved on, only to be followed by yet another group. These had the same clothing styles but in the main were congenital feeble minded. These too passed with no problems although their silly leers & inane smiles, their waving & shouting to and at us, soon stopped by their attendant, had me shaking in my shoes. I think I was the only one in our group who instinctively knew how close we were to some potentially dangerous people.

The Hall where the service was being held for the inmates was large, airy and well-polished, and had a stage upon which we, the choir, sat. Facing us at a lower level sat the segregated inmates. Some sat unnaturally upright, some slouched, others peered down at the floor, others up to the roof. A few held conversations between themselves BUT there was no contact between inmates. Each one was an island.

The service began and, doing what I loved doing the most, which was singing these lovely hymns and chants, I began to relax. And then.........A faint rumble started. It was rather like someone tapping their fingers on a table. The tension within the Hall was immediate. The attendants sitting around the Hall sides began to peer over the rows of inmates who were by now fidgeting uneasily. As the drumming got louder, the attendants converged into one area of the Hall, and as they moved in, the inmates in that spot began to slide away, leaving one sole male, who was identified as the drummer by virtue of his whole upper body moving violently as his feet pounded the floor. The attendants pounced on him; two had an arm each, the other two a leg apiece. Lifted high, the male was carried out screaming and cursing, pulling his legs back into his chest, then kicking out again with the utmost violence. How those attendants managed to hold on without letting him go I will never know, but it wasn't doing my overstrained nerves any good I can tell you!

Harvest Festival came around and we were back at the 'Looney Bin' with me kidding myself that nothing would happen to upset things this time. This time we were in the Hospital church. Everywhere we looked we could see apples, pears, grapes, sheaves of corn and loaves of bread, big enough to feed and sustain an army. I know I wasn't the only boy in the choir who longed to get his hands on some 'scrumps' (stolen apples), all grown incidentally on the 'Looney Bin's' own land and orchards.

'Come ye thankful people come...' we warbled, everyone singing at the top of their voices. It was great. We worked through the order of service, no problems. Now Vicar Pratt was in the Pulpit, and his voice and the warmth of the sun streaming in through the windows lulled me off and I indulged my fantasies, (Did I eat one of the red apples first or perhaps eat a pear?) until I realised another voice was speaking out besides Vicar Pratts! The Vicar's sermon was predictably built around 'God's Goodness,' especially to do with the harvest time, but the other voice had countered with 'God's Rottenness!'

Dear oh dear! Vicar Pratt's voice came straight back with a repeat of 'God's Goodness, which again brought forth from the heckler, 'God's Rottenness!' It went on for some time and then Vicar Pratt was allowed to continue. A draw I believe!

I think that of all the services I took part in, the one I always found most moving, the one I loved best, was the Armistice Day Sunday. Several of the choirmen were ex-servicemen from the Great War. I think one had lost a leg and another was on sticks as a result of his wounds. It was on this day that those in the congregation who'd served during that first holocaust proudly wore their medals, polished and burnished, shining and clinking as they moved. What a pageant of sight and sound and colour, as behind the flags and banners they walked to lay them upon the altar to be blessed. Widows and mothers could be seen wearing medals and Orders awarded to men who'd never lived to wear them; Kept in drawers all year through, and brought out, polished and wept over, as memories of what might have been returned. The whole nation wept for its dead. They were in the majority; they would never have the peace of mind knowing where their loved one was buried. So many like Our Mam's eldest brother who was blown to pieces. On the positive side, so much grief and pride was generated that even we little boys in the choir stood stiffly to attention like guardsmen as, at the end of the two minute silence, signalled by a distant gun or Maroon on a nearby park, the trumpeter, strategically placed within the church, sobbed out the heartbreak of the Last Post. Standing there, trying to keep my gaze forward, I would nevertheless allow my side vision to present to me a picture of the whole church, ablaze with the predominately red poppies, the flags and the standards. I would then see, as though through a dark glass, the strained and haggard faces of the medal bedecked ex-servicemen, many missing arms and legs, some with some of their faces masked off with pieces of felt, to hide the horror underneath. I would see the tears coursing down so many faces; tears with which my own contributed. The nation grieved, and I was proud to grieve too. Little did we know that within three years or less the carnage of war would recommence.

In those days the build up to 11am was palpable. In schools and collages bells would be set ringing, calling the classes to a central hall. In the factories, the workers would set their eyes to the clock. Those with medals had them close to hand. Cubs, Guides, Scouts and Brownie uniforms were decorated with red poppies. As the hands of the clock moved inexorably towards the hour, the processions formed up ready to move off after the two minutes' silence. Beautifully groomed horses, brushed until their coats shone, tossed their heads restlessly and champed at the bit, pawing at the ground whilst harnesses creaking leather against leather, shone as those on the battlefield horses never shone.

Did Christ on His Cross suffer as did they whose names were scribed on those all too familiar War Memorials up and down the country suffer? With the deepest respect, I doubt it. Here a man, there a woman, even children overcome with the build-up of tension and emotion fell, fainting stiffly down, as so many others had fallen into eternity, at Ypres, Passchendaele and on the Somme. There, a woman, a mother, broke down and wept unashamedly as realisation, yet again, reminded her that medals and certificates from an alleged grateful nation can never fill an empty chair. Is it time? Not yet; nearly.

The towns, villages and Hamlets held their breath. Men going about their business in the streets took out watches, held them to the ear, shook them; others took out medal clasps and pinned them on self-consciously. Some looked for clocks on public buildings or called, 'what's the time, mate?' House doors opened as men, women (some with a baby in their arms) came to stand half in, half out of the door, many shedding the first tears.

Those streets that had wayside shrines screwed to a wall, shrines that bore those names of the fallen from that street which were lovingly cared for, each had a shelf upon which most days of the year could be found a small meat paste or similar receptacle into which a few posies or wild flowers were placed. These have now been taken down and lost although one of the original shrines, circa 1914, can be found at the church at Queniborough. These shrines became a gathering point as neighbours called back to mind a familiar face of but a few years ago. Now, with only seconds left to the eleventh hour, tramcars and buses just stopped, even if by doing so a road or turn was blocked, for it mattered not; everything else was at a standstill.

A dull 'crump' a quick siren blast, a field gun discharged. A clock would begin to chime the hour. Gentlemen had already removed their hats; tram and bus drivers and passengers had already left the vehicle and stood in silence. Caught up in the emotion, some men forgot to remove their hat and, if witnessed, someone else, a complete stranger, would snatch the hat from the offender's head and throw it to the floor knowing this was one time retribution would not follow.

That silence, lasting for the two prescribed minutes, was emotionally terrible. I can think of no other way to describe it. I swear even birds stopped singing. As the world stood still, those who'd been sacrificed were remembered. Not a man was forgotten. Those two minutes lasted into eternity.

Finally, the Maroons sounded again. Hats were replaced; buses and trams moved off; the crowds dispersed.

For those two minutes the dead came back to life. They were paraded before us as we saluted them and then they went back to wherever they'd been before we called them.

I was to read much later on that the number plate of the car in which the Archduke Franz Joseph and his Morganic wife were travelling when they were assassinated in Sarajevo was 11.11.18! The hour, the month and even the year that terrible war ended.

Mary & Tony (ie Ron)

Ronnie finally left the choir because it was discovered he had a unique singing voice for a boy so, at Our Mam's instigation, he joined up with a partner (a girl who played the piano accordion) and they began to make money on the Working Men's Clubs under the title of 'Mary and Tony.' Not long after I too left the choir, for Bill Worth the choirmaster was testing boys to sing solo and I knew he had me spotted. However, Mam's view that 'Norman's got no confidence' had done its work and any confidence I might have had was now gone.

11: Life at a new house & more memories

Mam had found us a new house. It was on the cards of course because our present one contained too many memories. The house was no more than ten minutes from our old one but I hated it. Neighbourhood wise it was a much better district than where we'd been. Now, once again, we had electric light instead of the gas which gave off such a rotten sickly glow from the fragile little gas mantle which puffed to dust at the slightest touch and gave off its own familiar odour. It was never a light one could use for reading for very long, try as we might. All of us except Our Mam were avid readers. Now we had a switch to press down and the whole room was illuminated. No more the risk of holding a lighted match to the gas and whilst waiting for the familiar 'pop' inadvertently push the match straight through the mantle, necessitating a trip to the corner shop for a replacement. The old house on Morton Road had a reasonably sized back garden to cultivate or play in, even though that amenity was spoiled by the slaughter house at the bottom. Now we had a paved yard with a pocket handkerchief sized garden that was too sour to grow anything. To be fair though it did throw up a square piece of brass plate, about 10 x 10 inches, and at each of its four corners were Wedgewood ovals of the 'Three Graces' in various poses, with a much larger one slap bang in the middle. Mam took it to the museum to see if it could be identified but they hadn't a clue so she sold it to a chap on the market. I think she got 10/- (50p in today's money) Today it would probably fetch a lot of money.

So, our new home was a terrace. Gone was the little front garden which provided a buffer between us and the road. Gone were the iron railings that we and every other kid in the district could 'tiss' over and gone was the cast iron lamp post which gave the local boys so much pleasure! And the railway embankment and trains? Not so much the goods trains although we would stand and wave to the driver, fireman and guard (who always waved back) but the excursion trains to the East Coast with Mums, Dads and kids all hanging out of the windows, waving like mad until the smoke and smut from the funnel drove them back inside, slamming the windows and shutting us out. Oh yes, our new house was much better.....WAS IT HELL!

We didn't have fairies at the bottom of our garden, oh no, we had a shoe factory whose employees seemed to be working all hours of the night if the noisy whine and clatter of the machinery was anything to go by. We also had another factory going full blast across the road at the front!

Our Ted was still working, as was Maisie now, and Mam was on full time at the place she'd worked for years. As the pressure was off financially Mam now set in motion the grounds for Divorcing the Old Man. This was granted in 1939 on the grounds of excessive cruelty. He didn't have the face to contest it. The upsets of his coming round late at night, often the worse for drink, came to a full stop. Now all we had to do was consolidate our ground. (Like hell it was!)

Mam started going out at night to the Working Men's Clubs with a small group of friends whilst Ron and I were left to Our Maisie's tender mercies....... and believe you me, she wasn't tender and she showed no mercy!

Now, Mam liked a glass of beer but I can honestly say that never, in all my life, did I know her to have too much and get tipsy. No, she was purely a social drinker. She loved company and after the previous 20 or so years, who could blame her. Certainly not me! She'd always had compassion for the underdog and was always a sucker for a hard luck story, and one in particular sticks out in my mind.

One night Mam arrived back with a young woman carrying a baby of no more than a few months who she'd found wandering the streets. No lodging money was asked for or given. For the next week or so the young woman disclosed harrowing tales of the husband's cruelty, not only towards the young wife but to the infant as well. Naturally, as Mam knew all about cruel husbands, that pair were home and dry until.........

We always had a large fire guard around the fire, and when a pungent smell was noticed around the house it was traced to the old towelling cloth we'd donated in lieu of nappies, being dried, unwashed, around the fire. Mam told the young woman she needed to wash the baby's items before drying, but suspicion was aroused as the nightly horror stories recounted by our boarder, rang less and less true. Matters came to a head when Mam suggested it was time the bed linen on the mother's bed and cot were washed.

'It's alright, I've done them while you were out at work' she told Mam.

Even so, Mam wasn't going to swallow that one.

'The sheets can't be dry' Mam said, and brushing aside the mother's protests Mam went upstairs to the bedroom we'd vacated for them.

Had we but known it, the young woman, knowing the game was up, was shooting out the back door with the baby in her arms. Then we heard Mam calling,

'Oh my Christ, just come up here and look at this! That dirty bugger, that poor little baby!'

Up we went and, oh dear, oh dear! Mam was close to tears.

'Oh that poor baby,' she repeated 'Just look here!'

We did so. The cot, mattress and bedding Mam had scrounged for the baby was so wet with urine it was practically steaming. It was hung around the four sides of the cot, soaking wet with urine and stained with faeces which had been scraped off before being put there to dry. That blasted woman was too idle to wash them even though they hadn't cost her a single penny. Mam had scrounged them all from friends and neighbours. In the wardrobe lay further evidence; dirty unwashed baby and adult clothing plus used (although I didn't know what they were at the time) sanitary towels. The whole room stank. Raging with temper and calling the young woman all the names she could lay her tongue to, Mam ripped back the bedclothes from the single (loaned) bed. It was as bad as the cot. All the cot and bed linen was thrown out of the window into the yard. I swear that if the young woman had been around she would have been thrown out with them. Nothing was salvaged; all were burned. The follow up to all of this was that although we never saw her again, that night a knock came at our front door. Answering it, Mam found a reasonably dressed young fellow. He was rather nervous but he stood his ground and demanded his wife's and baby's clothes. Mam invited him in and, although it was plain he was reluctant to do so, in he came. Mam explained that his wife had nothing when she came to us, but then handed over a few of the baby's things which she (Mam) had scrounged and washed for the little mite. She said he could have them with pleasure. Even though she didn't have to, she also passed over items for the wife that'd been brought across that day by people who didn't know what'd happened.

'All the baby's items are clean and well aired, Mister, and I've put a few extras in for him.'

Now Mam always did have a lovely personality and way with her and, as she talked and explained things to him, showing him the things that'd been donated, he visibly relaxed, looking with interest around our ordinary but spotless home. Suddenly he blurted out,

'I don't understand it Missus. From what my wife said after she returned home at dinnertime, I thought I was going to have to threaten you with the police to get her stuff back, and now you're telling me that all of this is what you got for her and the baby from your neighbours; but you've been so kind!'

(These are sentiments I've heard echoed time and time again by people when they've spoken about her)

Mam looked hard at him,

'Well, now you've seen for yourself, haven't you, and just for the record, Mister, you don't look the sort of bloke who would throw his own baby through a glass window!'

Our visitor was aghast.....'Glass window!! But I never......'

'Exactly' said Mam 'which just goes to show what a wicked, rotten bloody liar your Missus is, don't it!'

The move to the new address was hard for me to come to terms with, for although only two or three stones' throw away from 1 Morton Road it was streets ahead as regards people with jobs. Here, when the factory hooters sounded 15 minutes to clocking on, the streets came alive with men and women racing to work, and in those times people didn't walk so much as race to get in on time, then, within 5 minutes, they were all gone, apart from the over sleeper dashing from his or her house, putting a coat on with one hand and eating a round of bread and dip with the other. Eggs and bacon, but not both, were reserved for Sundays only.

Once the workers were gone, those wives, widows and other women not in work would emerge with a scrubbing brush, bar of hard soap and basin of water and, kneeling on an old piece of sacking, the front step was scrubbed, rinsed with clean water and, if not satisfied, scrubbed again, for a dirty step meant a dilatory house wife! God help any dog that cocked its leg up on the pristine, fresh step, for not only would it be chased and doused with a bucket of dirty, sudsy water but its owner would be visited and roasted in front of the neighbours. These scenes were always referred to as a 'good showing up.' In extreme cases of child/ wife beating, stealing from neighbours etc the women of the street wouldn't be averse to standing outside an offender's house and bashing dustbin lids with copper sticks. (These were used for picking clothes steeped in boiling water from the copper) The usual outcome to this was the offender and family moving without leaving a forward address.

As Mam was a very attractive woman, and with her going out with friends in the evening, she'd been asked by several gentlemen if she would consider going steady with them. Now, for the first time she brought one home to meet the family. This chap's name was Robert, shortened to 'Bob'. Unfortunately, 'Bob' later proved that Mam just couldn't pick a reliable bloke. On the surface 'Bob' should've been alright, come to think of it though, so should the Old Man, but 'Bob' was just as bad even though he wasn't married to her. His history as far as I know was that he'd been a regular soldier, served in India, been discharged and now worked as a painter for the Local Council. He was medium height but had eyes and a ruddy face that gave the game away immediately. He was a heavy smoker and drank. Within a very short space of time the jealous scenes started up because he was just too possessive of Mam. I think to prove to the world in general that she was over the Old Man for good (which she wasn't) she twinkled and sparkled to any man who paid her attention, and believe you me, there were many. To try and put a 'reserved' sign on her 'Bob' deposited at our house various pieces of brass ornaments that he'd picked up on his travels.

It was also at this time Ron, who would be about twelve years at the time, was discovered to have a phenomenal tenor voice. With her contacts Mam got him an audition on the Working Men's Clubs, and the Entertainment Secretaries fought to get him booked for their peak concert times which were Saturday and Sunday evenings.

I have to say at this point Mam, Ted and Maisie were all working and Ron was earning good money on the clubs.....which just left me. I was 10 - 11 years old at this point and, from then on until I left school at 14 years I went to school looking very neglected. I was the fly in the ointment in so far as when the family went out in the evening no one knew what to do with me, but more of that later.

Pubs were visited by children with the same eagerness their parents displayed but for completely different reasons. Our goal was the gratings at the side of the pubs because we very often found that customers, having had more than their fair share of beer, would accidentally drop loose change down the grating which could easily be seen but remained unreachable unless one lay full length on the ground peering into the darkness below. Before assuming the prone position we kids would always check the ground was reasonably clean for in those days spitting was common place or, as hankies were few and far between, noses were cleared by placing the finger on one nostril whilst blowing hard through the other! With a coin identified, out came the tools of our trade, that is, a piece of soap and a length of bamboo cane. First, the soap was moistened by spit thereby making it reasonably soft. It was then pinned to the end of the cane. By pushing the cane down the grating hard, the coin would become tightly stuck on the soap. Next, the cane was carefully extracted from the drain complete with soap and coin. We always ran like hell afterwards! This was because the retrieved coin, sometimes as much as half a crown, may have been reported as lost by the looser to the landlord who'd made the loss good until such time he could go to retrieve it.

Last Sunday School Outing at the Mission Hall:

I embarked on what was to be the last Sunday School outing from the Little Mission Hall before I ceased going there due to our change of address. After the usual games and treasure hunt in the fields about three miles from the city centre, we were given tea and then came the prize giving, although what the awards were based on I haven't a clue. My prize was a yacht, about one foot long, complete with sails very like one of those illustrated on the front covers of children's books, being sailed by, to my mind, a soppy kid with curly ringlets and wearing a blue sailor suit. I think it was this conjured up picture that decided my next move....swapping. On the bus during the return journey the swap began and, in the time it took to get back to our alighting point, in place of the yacht I was the proud possessor of a piece of string on the end of which was a gadget.

When the string was swung round vigorously, the gadget made a warbling sound. Mam was not best pleased when she found out what I'd done!

At the bottom of the road to where we lived was an Eldorado Ice Cream depot. Every day, early in the morning, be it winter or summer, the ice cream sellers would set off into the streets on their tricycles which had huge 'cold boxes' mounted on the front. In these the paper wrapped oblongs of ice cream (or as we called it 'hokey pokey') were kept chilled by dry ice chipped from huge blocks. The dry ice was delivered on the back of an open back in huge squares, which a man picked up, or rather pulled along the ground to the cold store by huge pincers. Whilst in transit the only cover from the sun was old clothes, discarded sacking or sawdust. Each evening during the summer the local kids would wait for the ice cream sellers to return to the depot. You see, the ices were in paper wrapped oblongs which cost a penny each, however to boost sales the salesman was allowed to cut oblongs into halves; these were then sold for one half penny. Now, on returning to the depot, the halves could not be returned to stock therefore the men would, if in a good mood, answer our cries of 'got any halves, Mister?' by giving the odd half to us for free.

Further up the street and just across the street from our house, was the lamp lighter depot. At certain set hours, winter and summer, we would see the lamplighters arriving to report in. Soon after, the men would emerge carrying a long pole on the end of which was a metal container, quite small in diameter, which gave off a small flickering flame about an inch long. Just below this was a hook. As each lamp was approached the pole was pushed up under the lantern of the lamp and the hook engaged to pull down the small lever which turned on the gas that the small flame then ignited. Our man would then pass on to the next lamp. Gradually, as he went on his way, the streets would be illuminated by the ghastly yellow, gas given illumination. At near dawn the next day the procedure was reversed. One of my most abiding memories is of the bobbing up and down, flickering gas/ lamplighter's dance light slowly fading away the further the man walked down the street.

One might have thought that the street 'naughty boys' would've shinned up the lamp post after our hero had passed by and switched the light off again but strangely enough this rarely happened for, if caught, they would get the hiding of their life from their parents or, what we all dreaded, the police would be involved.

Unlike the children of today we were involved in and interested in all that happened around us, and much of what we term local and national events were put to music using popular songs of the day. Perhaps this is what gave us the feeling of involvement within the community which, so far as I can see, the kids of today don't seem to have. For example, the abdication of the Duke of Windsor was discussed at great length over the breakfast, dinner, tea and supper table. (if you could afford all of these meal times, that is) Information was gleaned by word of mouth usually because not everyone had a wireless; daily newspapers were a near luxury item and television lay some ten years in the future. From the bits of information emerging from that unhappy love story, a ditty went the rounds and children sang it more as a social commentary rather than out of disrespect. This was sung to a 'rag time' melody and went....

"Who's this coming down the street?

Mrs Simpson's sweaty feet.

She's been married twice before,

Now she's knocking on Edward's door!"

Another one was sung to the tune of 'Red Sails in the Sunset:'

"Red stains on the carpet,

Red stains on the knife,

Oh Doctor Buck Ruxton,

You've murdered your wife!

Poor Mary was watching,

So you murdered her too,

Oh Doctor Ruxton,

The devil's in you!"

Voting Time:

Voting time was always a wow. (Polling, what's that?)

Placards were pasted to walls and every kid, depending on what mum or dad had said, shouted out the favourite name. Punches were exchanged and gangs of small boys paraded around the town singing....

"Vote, vote, vote for Mr Hoggar,

Chuck old thingy in the sea.

For Hoggar is our Man, and we'll have him if we can,

And we won't go voting anymore."

During the summer months the flies would nearly drive us mad. A contributing factor to the number of these pests could well have been the large amount of horse dung in the streets, for milk, bread, coal, groceries etc were all delivered by horse & cart. On the credit side, the collection of this manure by home-made barrow, earned many a small boy a tanner from his granddad who wanted it for his allotment.

It was still possible 1937 – 1938 to purchase milk loose. One man in particular sold milk from huge churns carried in a small, highly varnished tub cart. The horse too was small, and the cart leaned back to an alarming degree, so much so that at times I expected that tiny horse to be lifted high into the air by the sheer weight of the milk and cart.

The milkman would measure out from his churn using long handled ladles which had copper scoops on the bottom, giving different measures of milk into jugs presented by the customers. The discerning milk customers, once the milk had been ladled into their jug, would cover it at once with small squares of muslin, often prettily trimmed with coloured beads or lace, to stop the flies getting in.

Really, the flies got everywhere. They were to be found in freshly poured cups of tea, in sugar basins, stuck in jam, around babies' mouths & eyes, and condensed milk tins. (I loved to suck the thick sugary condensed milk from my finger after poking it in the tin)

Pesticides, apart from 'flit' which was sprayed onto the brutes, were few and far between, so the universal fly catcher was the common or garden fly paper, and very effective they were too. Actually, a rolled up newspaper settled a few fly problems too but a squashed fly made a dreadful mess on windows and tablecloths!

Flypapers were tightly rolled cylinders of a specially treated paper, covered in a treacly sticky gunge which didn't dry out. Holding the small tag at the bottom in one hand, and the string at the top, one pulled steadily until the whole sticky surface was exposed. The whole exposed length, (about 14 inches) was then attached to the electric light or gas mantle. Another favourite spot, depending on how tall the occupants were, was to drawing pin it to the ceiling. It was magic, for in seconds the first flies would be stuck to its surface and, once on they had no chance of ever getting off again. Buzzing and struggling, they stayed attached until dead. In a hot summer they would catch so many flies that a new fly paper would be needed practically every week. The effectiveness was such that new arrivals alighting on an already caught comrade, would be stuck fast as well. The fly papers did have one unfortunate drawback though; should the string holding it break, or should some unfortunate visitor be taller than the norm, or should it be carelessly handled at disposal time, then the swearing and cussing as the unfortunate tried to tear it loose from hair or fingers, bore testament to the fact that 'our flypapers stick around forever.'

New School:

For some reason my new school (for we now lived in a different catchment area) seemed more relaxed & reassuring. The new Head, Mr Boreman, (I think that's how his name was spelt) was kind and had a ready smile for all. I never, ever saw him cross, and my male class teacher (Mr Belton) was also a lovely man. Years later I met Mr Belton and told him I was a former pupil of his.

He asked me my name and when I told him my surname (Hastings) he immediately replied, 'Norman'.

In the classroom was a great cast iron, pot-bellied stove, surrounded by a child proof safety guard, to boost what I imagine to be inadequate heating during the colder months. I don't remember a lot about the first few months except the school caretaker would periodically pop in to replenish the coke for the stove, and how we would sit reciting our tables. Before I was ten years old I knew my tables up to 16 x 16. Unfortunately, and there was always an 'unfortunately' for me.....because my birthdate fell on 5 August and each class went 'up' on 1 September, I was always handicapped by having to compete with classmates who were sometimes nearly a year older than me.

A New King:

With the abdication of David, Duke of Windsor, out of the way, the crowning of his younger brother, Prince Albert (George VI), was awaited with interest. The old King George V, no matter what is said nowadays, wasn't the sort of man to catch the public's imagination. He was too remote, too impersonal and besides, the generation before mine who'd fought in that terrible War of 1914 – 1918 couldn't forget how the instigator of the slaughter, 'Kaiser Bill', was safe and sound in Holland, and it was popularly believed this was because he was King George's cousin and that King George had vetoed any attempt to bring the sod to justice and hang him. Furthermore, our Royal ancestry was Germanic, and it was well-known many of the princes and princesses were retarded and handicapped. What was the matter with King George V's son, John? He'd hardly ever been seen with them yet he was only a boy of around 12 years when he died.

And hadn't Queen Mary been betrothed to King George's brother, the Duke of Clarence? Then there were rumours that Queen Mary wore high collars around her neck to hide something....... but WHAT? It was a fact even King George's grandmother, Queen Victoria, regarded him with suspicion, so much so his early death from seemingly unexplained causes was regarded as a blessing rather than a tragedy.........there were even rumours King George had somehow been involved with Jack the Ripper!!!!

It was popularly rumoured at the time that the Princess Royal, daughter of King George V, was forced to marry the Duke of Harewood to gain access to Harewood's money. Now, Prince Albert was going to come and take the throne, because his elder brother David had cleared off with his fancy woman, and yet, wasn't Prince Albert, (who was going to become King George VI) a bit peculiar too? There were some who said he was feeble minded and couldn't even talk properly! Some who'd seen the Royals close up, be it men or women, said they wore make up like a bunch of tarts!!

For the Coronation, we children were given a slim book which showed the Crown's Royal Regalia and described the actual Coronation Ceremony. I'm not sure but school children may also have received a mug. As for myself, I found details of the Old King's funeral much more interesting.

Great efforts were made to popularise the Royals at the time. The new King's daughters (Elizabeth & Margaret) were rammed down our throats yet up until then, with limited communications, I doubt many people knew who they were, and I suggest that had it not been for World War II King George VI would've gone down in history, not as George the Good, but rather George the non-starter.

Cinema:

I was passing the local 'Bug & Flea pit' as our local picture house was called.

It was a hot summer evening and must've been the interval for the doors were wide open. Attendants were close at hand to stop us kids nipping in free gratis. A record was playing and I paused, savouring the smell of the place. It was a smell peculiar to all cinemas, with cigarette smoke predominating, followed by the scent of cheap perfume. (California Poppy, Ful Nana etc) Next came face powder, warm air, dusty drapes and the final ingredient, 'The Flea Killer Spray'. This was indeed what it was known as by all and sundry, and until I am told differently, this is what I shall continue calling it. It went like this....

At some time during the performance, one of the attendants would walk down the aisle with what looked like an Aladdin's Lamp with knobs on. The gadget worked on the old tilly lamp pressure principle and, as the attendant progressed he, or rather the lamp, would emit a loud hissing noise. At the same time, a fine spray of whatever mixture was in the lamp could be felt by the customers. The spray was moved slowly from side to side otherwise things could, and would, get rather damp. When this happened some Wag would call out with the suggestion, 'waggle it about mate, cos sitting here it feels like I'm being pissed on!' This had the rest of the audience in stitches. We were a common lot! The smell from whatever mixture was in the spray was not in the least bit unpleasant, and whether or not its purpose was to kill any lice, remains for me a matter of conjecture.

On this particular early evening the lady in the cinema pay box hailed me with, 'Go to the tripe shop and get me some tripe, will you sonny!'

No problem. The tripe shop, Adcocks, was just across the road to the cinema and even if one didn't know where it was, the smell would guide you. Tripe was prepared & treated in out-houses in the back yard by people well known in the district for quality. I couldn't stomach the stuff when a child and no amount of 'It'll do you good' or 'you're not going out till you've eaten it' would convince me otherwise! With the lady's tripe wrapped in newspaper, I again crossed the road wondering, 'I bet she'll give me a penny for going.' Instead though, I was told, 'come here on Saturday and I'll let you in the Pictures for nothing!' The lady then took out a knife and, cutting the tripe into strips, began to eat the stuff raw!! Ugh!

On the Saturday afternoon I stood where the lady might see me, too shy or nervous to go and remind her of her promise, pleading with my eyes to be called forward, but it wasn't to be.

Syston British Legion:

Unfortunately, Mam's new boyfriend had developed the same traits as the Old Man and once again the peace of the neighbourhood was disturbed late at night by his yelling and veiled threats of abuse. I well remember Our Ron had a singing engagement out of town and this was one occasion I was taken along. In this particular Club (The British Legion, Syston) I was allowed to sit with Mam and her boyfriend in the concert room. As the evening wore on, what should have been an enjoyable night (for as usual Ron was great) began to go sour.

Bob, who liked his booze, was sweating and looking nastier by the minute as he'd got the idea Mam had caught some other bloke's eye and was playing up to him. The concert over, Ron's kit was packed up and we squeezed into the small car that was our transport. The car belonged to the parents of the girl who partnered Ron. She played the accordion and with everything packed in, it was a very tight squeeze! As I think about it now, me being taken along might have been part of the problem as Bob had to make his own way to and from the venue. Anyway, just as we got settled Bob appeared and, with no prior warning dragged the car door open and lunged at Mam. To get to her he had to lean across me and I can still feel, all these years later, my thumb sticking into his throat as I, a ten year old boy, tried to protect Mam by strangling the bastard. What a bloody life!

Last year of junior school:

As previously stated, my male teacher was a lovely man but now, as I moved into my final year of Junior School, my new teacher was a woman, a spinster, and to my mind anyhow, a snob with a capital 'S'. One of those teachers the run of the mill kids called 'Snappy.'

I swear that from the first day she had me spotted as a kid she wasn't going to like, just because I went to school looking rather poor. To be fair though, she wasn't deliberately unkind she just made it quite clear that if I kept away from her, she would pretend I didn't exist. Her favourite kids were Alan, Keith, Olive and Jean, but with me, well, she just looked away. Her favourite position for us kids to be in, was sitting with our hands on our heads, or sitting straight up with our arms behind our backs. It didn't half make your muscles ache! Our teacher took us into the hall for music which was a traditional type of singing: 'Three Gypsies Stood at the Castle Gates, they sang so high, they sang so low.....' which I knew was a load of old baloney because any Gyppos around where we lived wouldn't be singing, they'd be nicking the Castle Gates!

One of the teacher's pets was a big heavy girl of about ten years who went to tap and dancing lessons. Of this fact we were repeatedly reminded until one day we were told that as a special treat we were going to see a performance. 'Aren't we lucky children?!' What else could we do but chorus back, 'Yes Miss!'

A chord was struck on the piano and the girl went into her routine, tapping her tap shoes and kicking her legs in the air, showing lots of leg and knickers as she did so! I don't suppose it did much for the girls who were probably fantasising it was them out in front but I do know from comparing notes with the other lads afterwards that we boys found it all very stimulating! The dancing display became a regular feature to our singing lessons and one we boys looked forward to avidly.....you see we had to sit on the floor during the performance and every time the girl kicked her legs or swung around, her short dancing skirt flew up into the air! By golly, the way we applauded must have convinced her she was another Pavlova! I tell you this, it wasn't the cheering and near standing ovation she got that made us all red faced and breathless, and if our snobby teacher had known, she would've gone spare!

Years later, whilst sitting in the cinema watching dancers such as Ann Millar tap dancing and waiting along with the rest of the men (and perhaps a few women as well) for Ann's skirt to flick up, giving us a quick flash of the tight black knickers she always wore, my mind would flash back to that school hall.

12: 1938 The War Years

It was clear things were boiling up in Europe although 'war' was rarely mentioned. By 1938 and soon after Our Maisie had started work, we'd progressed enough financially for Mam to buy a new wireless to replace our second hand one. It's hard to believe now but my mind is quite clear on this point: if ever Herr Hitler was due to make a speech to the German nation, the wireless knobs would be twiddled up and down the country in an attempt to pick up his German station. Even though we couldn't speak a word of German and neither could millions of other English people, that wireless would stay tuned until Herr Hitler had finished. He fascinated us, and strangely enough I don't remember him ever being presented in the media as a threat. I can hear that voice now. He would begin to speak so calmly, almost gently, lulling his audience along, and then gradually his voice would strengthen and he would, without appearing to be shouting, ram whatever point he was making, down his audiences' throat. By the time he'd finished we were emotionally drained, yet still couldn't have told you what it was all about.

Many of the young men in the street belonged to the Territorial Army. I can see them now in their uniforms, their legs swathed in puttees (as per 1914-1918) up to their knees, clattering and clashing, their steel studded boots throwing out sparks as they slipped and skidded down the entries to meet in groups before going to the Drill Halls. Had only they known that in less than two years they'd be trapped on the beaches at Dunkirk, immediately prior to being taken prisoner and marched off into captivity for five years; victims of our nation's incompetent leaders.

In the meantime, and to bolster morale, cigarette cards showing aspects of A.R.P (Air Raid Precautions) were being swapped in school yards. Every boy tried to collect them all and there were 48 in a set. This meant any man or woman foolish enough to open a fresh packet of cigarettes in the street would be accosted with cries of,

'Got any fag cards, please mister?'

We were treated to the spectacle of Searchlight Practice when an old Biplane droned around the night skies whilst a searchlight tried to pick it up. I think it was a searchlight although it might have been a kid in the next street with his new torch. Goodness knows, the plane was slow enough and low enough!

All the same, for millions of people it was business as usual, and in those days it meant just that. I remember one Sunday evening being taken by Mam on a bus ride with Ron. It was around 8pm and we were miles from home when I developed a raging toothache. It was agony and I was whimpering with pain when the bus driver, with no ado about it, said, 'Here's a dentist's sign!' The bus was stopped, the door was knocked and the dentist, with no hesitation whatsoever, took me and Mam inside whilst the bus waited. I was sat in the chair, injected, and the offending tooth extracted at no charge! We then continued on our merry way. I expect today we would have been told to 'clear off, I'm watching the telly!' Truly, the Hippocratic Oath has become the Hypocrite's Oath.

Scholarship time:

Suddenly, for me as well as for thousands of other boys and girls in 1938, scholarship time arrived. For weeks we'd gone around with the shadow of the 'Scholarship' hanging over us although we continued to do our school work as usual. No extra work was given out and neither did we have hints dropped that we were expected to do better than other schools! The very high scoring children were scored as 1st class scholarship. These children went to the Grammar Schools. 2nd class went to the Intermediate Schools which were below Grammar Schools in what was expected from the children performance wise. Other children who sat and didn't pass 1st or 2nd, went to the standard Senior Schools BUT LET'S BE CLEAR ABOUT ONE THING, these children were NOT classed as failures and continued movement between schools was normal for it was realised some children never showed academic aptitude during formal testing. Opponents of testing (Scholarship) never take into account that if you abolish testing at any age there will always be children who cannot cope, or cannot keep up with their peers and feel disadvantaged. Selective testing ensures the different levels of ability are put into different groups where they can compete at their own pace and level throughout all their school years without feeling a failure.

On the appointed day along with the rest of my class, I took my place in the school hall. We sat alone at our desks and were warned about 'looking over and copying.' In front of us lay the Scholarship papers, face down. Further instruction was given, mainly on 'looking up; looking around' and sitting with arms folded, staring straight ahead when finished. Now we began, hearts pounding. I'd already decided I'd fail on simple logic ie......if Our Ted, Maisie and

Ron couldn't pass, then I had no chance! I turned the paper over and got the shock of my life. It was easy. All I had to do with the first page was to match shapes, fill in the missing lines and answer A, B, or C to certain questions. My mouth stopped being dry and I no longer had a tense tummy. I worked steadily, subconsciously noting as I did so that the questions were getting progressively harder 'but they weren't worrying me one little bit!' Several weeks later there was great excitement in school for the results had arrived. After playtime, we filed into the classroom, pushing and shoving and assuring anyone who might care to listen that we were sure we'd failed. Our teacher began:

1st Class Scholarship Awards first: Dear Jean, Yes Keith (these were the racing certainties) beams and smiles, even the odd tear or two whilst teacher beamed fondly on her favourites, but let's be fair though, these first class awards were taken by kids who came from really wonderful caring homes in the main, or from homes where, although money might be short, the parents were ambitious for their children and gave them extra tuition. I came from neither. The only time I knew Our Mam to know anything about me and school was when she sent a note to the Headmaster asking if I could leave school ten minutes early to put the dinner on so it was ready for them coming home from work at 12:40. (By this time Ron was at the Open Air School)

Teacher had now worked down to 2nd Class results: Michael, yes, Olive, Yes, Peter, Yes, Alan, Yes......suddenly, half asleep and quite confident I was going to follow my peers into the Duffers' Senior School, I jerked up! Miss was positively glaring at me. Miss looked again at the paper in her hand. I'd won a Second Class Scholarship!

The shoe mender:

During the last few months of junior school, one of my class mates asked,

'Do you want to come with me to see Mr Handler?'

'Who's he?' I asked.

'He's the shoe mender. It's alright, we go into his shop.' (Who 'we' were I never did find out)

We stopped outside a shop where local shoe repairs were carried out.

'Come on then' said my chum, and in we went. We were in a tiny serving area with the counter in front of us and a closed door into the shop on our left. A tall, middle aged, miserable looking man appeared and, seeing my chum, nodded towards me and said,

'Who's he?'

'He's alright' came the reply and, seemingly satisfied, the man disappeared out of sight.

The sound of a bolt being withdrawn was heard then the door into the workshop was opened, and in we went. Machinery was humming and the air was heavy with the smell of leather and rubber but I rather nervously realised that something just didn't add up. We were told to sit down on a bench seat against the partitioning. The man then reached down an empty tin. Without further ado he undid the front of his very dirty brown smock and the fly of his trousers, took out his penis and began urinating into the tin. He made no attempt to hide himself. Finished, he unbolted the door and went out into the street where he poured his pee into the gutter. He returned, first checking that the shop bell worked properly before, as it were, bolting us all into his workshop again. My chum asked the cobbler,

'Have you got any?' (Got any what, I thought)

'No,' was the man's reply, 'but listen to this,' and at that he reached down a thick book from a high up shelf and began reading from it. The gist of it, from what I could gather, was that two young boys from a well to do family were cared for by a nanny. One at a time she would take the boys into the bedroom and making them remove their trousers, she would cane their bare bottoms. When finished, and their bottoms were glowing from the caning, she would slip her hand between their legs and fondle their testicles. I'm afraid (or glad) that it all went over my head but my chum and his cobbler friend discussed the matter at great length. Next the conversation turned to masturbation, a subject I understood because it was addressed in the most basic of 'boy' terms. Then my chum, admitting that he liked a particular girl in his street, was invited to 'bring her to the shop and I can hold her down while you fuck her'......I may have been only ten years but I knew instinctively this man was deadly serious, and these were very murky waters indeed. Soon after, we left, and I never went back. I don't know about my chum as we never spoke of the visit again. I now know of course the man was a Paedophile. He must be long dead by now. Forty five years on when talking to a work colleague, he confided to me that lots of youngsters visited the cobbler. They were initiated into group masturbation or would have sex with little girl classmates whilst the monster looked on, condoning and encouraging.

Ted:

Our Ted at this time was very remote but always beautifully turned out. Clean shaven, hair parted down the middle with never one hair out of place, and was never short of a shilling or two. His temper, as always, was 'hair trigger' and, as I've said before, when addressing me, he rarely said a kind word if an unkind one would do.

I remember one dark night he ordered me to go and fetch him a razor blade from the Barber's shop on the corner. I was on Our Ron's roller skates and sped like a bat out of hell down the entry in case some ghost or madman might be after me. (Really, that's how my mind used to work) At the bottom of the dark passageway on my return I put my hand out to stop myself, forgetting that this was the hand holding the razor blade. It went in deep. I can see the scar now, running diagonally from my left middle finger towards my little finger, about an inch long. Sympathy? Anxiety that I might have cut the guide? Go to the doctors for a stitch? Don't make me laugh. All I got was a rough bandage of discarded rag which was soaked in blood in no time and a warning that if I'd blunted that 'bloody blade' I'd get a bloody good hiding!

Mam would take my part though if she felt it was warranted. Just down the street to us lived a boy who was inclined to be a bully. He was about thirteen years to my ten. For some reason, after dashing home and washing the dinner pots and getting the table laid for tea for when the others came home from work, I'd gone into the street and 'laddie boy' started to punch, and I mean PUNCH me. I think he thought it would be alright because with no man in the house apart from Ted (whose attitude to anything involving his little brother seemed to be, 'let him get on with it; it'll do him good and toughen him up a bit') retribution would not follow. I remember to this day the sadistic pleasure this lad took in beating me to a pulp. It seemed as though the more he hit me, the more he wanted to. I tried without punching back to get away but he pasted me. I was still sobbing when Mam came home from work. I can see her now getting more and more worked up and to Our Ted's unsympathetic, 'he probably asked for it' she snapped 'you keep your nose out of it. Can't you see he's been badly hurt?!'

Mam questioned me more closely....'What did you say to him? Were you cheeky? How old is he?'

My answers satisfied for, eyes blazing and white of face, she took me by the hand and with me still sobbing, I was taken off to identify the boy's house. Up his entry we went and she knocked on the back door. The boy's dad, a decently dressed, respectable looking, ordinary bloke answered the door. Voice trembling with anger Mam said,

'Look what your son did to my lad! He's beaten him as if he were a dog! God's truth Mister, your son's thirteen years to my boy's ten and twice his size! I go out to work to keep my kids and come home to this! Tell the bullying bugger to keep his rotten hands to himself!' Then Mam issued the ultimate threat......'Or I'll go to the school about him!'

The father turned,

'Les, come here!'

The boy, who I'd spotted listening behind the living room door, emerged white and trembling, cringing at the anger in his father's eyes, like an already beaten dog.

'Did you do this?' he asked pointing to my red eye and tear stained face. (I sobbed all the harder)

'It wasn't my fault, Our Da....' Matey began, but his dad cut in with, 'Did you hit this little boy?'

'Yes Dad, but'.... His father stopped him once again...'Get inside!'

The dad then turned to Mam,

'I'm ever so sorry Missus, but I promise you it won't happen again!'

Now both he and Mam were white with rage; they'd have made a good pair of book ends.

As we turned to go I saw the father fumbling with his belt, a thick leather job. Halfway up the entry the son started to squawk,

'No dad, don't hit me!'

Then the sound of the first blow and before we'd got out the entry the boy was screaming and crying as his father laid into him. I couldn't feel any pity though, nor apparently could Mam as she said,

'Serves the rotten little bully right!'

The warning went out to every kid in the district who'd been using me as a punch bag. HIS MAM BITES!

Parental discipline in all the homes around us was rigidly enforced and supported in and out of school by Heads and teachers, near adult siblings and parents, but in the main, fathers. The cry heard more often than not was, 'You just wait till your father gets home!'

Our Mam had to be the arbiter of rewards and punishment in our house and one of her sayings years later on the subject of discipline was,

'If I couldn't hit them hard enough, I'd kick them and, if that didn't sort them out, I'd take my shoe off and hit them with that!' She didn't really, but you get the message.

The Old Man may or may not have been given access to me and Ron when the divorce of our parents came through. I don't know. I do know that if he decided to come round to 'pump us' as to what or where Mam was going and doing, he would stand at the bottom of our entry and give a piercing whistle using two fingers stuck in his mouth. Ron and I would then be sent out to be given a copper or two whilst we were being questioned. As Ron was on the Clubs and earning good money he didn't really need it and gradually it was just me that went out.... complete with a list of instructions such as, Norman needs new shoes, trousers, vests and shirts, and ended with,

'Mam said you're a rotten stinking sod and she hopes your fancy woman poisons you!'

Now, I ask you, what sort of thing is that to be told to say to your Old Man? He'd just laugh though and send back an equally insulting reply. You've heard of piggy in the middle, well, that was ME!

I was still being subjected to his big smacking kisses and, probably due to him only using a cut throat razor his cheeks were rougher than the roughest abrasive paper. Tales were filtering back about him from all sorts of sources, the most recent being that the other occupant of a house he was sharing, had returned home to find the Old Man lying in a pool of blood. It was suggested some cuckolded husband had gathered with friends and worked the Old Man over. Our dad did love the ladies!

13: Moat Boys Intermediate School

I was allocated to Moat Road Intermediate Boys' School under the Headmaster Mr H M Purnell. This was an all uniform school and at interview sitting cross legged in 'Nelly's' study (this was the nickname given to him by Moat Boys) each of us was given a sheet outlining what the uniform consisted of: a navy blazer with school badge, grey flannel trousers, grey or white shirt with a Moat tie and cap with a miniature of the blazer badge. I started my new school resplendent in my new school uniform but unfortunately my luck was running true to form because on the first day my cap was pinched and never seen again. (The same thing happened to my own son but with his craft apron on his first day at senior school. However, it mysteriously reappeared on his desk the day he was leaving aged sixteen years.)

We also needed gym shorts, a singlet and football boots. I must add here that the Headmaster would often tell us,

'Any parent who cannot afford a uniform is not to worry. As long as a boy is clean, polishes his shoes, combs his hair and wears a clean shirt collar, then that is perfectly acceptable in my school.'

I only know of one boy who did not have a school uniform. He came from a large family and all his siblings were girls. John was always neat, tidy and spotlessly clean in his person. The feeling of togetherness in and out of school was such that when, on a particular day John came to school wearing a pair of his sister's shoes, every boy in the class ignored them and rallied around him to show it didn't matter at all.

I don't know if the Old Man paid anything towards my finery but I do know that until I left to go to work at fourteen years, my school uniform were the only togs I can remember being bought from new during my senior school years! Actually, tell a lie, two years after starting my new school I was told I had to make do with a blazer that wasn't in the school navy blue, so I stuck out a mile to every other kid. When this was pointed out long after I'd started wearing it, Our Mam purchased some traditional blazer coloured material from the market which some woman she knew, 'made up' into a blazer for me. Unfortunately, there wasn't enough material so the body of the jacket was shorter up the back!

After someone lent Mam some hair clippers, she decided to try to cut mine and Ron's hair. She'd overlooked the fact however that Barbers served an apprenticeship. On completion, we both looked as though a basin had been put on our heads and the hair cut around! If you've ever wondered how it is to walk around in the summer with your coat collar pulled up around your ears, then take it from me you feel pretty silly! She relented in the end though and the Barber at the corner was able to put right most of the damage.

I was to find a lot of kindness in my new school but I think they were puzzled as to how this new first year boy who'd passed the Scholarship with such good marks (did I tell you I was borderline Grammar?) was now failing abysmally and was consistently bottom of the class. Anyway, several months later, along with a number of other boys and without prior warning, we were called for a retest. Yours truly, bottom of the class three times in a year, was again found to be borderline Grammar School material. What the heck??? I could've told them why but nobody thought to ask me. It was because I just didn't have any confidence! I knew this was true because Mam used to tell people at least once a week in my presence... 'Our Norman daren't go upstairs on his own because he's got no confidence; Our Norman won't sing like Ronnie because he's got no confidence; Our Norman won't tell the Old Man he needs some new shoes for school because he's got no confidence!' Mam was quite right of course, I didn't have any confidence BUT MAM, WHOSE BLOODY FAULT WAS THAT!

I would shut the classroom and 'here & now' out by letting my mind wander. I slew dragons, climbed mountains, won the Victoria Cross. There was no need for any of it. All I needed was a little love, attention, encouragement but I got none of these, and so I came to terms with my life in the only way I was able to. I shut off. I DON'T BLAME YOU, MAM!

My first form master was George Page, always nicknamed 'Doughy' but I have no idea why. He was the music master and a very good violinist, playing in all manner of orchestras.

'Doughy' was small in stature and in my opinion no disciplinarian. Of course he didn't have to be as his class were all first year 'fags.' I cannot ever remember him using the sanction of the cane against any boy, or even needing to use the threat of it, but I do remember the near hysteria when he tried to chastise 'Our Albert!'

Albert Driver was a very tall, well-built boy who towered over Doughy.

'Driver, take that silly smirk from off your face,' thundered Doughy, but this made Albert smirk all the more.

'I've warned you,' he continued and tried to smack Albert across the face.

From then on it was pure farce for every time Doughy tried to get a smack in, Albert just tilted his head back and so it finished up with our teacher jumping up at full stretch and never once connecting. We were all doubled up with laughter!

For a few months Albert and I were chums. One day I visited his home and his dad, who was a railway train driver, (Driver, Driver) pulled out a weird looking machine with two round pendulum type clock weights hanging from it. I was invited to hold these, one in each hand, which I did. (silly boy) Albert's dad then turned a crank handle, and I swear my hair stood up on end as I received a fair old charge of electricity. I believe the gadget was to help arthritics. Driver Driver thought it hilariously funny but I didn't!

Albert's mum was a lovely woman who'd send me and Albert picking stinging nettle flowers so as to make wine. When she made a brew she'd send me home with a bottle. Hardly allowing it time to stand and work fully, greedy me would guzzle the lot then go off to school – or at least I think I went to school, for I cannot remember!

One day, Albert told me that his cousin was Betty Driver, the singer on the radio. I knew who Betty Driver was as we used to listen to her on the radio variety shows. She had a lovely voice. Television, what the heck was television!? In 1940 a television was a new- fangled gadget dreamed up in an H G Wells book! Today of course we know Betty Driver better as 'Betty Turpin', the barmaid in 'Coronation Street.' Albert, well, when he grew up he joined the Leicester Police Force and retired as a senior officer.

When Doughy found out that another boy and I could strum on the Ukulele, and another boy named Ball could play the piano accordion with him on the violin, we had our own little orchestra at music time.

That last Christmas before war was declared the school put on an exhibition of work. One section was a commentary on world events. I remember one display was to do with the Russian/ Finnish war. There was an excellent caricature of Joseph Stalin and the verse below it went....

'Take no notice of old Joseph Stalin, for when smiling he's nobody's darling. But what's got his goat, is a Finn in the throat, and now he's forever snarling!'

Christmas Dance:

Although sharing the same building as a school we were kept strictly separated from Moat Girls with them on the Ventnor Street side and the boys on the Orson Street side. When crossing the school hall should any boy so much as dare to call across to a girl or wink he was regarded with great suspicion and warned off as a sex maniac in the making. We were told a school Christmas dance was to be held and the girls would be brought into the hall. Of course none of the boys had any idea how to dance and so we were given basic instruction on the Waltz, Quickstep and Foxtrot by Mr Neal, the French Master and the girls' gym mistress. (They eventually married) Unfortunately, although I'd filled in my dance card, on the night the dance was to be held I had to cry off as my school trousers were dirty and I had no time to wash and press them. I had no others, these were my only pair. I was a neglected child, and to think I used to feel sorry for John in his sister's shoes.

14: 1938 67 Asfordby Street Leicester

67 Asfordby Street, Leicester (Centre)

The year was 1938 and movement was afoot in Europe. A van pulled up outside our school and we were set to, unloading cardboard boxes the size of a shoe box. Gas masks, although our Headmaster, H M Purnell, insisted that in school we always referred to them as respirators. Each boy from our class was called out and the rubber smelling monstrosities were tried on over the face to determine the size needed.

What simple pleasures the gas masks provided, for, as one breathed out, the air escaping from the tight rubber close to the side of the face, made hilariously funny farting noises! The class were convulsed with laughter! The next thing timewise was a questionnaire which wanted to know 'do you have any relatives overseas (I think the emphasis was on Canada) and in the event of War would your parents wish you to be sent to that colony to be in a safe place?' Children who put their names down to go to Canada under this scheme, wore a green arm band, and for a time were a novelty, but when a passenger liner carrying many women and children to that country was torpedoed resulting in many lives being lost, the arm bands disappeared. The Old Man, having so many relatives in that country (although by this time his parents were dead) tried to get me to agree to going over there with him, but as I'd been afraid of him for so long, no way!

Moat School prided itself on the correct usage and pronunciation of the English language and our Headmaster seemed to go over the top with the subject but I realise now he was getting us ready for when we left for the 'outside world.' Everyone was expected to learn poems and know how to deliver them slowly and clearly. Tone poems mainly:

- Not a drum was heard, not a funeral note, as his corpse to the rampart we hurried
- Full fathom five thy father's Lies, of his bones are coral made
- Quinquireme of Nineveh from Distant Ophir, rowing home to haven in sunny Palestine'
- Softly, silently now the moon, walks the night in her silver shoon

Reading them as printed does not sound very hard but now say these words slowly, pronouncing every word almost as a chant.

15: More school days & living in Dorothy Road

That first year in Intermediate School was memorable in more ways than one for, in the early part of 1939 we again changed our home. It was the year of my first cross country run. All the first year boys were put at the front of the line-up, then came the second year boys and then, to us, the big boys from the final year - and some of them were very big!

All of us were milling around, tightly packed together, when the 'Off' was sounded. At once, every big boy at the rear shoved forward hard, and I went 'arse over tip.' Whilst down it felt like I was trodden on by every one of the 300 runners behind and when I finally got to my feet I was a mess, for both elbows and knees were ripped and bleeding. 'Sod this' I thought, 'I've had enough' so I set off for the changing rooms.....via the 5 mile course! The blood running down my limbs began to congeal, forcing me to lope along like a stick insect the harder it set but gritting my teeth I kept going, passing boy after boy. I clearly remember one of the form masters acting as a steward catching sight of the blood caked apparition passing him at a rate of knots and shouting,

'Your arms and legs; you can't run like that!'

As he didn't produce chapter and verse, plus a rule book to support his statement, I just ignored him and kept going. I was in my element and could have kept going all day. I'd like to say that I won that first year, but it wasn't to be; not for another two years in fact, the war you know. Instead, I came in 35th. That tumble had ensured most of my fellow pupils were out of sight by the time I'd regained my feet and sorted myself out. To this day, I maintain that I was going so strong at the finishing post that had it been a six mile race I would've been in the first five. What with the bandages I was walking like an automaton for days afterwards. Why was I such a good runner? Easy, I was such a nervous kid that I dare not go to bed, even when I was fifteen years old, unless there was someone else in the family already upstairs or going to bed at the same time. No way would you get me upstairs on my own to fetch something if it was dark even if one of the family were to stand at the foot of the stairs. My daylight routine for fetching something from the bedroom was: Inform the family, open stair's door; check that no ghosts are peering down the stairs from the landing; prop stair's door open with a chair leg ignoring cries of 'shut the blasted door, we're all freezing in here', run headlong up the stairs, along the landing and crash through the bedroom door, grab whatever was required then, still without stopping, spin around at full speed and reverse the route. Jump the last five or six steps and burst back into the living room. This was all done with the eyes tightly shut!

I really developed my racing skills, or should I say honed them to perfection, when we moved into this new house of ours. The house was in an even better neighbourhood and the rooms were much, much bigger. It was half passaged up and down, and we had a proper bathroom, but the garden was miniscule and the local kids were a little more standoffish to what I'd been used to. I could cope with this but for one thing......between our house and the corner shop which we patronised, was a piece of waste land upon which could be clearly seen a brick structure in which a man had committed suicide by hanging himself. That was the first thing, the second was that we moved into the new house during the dark nights and I, being the youngest, was the one sent on errands to the corner shop AND I HAD TO PASS THAT CURSED PLACE!

The routine went something like this:

Mam: Go and get a loaf of bread.

Me: Can I go in the morning before I go to school?

Mam: Just do as you're told. We need the bread for supper and breakfast.

Me: But Ma.......

That would be as far as I got before the money was pushed into my hand and I was ejected through the front door with the promise it would be left on the latch for my return.

Me: And leave the light on as well Our Mam! (No way would I go up our dark entry)

Thus, I would set off, walking in the middle of the road, casting nervous glances, right and left, before and behind me. Should there be another pedestrian walking along that self-same road in the direction I was going, GREAT! If not, proceed with caution. Nearer to the suicide spot my pace increased, first to a trot and then to a flat out gallop, until at the moment I came abreast of the place I was going full speed ahead. I was determined that if the suicide came back from the dead he'd have no chance at all of catching me. Still at full speed I'd dash into the shop, nearly knocking the door off its hinges in my haste and frightening the life out of any customer who may be inside waiting for service. The return journey was simply a reversal of the journey out, except the nearer I got, the more I broke into a cold sweat at the thought the front door might be closed against me. If it had been closed then it was a case of 'open up' quickly before my hammering and screams brought the neighbours out to see who was being murdered.

One of my playmates lived at the top of the street in one of a row of terraced houses. Because most youngsters in those days had their noses stuck into comics and 'tu'penny dreadfuls', we used to swap or exchange these items. One day I was loaned a marvellous magazine, full of the most colourful pictures of a nature setting. Birds, animals etc. The owner of this and many others like it was a young chap who lived in another of the terraces. He was a Salvationist, married with a wife and baby. He was most affable to us kids and would loan us the books on request. He wasn't in work but his wife was, and during the day the baby was minded elsewhere. Calling one day to get another book or two on loan, I was invited to go into the middle bedroom and 'help yourself.' Upstairs I went, not really liking to do so, but I was hooked on those books as was everyone else in our house. I'd selected those books I hadn't read when the young chap came into the bedroom and pushed me hard onto the bed. His hand went straight to my flies as he said, 'let's have a look at you!'

I was up off that bed, down the stairs and straight into the street in seconds flat and, unlike General MacArthur, I did not return. I said nothing of this to my family. I wouldn't have known how to, and in any case, I'm sure I would've been blamed.

Weekends for me were Hell. By 7pm Ted would be out courting, Maisie would be out dancing and Mam and Ron were out fulfilling singing engagements. I would be on my own in that, still to me, strange house. Every week the routine was the same as were the words of reassurance,

'Now, you'll be alright; lock the door after we've gone and nobody can get in.'

This last bit always got my mind working overtime. Who won't get in? Why do they want to get in? More important, WHAT WILL THEY DO TO ME IF THEY DO GET IN? By the time the last to leave had gone, I was a mass of nerves. I wasn't quite twelve. To keep me company (they said) the wireless had been left playing but how could I hear if THEY broke in and came for me over the sound of music!? The back door was locked, or so I'd been told, but what if it wasn't locked properly? I could go and check but what if THEY or IT was peering through the window at me. Ah well, nothing else for it.....head down, run like hell out through our middle room, speed through the hall, tear at the Yale lock on the front door and, leaving the door wide open, speed out into the near deserted dark streets and walk around non-stop until 10:30pm, at which time I knew the first members of the family might, just might, be on their way home. Usually though, it was after 11pm. I must have been followed by more dirty old men than any other kid in the city. Rarely did my family find out about my nocturnal walk arounds. If they had, I'm sure they would've tried to reason with me, encourage and reassure me. Some hope! I hate to say it but all they ever thought about was themselves. As it was, my nerves were my own private Hell.

I lost so much sleep that more often than not I was dozing off at school and falling further and further behind. I realise now that had the Authorities known what a skivvy I'd become, with no messing about, I would've been taken into care. Looking back I think it would probably have been better for me if I had. I don't think my family ever saw me as anything but a passenger. The only difference it would've made to them was they'd have lost an unpaid skivvy. I was the youngest and the only one not at work so I had to earn my keep. This was my weekday routine:

I'd wake with a start to the realisation that the house was quiet. Everyone had gone! I'd fallen back to sleep as I was so tired. I'd go downstairs and grab a slice of bread. I'd look for a comb but wouldn't find one because it was probably in Mam's bag. I'd comb my hair as best I could using a fork then rinse my hands and face with water. After dragging a big bundle of dirty washing tied up in a sheet to the washer woman (praying all the time I didn't see anyone I knew) I'd go to school.

At 11:45am, I would remind the teacher I needed to go early so I could put the dinner on. I'd race home and light the gas. I'd unset the breakfast table and wash up the breakfast pots. There was no washing up liquid in those days so I'd use bar soap in hot water to work up a lather as best I could. I'd check the saucepans were simmering, making sure the water hadn't boiled away then reset the table for dinner. At 12:35 Ted would return home. I could hear the click of his bike gears. He'd be closely followed by Mam and Maisie. (They worked together) Ron was at the Open Air School so didn't come home for dinner.

Mam would serve out the dinner and once eaten she'd make a flask for work. Ted would be fast asleep at the table with his head in his hands. How on earth did he do that?

At 1:30pm the factory hooter would sound and they'd all leave with hardly a word to me. Mam never kissed me goodbye. I would survey the debris with a sigh and decide to leave clearing up until I got home for tea. I'd then leave for school.

With school ended for the day I'd arrive home. In winter my first job was to try and light the fire, knowing full well it would take several attempts to get it to catch. I'd use the last of the matches and look for more - none. I'd dash out and ask a neighbour if she could help. Finally, with tears streaming down my face from the wood smoke, the fire would catch and I'd then unset the table from dinner and start washing the pots using the bar soap and hot water to build up a lather. I'd then reset the table with the pots for tea and put the kettle on a low light ready for the family to return home.

Oh yes, instead of a pudding at dinnertime we'd have some shop bought cakes. Our Ted wouldn't eat his then but save it for tea time. I was always given a dire warning, 'leave that bloody cake alone. I'm having it at tea time. If you dare touch it, I'll give you a bloody good hiding!' Cramming the last few crumbs of said cake into my mouth, I'd greet my just arrived home from school brother, Ronnie, with, 'where have you been? I've had to do it all on my own again!'

Ronnie would tell me some silly tale about missing his tram connection in town but I knew full well he and his mates had been riding up and down the lift at the newly built Lewis's store in town, but I didn't argue. There wasn't any time anyway. The work was done, and besides, he was earning money on the Clubs. Me? I was Cinderella!

War Refugees:

With the Spanish Civil War over, the Basque children who attended our school as political refugees were repatriated and we had our first refugees from Germany or Austria. One boy was Jewish. I hope he wasn't representative of his people because I've rarely met a more obnoxious kid. I think it was true to say that within a very short time we were queuing up to dislike him. He didn't stay with us for very long in fact he went off the scene very quickly to sit out the War (which could be clearly seen around the corner) overseas.

Air raid cellars and the school air raid shelter:

The school cellars were converted into Air Raid Shelters and we practised drills for when the Sirens sounded.

'When the school bell rings three times you will stand up, file out of the classroom with your teacher leading carrying the school register and you will file down in an orderly fashion to the Plenum System. Once seated, the master will call the register. You will sit, and may talk quietly amongst yourselves, until such time as the All Clear is sounded.'

The shelters were easily accessible and they gave us our first whiff of scandal.....to explain:

Our school was divided into three sections: Infants downstairs and Senior Boys and Senior Girls upstairs, although segregated with boys on one side and girls on the other. We, that is the boys, were called into assembly, as I am sure the girls were, and from the stage the Headmaster addressed us.

'Boys, I have to tell you there has been some goings on in the Plenum System. (The cellars cum air raid shelters)

Without expanding on what he'd just said he warned us just what would happen if we even looked at the cellar entrance without his permission. We were all agog and later found out that one of the 13 year old boys plus one of the 13 year old girls had been found down the cellar going at it hammer and tongs! They were both expelled. Frankly, as far as we were concerned, that place could hardly have been put to better use.

Ron's voice broke and soon after he started work for a wet fish merchant. Now my sufferings were added to because Ron and I were sharing a double bed, Ted now having his own small bedroom and, no matter how well he washed, he always stunk of fish! I think was born to suffer!!

Ron's boss, the fish monger, was quoted by Ron many times as saying, 'there won't be any war, 'it's impossible', which just went to show what a right ruddy know it all HE was!!

Smoking:

Along with all the kids my age, I used to try the odd 'drag' on a cigarette when circumstances permitted. To feed his image Ted was smoking a pipe. When any opportunity presented itself I would slip into his bedroom and, pinching some of his pipe tobacco, I'd roll it into a piece of newspaper and try to smoke that (not very successfully, I might add) but then I discovered a smoking material that was more freely available. Bull rush stems!

In the front room we had a vase containing well dried out Bull rushes. We found that if we snipped off the bottom inch, stuffed a needle down the centre and then ignited it with a match (quickly blowing out any flare up of flame of course) that we could draw in and inhale the acrid smoke. Mam would puzzle over her shrinking Bull rushes, and what started off as two foot long stems eventually disappeared into the vase itself.

Mam's friend Bob and visiting the Old Man:

Mam's friend, Bob, was regularly making scenes now and gradually she was offloading him. I hated him. In the meantime I was being sent to see the Old

Man straight from school on a week day. This meant a journey into town to his place of work. It was up a small gateway and I would stand looking at the grim and grimy looking factory windows behind which were the bank of looms he operated. Within a moment or two I would see a hand rubbing away at the grime inside and then his face would appear. A second or two later he would come out, hitching at his trouser waist as he did so, for he would never wear a belt. First he would take my head in his hands and give me a big smooching kiss. With that out of the way he would begin to question me, always about her, Our Mam. He never asked me how I was or if I was happy. After a short time and satisfied I could tell him no more, he would give me a big block of nut chocolate and a few coppers, which I never declared. In fact the chocolate would be devoured on the return journey home.

When Mam came in that night, the counter pumping would begin! (As if I could tell her anything!!)

I realise now that these two loved each other so much so, that love had turned in on itself and become a destroyer.

That Christmas, the Old Man gave me a pound note to buy myself something, his attitude being, 'you're the only one coming to see me, therefore you're the only one I'm going to give a present to.'

When Mam found out she took the pound from me saying, 'I'll look after this for you until you've decided what you're going to spend it on' but when I'd decided and asked her for it back she refused to give it to me. Her logic was, 'I have to keep you, so this bugger's mine!' I think it was then I hated her for the first time, really hated her. You see I had a brain and could reason, and my reasoning went like this.......Ok, so I don't go to work and bring in any money, but I'm the one who runs all the errands, does the housework and even scrubs the bedrooms in the school holidays. ME! And perhaps you do, as you say, 'keep me' BUT how well do you keep me???? I'm the most badly dressed kid in the school, I don't have any football boots or kit and do it in my vest which I wear all week, and because I sweat a lot, the under arms are thick with caked sweat. You bought me PE shorts but they got to be so tatty I had to beg some out of the 'tat' cupboard at school. This was allowed because we weren't permitted to do PE in our school trousers. You never bought me underpants so I couldn't even sew the fly up and use them and, on top of that, you never supervised my hygiene so I must have smelled. YOU KEEP ME....that's a laugh! I even used to darn my own socks with cotton.

(Well, I did say right at the start I would tell you the story of me and Our Mam, THE GOOD AND THE BAD, didn't I.........but I loved my Mam, and I would have died for her, cheerfully or tearfully.

Pre War Years - Cleethorpes:

In August of 1939, during the last peace the country would enjoy for nearly six long years, Mam took me and Ron to Cleethorpes. I don't know where Our Ted went for his holidays but I do know he was courting strong, and Maisie went with her current boyfriend's family to Portsmouth.

I enjoyed Cleethorpes. It was possible in those days to slowly work one's way along the front, seeing a different show being performed on the sand every few yards. There was a Magician, a Sand Artist, a Punch & Judy Show and, best of all, The Super Follies!

(Life Begins with super follies, when the busy day is done. We don't care how much they work us, just as long as we have fun. Georgie and Tommy are a couple of lads, they keep us smiling. It's best to keep on always smiling, so life begins........)

I can even remember the tune!

In those days only breakfast was eaten in the digs; all other food was eaten out. Sometimes lodgers were allowed to bring food back to the lodgings where the Landlady would cook it but, come rain, hail or snow, lodgers were not allowed back in the digs until bedtime!

I'd managed to save a few shillings and one of my first seaside buys was a pocket watch for half a crown. (12½ pence in new money) That year the Old Man had treated me to a wrist watch, mainly, I think, to try and entice Our Ron to go and see him but within the first few day the watch glass was lost through no fault of my own, and whilst unprotected, one of the hands was snagged and pulled off. The Old Man was disgusted with me but honest, it wasn't my fault. Unfortunately, as I had an enquiring mind I had the watch in pieces on the beach within an hour. Sand, being a poor lubricant, it then ceased to work, for good.

Apart from the Super Follies, the sand shows had no seating as such and so the audience stood on the promenade (until the collection plate was passed around) then they moved to the next free show.

We later learned Maisie's holiday was 'ruined' for the highlight was to have been a day trip to France. In fact the ferry did take them to the French coast but they weren't allowed to disembark as the French Army was mobilising and they had to turn back without landing.

Ron: fishmonger, clicker and Mrs Besom's farm:

By now Mam and Maisie had plenty of work in the shoes, and Ron was working, first for Mr Bown the fish monger on East Park Road. Mam had always said that when each of us left school she would buy us a bike, and on leaving school Mam bought Ron a new one. Of course there's always one exception to every rule, and that exception, when my turn came for a bike, still lay in the future. Ron's bike was a smashing red racer, and at times when he was at work, I was alone at home. TEMPTATION! I wheeled it out and started to race – after all, it was a racer, wasn't it! I remember tearing down Chesterfield Road at speed, then the next thing being upside down with my head stuck between the engine and bumper of a lorry that had pulled out in front of me onto the main road. The driver admitted later he couldn't understand why I'd not been killed. Three inches either way and I would've been. The bike was a mess; the front wheel was ruined, a front fork smashed back, frame dented. Now, I knew that by pulling out onto the major of the two roads the lorry driver was at fault, but he got away with it for he claimed there was no HALT sign on his road. The bike was repairable and he paid half; I got warned, and that's about all because Mam realised I'd learned a valuable lesson.

Ronnie finally left the fish trade and began working at a shoe factory (Hendersons on St Saviours Road) as a trainee clicker, but he wasn't happy and eventually got himself a job on a farm on the outskirts of Leicester. I missed him terribly.

In the beginning he went out with the farmer's daughter delivering milk by horse and cart. After a few weeks the foreman's wife, Mrs Besom, asked him if he thought he could do the milk delivery on his own.....Oh Yes! So, a routine was established. Each morning he was given a 'float' in small change before setting off, and each morning he would count this money at the top of the farm lane to make sure the money was all there...£1/ 5 shillings. On this particular day, on counting the float, Ron found that Mrs Besom had only given him £1/ 2 shillings and sixpence, therefore he was 2 shillings and 6 pence short. (Half a crown) Ron completed his milk round and returned to the farm where he handed the cash in before washing ready for the evening milking. Mrs Besom sent for him:

'Turn out your pockets' Mrs Besom ordered, and Ronnie complied. After pawing through what he'd turned out Mrs Besom asked, 'where is it?'

Very puzzled, Ronnie asked, 'where's what?'

'You've stolen half a crown; you're half a crown short!'

Upset, Ron said, 'Please Mrs Besom, you gave me half a crown short in my float. I know you did because I always count what you give me before I go out onto the main road. This morning you only gave me £1/ 2shillings and 6pence.'

'How dare you!' screamed her ladyship. 'How dare you check I've given you the right money!'

At this point the eldest daughter broke in. 'Ronald is quite right mother. Don't you remember this morning when you said you were out of change and could only give Ronald £1/ 2 shillings and 6pence?'

Ronnie said afterwards that old Besom never admitted she was in the wrong so he left as soon as possible.

3 September 1939 – declaration of war:

It was a few minutes to 11am and Ron and I were returning home as fast as we could because momentous events were afoot. We charged down the street and rushed into the house. The wireless was on and I heard the words gravely spoken,

'As no such guarantee has been given (or was it received), this country is now in a state of war with Germany.'

I think it was Our Ted who spoke first,

'The best thing I can do is volunteer for the medical corps. There's no way I want to get pushed into the infantry to be shot at!'

Once Ted had received his papers for the Army (in January 1940) a date was fixed for his wedding.

On the morning he was to marry Elsie Cartwright the snow lay thick on the ground and about 11am the Vicar came knocking at the front door,

'Mr Hastings, if you still want to get married this afternoon you'll have to get some help to dig a pathway through to the church, otherwise you'll have to set another date.'

Ted managed to get some of his mates to help and they finally cleared a pathway to the door. The wedding went ahead.

Two weeks later Ted was in the Royal Army Medical Corp and four months after that he was in Dover evacuating the dead and badly wounded soldiers from the holds of the rescue ships after Dunkirk. What we didn't know, until much later, was what the nature of this work was:

Wearing a rubberised groundsheet over his clothes he and other Medical Corps men would go onto the evacuation ships, climbing up and down the ships' ladder with dead and wounded men over his shoulder. If you doubt this then go and look at the size of the hatches leading into the bowels of a ship. Ted later told us there was often so much blood his uniform was soaked through to the skin and as he walked, the blood in his boots spurted out through the lace holes.

But the horror did not end there, for ships that had been bombed had dead men aboard with limbs etc blown off and scattered about. In the makeshift mortuaries, armed with long metal clips and staples, the severed limbs and heads were clipped back on, all the time hoping this was the correct arm, leg or head. By the time this duty was eventually over Ted, a non or virtually non-smoker, was smoking packet after packet of cigarettes.

Ted's wife (Elsie) was living just up the hill from us and I clearly remember one day, as I was going home from school, seeing her and her parents almost running up the hill, obviously in a great hurry. I found out why later. My sister in law had a brother, young Bob, who'd been brought back by his army mates from Dunkirk, very badly injured in both legs. Sadly, by the time he arrived at Dover hospital, gas gangrene had set in and there wasn't much hope. Both legs were amputated and he was sinking fast, thus the haste of his family.

When his family arrived he asked his mother for a glass of beer but an officious nurse or Sister had commented,

'Beer is not allowed on the ward!'

At this, young Bob's mother had stood up and said,

'If my boy wants a glass of beer, then he'll have a glass of beer!' and with that she went out and got him a bottle of beer. His last wish was fulfilled.

Young Bob died soon after, still in Dover hospital.

The family were told that if they wanted Bob's body sent home for burial they should arrange for the local undertaker to meet the train at London Road railway station at a prearranged time; the coffin would be sealed and should not be opened.

Preparations were made and at the appointed time the train was met......no coffin! A mistake had been made and Bob had been buried in Dover cemetery. With this news, the family decided to leave Bob in Dover with his mates. Young Bob, R.I.P.

After Dunkirk Ted worked in the War Office, London.

16: The War Years

The Sunday evening World War II broke out, Mam, Ron and I went into town, as I imagine did many of Leicester's inhabitants. We were walking along one of the main shopping streets but because of the blackout not a body could be seen, and yet we could feel crowds of people pressing around us as we were forced along. It was eerie. From somewhere our little family group had managed to obtain an 'illuminous' badge which was a disc approximately 1 inch diameter. If it was held close to the face and a glimmer of light fell across its surface, it was possible to see a green glow emanating from it but that was all. Certainly, the people in Granby Street, some going one way and some going the other, sensed rather than saw their way along and had no idea where other people were until they collided. Were people seeking comfort and confidence from the close proximity of others? Then someone struck a match to light a cigarette, forgetting! At once the cry went up that we were to hear so many times during the next few years: PUT THAT BLOODY LIGHT OUT! THE GERMAN BOMBERS CAN SEE IT! which struck me as rather odd at that moment as there weren't any of the dreaded Hun above us!

Mam later managed to buy an old wind up gramophone with one record by Vera Lynn. I remember the 'B' side was 'Somewhere in France with you.' I wonder who else nowadays would remember this song!?

1940 War days and Half days at school:

Our school midsummer holidays were extended that year and when we did return to school it was on a half day basis; mornings one week and afternoons the next, with the girls' side fitting in on the alternative half days.

I cannot remember whether it was one of our half days of schooling or whether it was a Saturday but certainly a school chum and I, whilst standing at the Spinney Hill Park entrance close to Park Vale Road on the Mere Road, heard an aeroplane. We ran to the top of Derwent Street (or was it Darley Street) and looked out over the said street which sloped down towards the main Charles Street/ London Road railway station. There were no high rise flats in those days and we had a grandstand view of a plane in the near distance, droning steadily along.

'That's a Wellington bomber' said my companion!'

'No it's not,' I replied, 'I think it's a Defiant bomber!'

At almost that exact moment, the plane's nose dropped. It casually dove down quite a way and then up came its nose as it regained its former height and continued on its way. Several moments later, or should I say several explosions later, we were both proved wrong. Cavendish Road had become the first place to be bombed in Leicester. Oh yes, the air raid siren did go off.......but later. The War had arrived and for us the Phoney War was over!

When attending school we always carried our gas masks or Respirators, as decreed by our Headmaster. To forget would swiftly bring down the wrath of HM Purnell upon our heads.

The first of our Masters to go off to war was Mr Morton, a very tall young man forever remembered by most of the Moat Boys of that era for screwing one eyebrow up much higher than the other whilst teaching. It was a feat most of us tried to copy but which left us screwing our faces up into the most awful grimace thereby convincing the locals that the pupils of Moat Boys suffered from the most appalling malady. Happy days!

17: 42 Eggington Street – More war years

In April 1940, the family, minus Ted (who was in the Medical Army Corp) moved house again to 42 Eggington Street, Leicester. The house was a small terrace and, as far as I was concerned it was a move for the better. I loved it.

At school various things happened: We were visited by a Chinese Nationalist Senior Officer who seemingly had no English. I don't think our French Master, Mr Neal, understood Chinese so all in all that was a waste of time.

The last progress report Mr Neal made upon me were the words 'I believe he does his best.' I think Mr Neal was trying to be kind.

With the news our French Master was to marry the Gym Mistress we boys were asked, as I suppose the girls were too, to contribute towards a wedding present. Soon after the new husband went off into the Air Force teaching the free Polish Airmen how to speak English, using French as the in between language. I remember how Mr Neal visited once and spoke from the stage, telling us how our Polish Allies had warned him that if he did not treat them better he would be taken up and thrown out of an aeroplane without a parachute!

For all that we were hearing from France where the British/ French and German Armies were facing each other, there might not have been a war, and on thus the phrase 'All is quiet on the Western front' came to mind, but then....

May 1940:

Mam decided to take me and Ronnie to Blackpool on a weekend holiday. All arrangements were made but then the German Army went into the attack and everything was cancelled. At first the news bulletins were full of optimism, for after all, were we not going to 'Hang Out the Washing on the Siegfried Line?' Sadly, it was the Germans who hung US out and within a few days the first evacuees from the defeated British Army were to be seen in tents on public parks whilst we school children were handling Francs & Centime coins; worthless now and strange to us then with their holes.

I should perhaps not recount this but this little story is indicative of the times, anyway, here goes: To finalise our Blackpool Trip Mam took Ronnie and me with her to confirm the booking. It was a Sunday, and in those days everyone had a 'Sunday Best' outfit, which in Mam's case was a grey two piece suit with a fox skin draped over one shoulder, across the breast and fastened on the other side. It was a hot afternoon and so Mam had loosened the fox skin and was carrying it draped down her front. Two men on bicycles passed by and I distinctly heard on of them say, 'She's keeping her tits and fanny warm!' Our Mam just laughed out loud; I pretended I hadn't heard.

1940 Messerschmitt plane & blackouts:

We knew all about the Battle in the Skies but it was not until a German Messerschmitt 109 fighter plane was displayed on the Victoria Park as a war trophy that the majority of our people saw a German aeroplane for the first time. It drew enormous crowds and most people were surprised how small it was. Personally, I was highly sceptical, for I was not convinced that the one small bullet hole through the back of the pilot's seat was what brought it down. Surely at the speed our fighters spewed out bullets there would be more than ONE bullet hole? If my memory serves me right, painted upon the side of the German plane was a caricature of an owl/ penguin (Mr Chamberlain) for he had an umbrella under one wing. I may be wrong.

The blackout was a pain. Let the smallest sliver of light shine through and as sure as God made little apples, the cry would go up....PUT THAT LIGHT OUT! Our windows were criss-crossed with sticky tape to hold the splintered glass, and the merest chink of light was frowned upon. It was years before we fully realised that with just the merest glimmer of moonlight, railway lines and rivers & canals showed up clearly, leading the bombers to one after the other of our cities.

Traffic through the streets was virtually non-existent. Bread and milk was delivered by horse and cart with just a sprinkling of electric vans and of course, the ever present tram car.

I can remember how, starting Gwendolen Road on my way to choir practice, rolling a tennis ball along the East Park Road, keeping it in the tram rail groove all the way to St Barnabas Church and never once having to get off the road or lift the ball because of oncoming traffic. There just wasn't any.

The street lamps, most of them gas, were dimmed out, thereby casting only a weak, cold glow downwards. Several boys discovered it was possible to stand directly under the lamp, tight up against the lamp post itself, and become virtually 'invisible' as the light made a ring around the base of the lamp post, leaving the centre in darkness. Jumping out gave many a poor passer by a near heart attack.

For some time Air Raid Shelters had been dug out on the Spinney Hill Park, steeply sloping off before levelling out. There was also a massive static water tank close to the East Park Road/ St Saviours Road corner exit; very big and very deep! We children used to watch the progress of the shelter construction with interest as we went to school and I remember that to cross from the swing yard to get to the exit we dare not cross the cricket pitch otherwise the park keeper would shout at us:

'THE PITCH IS FOR CRICKET ONLY. USE THE PATHS OR I'LL REPORT YOU TO YOUR HEADMASTER!'

This was a threat Moat Boys pupils would heed! Former Moat Boys will confirm that should any one of us misbehave on public transport, be it bus or tram car, and should this misbehaviour be reported back and the boy identified, then retribution would swiftly follow! No excuses accepted; the boy would be caned, HARD! In school or out, that's your lot, MATE!

'Nelly' however, was a very fair man....... I'd been having a very hard time at home due to being accused of telling tales to my father who'd deserted us many years earlier. I was forced to go and see him (the Old Man) and it all got too much for me; I played truant. Mam found out and took me into school. She told Nellie I was an ungrateful little beast; that she'd had to bring me up, clothe and feed me etc, etc (that bit about clothing me was a laugh!!) and I was a no good rotten little liar. After she'd gone, Nellie made me sweat for 3 days and then he sent for me.

'Your mother says you're a liar' he said.

I looked him straight in the eye, trembling at what might come, and said, 'No Sir, I'm not a liar.'

'Do you intend to truant again?' he asked.

'No Sir,' I replied.

He looked hard at me. 'If you do play truant again after saying you will not, then you would be a liar. This is your last chance. Next time I WILL cane you.'

I never played truant again. 'THANK YOU SIR!'

19 November 1940:

With the remnants of the British forces brought back to England the Germans started to bomb England into submission. Details of the Battle of Britain are plentiful and I pass over them until we come to November 1940. THAT TUESDAY NIGHT!

I was thirteen years old and alone in the house; We were still living in Eggington Street and all the others were out. I heard some rather peculiar noises, foreign to the night, and went to the front door. It was pitch black outside and all quiet so I went back inside. But more strange noises! After a few moments I went to the door again; it was as light as day! Strange! It was cold, so back I went to the fireside......then a whistling and a whooshing sound and a bang. It came again and again, each one seeming to come closer...boom, boom, BOOM! The penny dropped and I shot under the stairs! We were being bombed! I could've sworn that I, and I alone, was the target. The house shook, the windows rattled and within a short space of time the corner of Fairfield Street and Eggington Street became a heap of rubble. Fortunately the occupants escaped but were badly shaken and unnerved. They'd been under the stairs. I believe the family name was Broadhurst; Grandma, son and two boys. Under the stairs or table were favourite places to shelter as Anderson shelters were damp and often flooded but some people had brick built shelters.

Over the next hour my family returned. Our Ron literally fell in through the front door, quickly followed by Mam (who'd been at the Club) and finally Maisie. We all crowded under the stairs. Every time the desynchronised sound of the German bombers was heard overhead, we dived down. The German planes had a 'drum, drum – drum, drum' sound whilst the British planes were a continuous drone.

Time passed and we heard a frantic pounding on the front door. It was Mrs Marshall and her two girls, Hilda (14) and Nancy (17), from across the street seeking sanctuary. Mrs Marshall's husband, George, was still at work, and being of a nervous disposition she'd come to our house. It was pretty stuffy with seven of us crammed together, but also very funny to me as, no sooner had they all piled in, when a plaintive voice piped up, 'I need a wee!' Out we would burst and one of us would peel off into the kitchen to use the bucket. A tinkling noise would be heard and an accompanied sigh. Someone else would then shout, 'they're coming again!' The bucket would be dropped and we'd all pile back under the stairs. To cram us in completely, husband George turned up, as did a police officer, all steel stencilled helmet and all, to order us out of the house as an unexploded bomb had landed at the top of the street and we had to get out. (In fact it was an aerial torpedo)

Conditioned to obey authority, we grabbed our coats and dashed out, remembering to turn the lights off and leaving a near brimming bucket in the kitchen where it was. We rushed out to search for the nearest Air Raid Shelter and turned left towards Spinney Hill Park, passing as we did the still smoking ruins of the corner house two streets down.

Out of the house and left towards Spinney Hill Park at the end of the road;

Turn right towards East Park Road and the air raid shelters

On the park, we turned to the right towards East Park Road (it was pitch black) only to have an invisible voice scream out that we couldn't go down there;

there were unexploded bombs! Instead, we turned left, up the hill towards Mere Road, but only to be turned back with shouts of, 'those shelters are full!' We did the only thing we could do and headed straight across the middle of the park towards an underground shelter below the bandstand. We were in luck, they had room, and so down the steep slope we went, turning left at the bottom into what was to be 'Hell on Earth' for the rest of the night. We were seated on long wooden forms that ran the length of the shelter facing each other. The lighting was a sickly yellow and the floor, walls and ceiling were bare concrete leaking moisture. No one spoke, sang or did anything, apart from one chap who, every time we heard a bump or felt the shelter shake, kissed his wife and child goodbye.

Deep as the shelter was, sounds from above ground carried, and we heard a stick of bombs coming down. These were going to be close, VERY CLOSE! WHAM, WHAM, WHAM! The shelter seemed to stand on end. People were screaming and the big kisser and his wife seemed to have their lips welded together! You may find this hard to believe but the concussion of those bombs forced the water in the soil through the concrete of the shelter roof and it poured down upon us. We got very wet! From then on all was quiet and we heard no more big bangs that night.

Dawn came and the 'All Clear' sounded. We emerged into the cold light of day, grey and exhausted through lack of sleep, to the smell of stinking high explosive and to see a line of bomb craters just over the fence on the cricket pitch itself. We were very lucky people indeed. Up to the 1980s the different shades of grass where the bomb craters were, could clearly be seen..... and even up to 2000 when conditions were right.

Those who could go back to their houses did so, whilst the homeless by virtue of Mr Hitler's unexploded bomb were directed to the foyer of the local Evington Cinema. Unbelievable, but the Evington Cinema was used to receive people bombed or bombed out that night, through the night. Can you imagine the carnage had it received a direct hit!

Dopey through lack of sleep we and the other dispossessed souls, were eventually ordered out onto one of the buses brought to convey us to who knows where. I certainly have no idea except to say it was a Working Men's Club where we spent the day.

I suppose we were provided with tea and 'tab nabs', and sometime later the same day were in yet another Working Men's Club where our soldier brother Ted found us. But how did he know we'd been bombed out? Anyway, he gave me the pin from a hand grenade before disappearing.

In the late evening Mr Marshall told us that a lady friend who worked with him had a flat (apartment) in the Evington Road area, close to the London Road, and we could spend the night there. We all set off together and when we arrived, were made to feel very welcome. Hardly had we settled down in the large lounge though when the 'Whome, Whome' drone of the enemy planes could be heard, followed by assorted and distant 'Whams' as the bombs fell. There was no air raid shelter and, as the bombs or whatever seemed not to be so numerous, we sat back and relaxed. The night drew on and it seemed to be reasonably quiet. Mam suggested that as the double bed in the back room wasn't being used, that Hilda, who was my age, and I, should try and get some sleep for an hour or so.

We were tucked in, with the top sheet over her, and under me to maintain decency, and both of us went straight to sleep. Tired out!

An hour later, Mam came rushing in and ordered us up and out. She could hear a plane circling overhead! How right she was, for no sooner had we got under a table in the next room when the whole building shook with blast concussion. We all thought 'this was it', but in fact this ended the night's fireworks.

It was still dark when someone came to the door saying a landmine on a parachute had blown up the Pavilion on the' Vicky Park.' We had guessed it was a 'biggy' as when the bedroom was later inspected for damage, it was found the bed on which Hilda and I had been lying, was cut to ribbons and covered with broken glass.

It was still dark when Ron and I raced the few yards to 'Vicky Park' to explore the damage. The Pavilion at the back of our refuge had been completely destroyed, with a whole section hanging down over a huge crater. We could smell the high explosive in the air and I found a thick piece of parachute cord. I kept it for years. The Pavilion was torn down later and a large water tank for fire fighting installed.

Now we were back at the Railway Men's Club, still not allowed to return home due to the unexploded bomb. A billeting officer was talking to Mam and I recognised one of my school teachers, Mr Norton, who was a go between for the school and a Merchant ship which the school had 'adopted'. I can't remember the ship's name but her skipper was a Captain Griffith Jones. Mam, Maisie, Ronnie and I were taken in Mr Norton's car to a lovely, kind couple (Mr & Mrs Dawson) who lived in a beautiful house and had a son, Eric, who was in the RAF.

(Royal Air Force) Mrs Dawson belonged to the WVS (Women's Voluntary Service) and she made us feel very welcome, as did her husband.

Unexploded bomb or not, 'there's no place like home' and as soon as the furore of the bombing died down, we went back home. The Bomb Disposal soldiers were making use of the evacuated houses leading up to Mere Road whilst still looking and digging for what we were assured was an aerial torpedo but as fast as the Bomb Disposal soldiers dug down, so the bomb went down further into the soft soil. The Mere Road Post Office at 182 Mere Road was at the top of the hill and the authorities feared that with the depth the bomb had gone down that had it exploded it would have created an earth quake with devastating damage. Eventually though, we became so blaze about it we would stand at the top of Cork Street looking along towards the Post Office site where the soldiers were still digging down. Soon after, standing on the Mere Road/ Cork Street junction, I saw the barrier lift and an army lorry turn down Cork Street. It had an open back in which I faintly saw a long grey cylinder thing with a very muddy soldier using it for a seat. Was that it?! We were told later that after this bomb, the Bomb Disposal Team was dispatched to diffuse the bomb under St Pauls Cathedral in London. Whether this was true, I cannot say.

Saxby Street was heavily bombed as was Tichbourne Street, and the Saxby Street Methodist Church had to be demolished. I was told how a youth of 16 years or thereabouts, had lost a leg after being blown off his bicycle by a bomb, and then the ambulance in which he was travelling had been blown over by the blast of another bomb losing him most of his other leg.

Other tragedies were the bombing of Grove Road where police officers and civilians were butchered, and Humberstone Road/ Frank Street where, including two or three houses from Frank Street was a shop that sold the most delicious homemade Steak & Kidney pies in a lovely rich gravy. I can never forgive the Germans for losing us our Steak & Kidney pies.

On the home front we realised that we, as an island, were isolated, however, I have to say that we as children never realised just how serious things were. In fact the tragedy, if tragedy it was, that hurt us the most was sweets being rationed. Just a few ounces a month – terrible!

Apart from one other incident there were only spasmodic Air Raids on the City of Leicester and we weren't directly involved. This final incident had me and Mam standing on the front door step one evening listening to the sound of a German plane in the night's sky. Now, we knew that a bomb did not come straight down when dropped but travelled a fair distance forward before hitting the ground. This was proved that night for a bomb passed directly over our heads before impacting close by; I think it was Worthington Street. How do I describe the sound the bomb made? It was something like standing on a railway station platform when a high speed express train goes hurtling past. Both Mam and I fell up the step to get into the house but there was no need as the bomb was long past when it exploded.

I was still hopeless at school except for my written essay work. One incident that seems to prove this was that with so many male teachers going off to war we were getting young men and older women to fill their places. One young teacher set my class an easy essay to write, the subject of which now escapes me. Duly completed, our work was handed in. The following day I was sent for:

'Where did you copy this from?' was his demand.

'Please Sir, I didn't copy it' I replied, 'it came out of my own head.'

'I don't believe you; no child of your age could write this. I'm going to take this further!'

Well, if he did he was soon put right by my form master, for I didn't hear another word on the subject.

I was still hopeless at school and realise now it was possibly because I spent so much time day dreaming and thinking about 'what might have been.' In fact, I honestly believe that had it not been for my English work, good behaviour and interest in non-academic school work, I would have been thrown out and into an ordinary senior school. **OR** perhaps the record of every child going right back to infant school which was passed along from school to school, gave a true and accurate picture of what I'd had to endure virtually from being an infant. Without feeling sorry for myself I say to this day that everything rotten that ever happened to a child, happened to me!

I was surprised on returning home from school on this particular day to find Mam at home. This was unusual because she worked full time and had done so for many years as a shoe machinist at Smith Faires on the St Saviours Road. The routine usually was for me to get home around 4:30pm, wash the dirty dinner pots, set the table for tea and light the fire after laying out the paper, sticks and coal. Now all of this had been done for me and beaming alongside my beaming Mam was a soldier; a likeable 'at first sight' man.

'You don't know who this is,' said Mam, but I DID, for the CANADA flash on his khaki battledress shoulder had given me a clue.

'It's Uncle Bill from Canada' I warbled, and I was right! It was! I will explain....

My father had deserted us, his family, around 1933 and, although I knew little about the Hastings side of the family, what I did know was that the Old Man's parents and several brothers and sisters had emigrated to Canada (Paris, Ontario) in 1912. My father and one sister, Aunt Lucy, had stayed behind in England. More later but just for now I will explain that to try to get some money from the Old Man for my upkeep and clothing (some hope, usually) I had to go to see him at whichever house he lived. He was now divorced but remained unmarried. During one of these visits he mentioned that his brother Bill, a man who my mother had known through a short stay in Canada between 1916-1919, and always described as the 'best of the bloody lot,' was likely to come to England with the Canadian Expeditionary Force. Well, he had, and here he was. He was lovely. I only saw him that once as soon after he developed a stomach ulcer and was sent back to Canada to an honourable discharge. He was, after all, in his mid-40s with a wife and children. Later on another Canadian, Fred Hastings, came over with the Canadian Expeditionary Force, as did a nephew of my dad's, Johnny Ball, who was later killed in Holland 1944/1945.

1941 Cross Country – My last year at school:

In 1941, and in my last year at school, I notched up my only real success at Moat Boys; winning the county cross country race. I'd decided that come hell or high water, I was going to win it. I trained by running as many times as I possibly could around the Spinney Hill Park. Ten times, then fifteen times, never stopping or slackening off pace for hill or dale. Came the great day and no way was I going to be trampled as I was in my first year.

My ex form master, Arthur (Billy) Boden had been asked before the day of the race, to predict the winner. His reply was always 'Hastings, Form 8.' On the day all the school lined up at the bottom of the gravelled road. This was before the continuation of Ethel Road was built and in those days it was a large playing field. Crown Hills School lay years in the future and the line-up for the run was between where Mayflower Church and Mayflower School are now. I lay back at the start and then began to overtake the field as they thinned out. The last laps were over the Evington Golf Links and I saw my chance. I vaulted a fence and then I really ran. They tell me I was sprinting over the last quarter of a mile and the rest of the field stood no chance of catching me. Mr Boden's 'Well done Norman' as I passed the winning post so far in front of the other 300 runners is a memory I treasure and will treasure to my dying day. I was halfway to the changing rooms when the second runners came in. At last, I'd come first in something.

Arthur (Billy) Boden:

I now share a memory of Billy Boden who was a 'classics' man. In our 2nd year at Moat Boys, Mr Boden recounted how an ancient Greek (or whatever) sculpted a statue of a beautiful woman in marble which he fell in love with. Gilbert, who was seated next to me in class, leaned over and whispered,

'I bet he made a hole in her!'

Unfortunately for him (and I suspect for Billy Boden too) Billy had seen Gilbert whispering and had asked,

'What did you say Gilbert; stand up boy and repeat to the class what you were just whispering to Hastings!?'

Gilbert stood up, mute and silent, and I swear I could hear his brain cranking round. Again, Billy put the question to him,

'Gilbert, I'm waiting; what did you say?!'

Can you believe it; instead of saying ANYTHING THAT CAME INTO HIS HEAD, WHAT HE DID SAY WAS,

'Please Sir, I said I bet he made a hole!'

A lifelong bachelor up to his death, our Billy was too embarrassed and horrified to take it further and could only blurt out,

'Sit down Gilbert!'

If Billy Boden had gone into the wartime forces, that would have been the ultimate obscenity. One evening, Mam was reading the evening newspaper when she asked whether we had an A E Boden at Moat Boys School. When I asked why, Mam explained that an A E Boden had registered as a Conscientious Objector. The following day, every boy in the school knew that 'Our Billy' was a 'Conshy.' Now, you have to remember that most people had family members in the forces, and 'Conshies' usually received short shrift. (eg white feathers etc) On the Friday it was assembly and the tension was palpable when 'Billy' stood up to make Park House report. He was visibly nervous but needn't have worried because as he arrived on stage everybody clapped and cheered, and then gave him a standing ovation.

God Bless you Billy Boden. Wherever you are, you will have made it a better place just by being there!

The final story about school days and the one that makes me laugh the most, relates to an incident in the Science Laboratory just before register was called at 10 minutes to nine. As I'd been ill it was November before I started that term rather than the September with all my classmates. Seeing a microphone on a bench, and having just seen the then deputy Headmaster, Mr Oram, leave the room, I picked the 'mike' up and, assuming it was 'dead,' started to belt out a rendition of, 'We're gonna hang out the washing on the Siegfried Line'. Mr Oram chose that moment to return and, having only been in the school for ten minutes, I was caned. Surely that should have gone down in the Guinness Book of Records!

I left school in July 1941. I was 13 years of age as my birthday fell in August, but did I get a bike? Did I hell!

I was quite a nice looking kid, even though I say it myself, and in my last year at school a group of school girls followed me down the long entry at the side of the house and, in spite of my struggles (really?) they forcibly, and in turn, had long smooching kisses with me. Not that I minded, but elderly Mrs Thrall, our next door neighbour, came out and rescued me.....the rotter!

On that last school day for the leavers of three classes in which my age group fell, 'Nelly' our Headmaster addressed us thus:

'In the years to come you will look upon your days at Moat as the happiest and most formative years of your lives, and you will, all of you, wish you had worked harder'.

Inwardly, I was laughing but, Mr Purnell, you were right and I was wrong.

In the 1950s, 'Nelly' retired from teaching and entered the church (St Peters, Belgrave) as Curate. A few short years later, he died. I still visit his grave in Belgrave Cemetery. Up the middle path to the top of the hill and he is just to the right, 2 or 3 graves in/ 2 or 3 graves down. Inscribed on the stone are the opening words of his favourite prayer,

'Lead me Lord'

I still use that prayer twice a day. H M Purnell, RIP.

'Nelly' told us that once having left school should we ever go for a job interview we were to mention we'd attended Moat Road Intermediate Boys School; this would/ should normally gain us the sought for position. Once again he was right, as I can vouch for from personal experience

18: Into the working world

I was now fifteen years old. I'd left school and was at work. Just me and Mam were at home now and Mam was giving me spending money out of my wages. I think it was about this time the relationship between me and Mam began to get better, very much better. Perhaps it was because I was now bringing money into the house each week, or was it because I was now prepared to speak up for myself?

Just up the slope of the next street to where we lived was a family of youngsters with a daughter about my age. We were friendly but that was about it. Unfortunately, they had a young evacuee girl (who was a year or so younger than me) and her little brother, billeted upon them. I was always polite to the two newcomers but one day the daughter of the family came to me very embarrassed saying the evacuee had said I was having sex with her. (the evacuee) It was blatantly untrue and anyway I would've been too scared to ever go that far with a girl. I was at panic stations, afraid that the lying evacuee girl would be believed. What should I do? I decided I had no choice but to tell Mam.

Mam looked at me hard and asked if there was any truth in what the evacuee said; had I ever touched her where I shouldn't? I knew what she meant.

'No Mam, I've only ever said hello to her and her little brother who's always with her.'

Mam's face set hard as she said,

'Right, you just come with me!'

Up the hill we went to the girl's house, and up the entry. Mam knocked on the back door which was opened by the woman of the house.

'Now, I'm not here to argue with you missus, or you mister, but my son is very, very upset at what your evacuee child is saying about him and I want it stopping as of now! What she's saying is lies. I trust my son, and when he says he hasn't touched her, he hasn't touched her. He's no saint but he's no liar!'

We had reached a turning point in our mother and son relationship.

Soon after, Mam was to stick up for me again. It was a Sunday morning and I was feeling at peace with the world. Having got up early I was just standing about in the street close to my home waiting for the first of my chums to appear. At that point a young and officious policeman came around the corner. I smiled and said 'good morning' but if I expected a similar response, I was to be disappointed.

'Where were you at 6 o'clock this morning?' he asked.

Thinking this was a bit of a leg pull, I replied I was in bed fast asleep!

'There was a break in at the Spinney Hill Park Pavilion, and you match the thief's description' he continued. 'Well, did you do it?'

I could only stand there and look at him, speechless! I was just getting ready to claim non-involvement when the front door opened and Mam came out carrying an empty milk bottle to put on the doorstep. She could see I was flustered and that the policeman was obviously interrogating me, so she came across the road and demanded,

'What are you saying to my lad?'

The officer backed down straightaway and I realised later there had been no break in. The officer was just being clever, or trying to be clever.

'You just leave my boy alone, Sonny, Mam continued 'Decent young boys shouldn't have to be bullied by the likes of you; NOW CLEAR OFF!'

He disappeared, tail between his legs!

My first job interview was for a boy to work in an accounts office, but I didn't go as Mam had heard the accountant was a 'bit dodgy.'

Next I worked in the packing room of a shoe firm but my immediate boss was a sarcastic so and so, and so within a week he'd gone too far and I told him to stick his rotten job.

I then went to train as an Engineer but it was only a small firm and I was learning nothing, so 'bye, bye!'

I next got a job on the Co-Op delivering bread from a horse and cart. The chap I worked with was highly delighted with me and said I was the best, most reliable boy he'd had. I think the horse liked me as well!

My next job was as an errand boy. One day, the male cashier who appeared to be over me when jobs were being given out, called me into his office and asked if I knew where a certain shop was in Northampton Street. I did, as this shop was known to all my chums as being THE shop that sold 'men's things.'

The cashier gave me a sealed envelope with strict instructions to hand it to the chap in the shop unopened. I finished my main deliveries and then went on the final errand, looking around with interest. I had never been in there before and frankly it was a disappointment for there was nothing on display to see. The chap who took the envelope had awful eyesight for his nose nearly touched the note he found in the sealed envelope. My thoughts at seeing this were, 'you've been overdoing what all boys are warned about mate!'

The chap went into the back of the shop and, on his return, was trying (not very successfully) to reseal the original envelope, which he passed back to me. I threw the envelope into the basket of the carrier bike and set off up Swain Street to return to work. As I rattled along I saw that the resealed envelope had come open and the contents, a red oblong box, had juddered out and was now dancing around loose. Honestly, I had no idea what it contained but my curiosity got the better of me and I opened the box. There, reclining in a bed of French chalk was a thick, pink, rubber, washable, contraceptive which all boys, even today if I'm led to believe, called 'Froggies.' My goodness, it was a thick beggar and, as I knew what it was and what it was used for, it crossed my mind that wearing that thing for the purpose intended, would be like paddling in the sea whilst wearing wellingtons! When I got back to work his nibs was not in the office and so I just placed the still open envelope on his desk, sure that he wouldn't be far away.

I returned to my base in the packing room but was hardly settled when he rang down and told me to 'come up now.'

'I asked that this purchase be sealed and yet the envelope is open!' he demanded.

'I don't know about that' I replied, 'I handed your letter to the chap and he gave me this back, as you have it now.'

'Did you look inside the envelope?'

'Oh no Sir,' I replied truthfully, and I hadn't, for if you remember I didn't look inside the envelope as the box came out on its own!

I didn't stay long at that office; the men were stuck up and mainly Army Dodgers.

From working as an errand boy I went to work for a Bricklayer Boss. I soon realised though that I was just being used as war time sweated labour, and I do mean sweated! Mind you, old Jackie, the chap I mainly worked with, was a great bloke. Ex 1914 - 1918 Serviceman, and after a few weeks I was 'bang on' with the Great War Bawdy Ballads. The boss though tried to do me out of sixpence in my pay packet and so with Jackie's 'you told the bugger, didn't you, son,' I said goodbye to that job too!

I had always wanted to win a medal in the Army and so, seeing an advert for Boy Soldier Apprentices, and with Jackie's blessing, I went across to the Army Recruiting Office in Ulverscroft Road to put my name down. I stood in the main hall. Deserted. I shouted out, 'anybody home!' Nothing! I hammered on the desk; again nothing! For about 20 minutes I stood hollering & hammering, but nothing. So out I came! No wonder we almost lost the ruddy war!

Now, where to go for work!? I wanted to get into the war so I opted for engineering again. Unfortunately, I hadn't realised engineering was a reserved occupation, as I will recount later. Within one and a half years of leaving school I had managed to get myself 8 jobs, not bad! But don't get the wrong impression, I packed THEM in; I never got the sack.

Over the three previous years I found that items belonging to or loaned to me, would vanish. I have recounted one or two such instances but on one occasion I was left sick to the stomach. One of the chaps in engineering (Ron) had shown me an old book which he'd found in a house due for demolition. The book was at least 60 years old and I could only get him to lend it to me by loaning him a good book in return. Now, the only book I had that fitted the bill was a book awarded to Mam's youngest brother (Jack) who'd died in the City Cinema. My Aunt Annie was its custodian but it had come into my possession after being loaned to my brother, Ron. So desperate was I to read that old engineering book of my workmate, that I did a swap. My book was called 'Believe it or Not' by Robert Ripley. At home, I showed the old engineering book to Mam who said, 'I bet that's worth a few shillings.' Come the time to swap the books back though, to my horror, I couldn't find the book I'd borrowed! I asked Mam if she'd had it, but she denied knowing where it was. At this time though there were only the two of us at home, so you must draw your own conclusions. My workmate, quite rightly, refused and was adamant, 'you bring my book back and you can have your uncle's book back!'

I never did find that book and I never saw that Robert Ripley book again. If anyone should find a book by this author entitled, 'Believe it or Not' and inside is an inscription 'awarded to Jack Wileman of such and such Sunday School, I will happily buy it off you. Name your own price.

What made Mam pull tricks like this I shall never know as there was no need. She was getting good money in the shoes and I was tipping over my wages with only a few bob spending money kept back.

I know at one time I was put on boring repetition work on a Capstan Lathe. I worked so hard to get the piece work bonus that at night I was operating the machine in my sleep. By the weekend, I was exhausted. I'd earned over £4 which was good money for a fifteen year old kid but Mam only upped my spending money by a few shillings. But where did all the money go? By now she was rid of the Old Man. She was a free agent and I didn't have to go and see him anymore. Apart from one night a week, all her time was spent in the Railway Working Men's Club with her mates, all of them determined to have, in her words, 'a bloody good time.' My brothers and sister, did they but know it, were well out of it. If you dear reader think I'm being disloyal and a rotten son, well, it was always me that got the dirty end of the stick. As Mam was so fond of saying, 'you're just like (in looks) your bloody Old Man.' For Christ's sake, could I help that!?

The old man, Corah Street:

I don't know who it was of my parents who began a serious relationship first although I have an idea it was Mam, but by mid 1941 I'd stopped going to see the Old Man on a Saturday afternoon.

Before he remarried, the Old Man lived in the West Bridge area of the city in a little 'one up, one down' cottage in Corah Street which he kept spotlessly clean. The front door was the only entrance (or exit) to the place; the back of the property being a solid wall. Having no back door or yard you might ask where the toilet for the cottage was. In fact these were at the bottom of the small street and I seem to remember they were a row of four which were shared; one toilet to two or three houses. These were accessed by a key tied to a huge wooden bobbin so as not to get lost too easily.

I remember going to see the Old Man one Saturday afternoon but was delayed watching a parade to do with the war effort moving through the centre of town. When I finally arrived, oh dear, the Old Man was in a heck of a mess (and temper), for that morning he'd been to the dentist who'd done what so many dentists did in those days, and whipped out every one of the Old Man's teeth in one go. Gosh, his mouth was a mess, and his gums looked just like raw pieces of liver. I got a right rollicking I can tell you, but how the hell was I to know what he was doing?

'Go and tell your Aunt Lucy to come here; I need her' I was ordered, so off I went to Dannet street where Aunt Lucy lived. I told her I'd known straight away something was wrong for, as soon as I entered the house there was dust from the coal fire on his bits of furniture and the ashes hadn't been emptied from yesterday's fire. Aunt Lucy, good soul that she was, put on her coat at once and accompanied me back to his house. To put him back together I suppose. What struck me as incongruous however, was that all the way back Aunt Lucy was saying, 'It's all your rotten Mam's fault!!'

NO IT WAS NOT!

Now all of this is in the past. I never spoke to the Old Man again but I did see him at a distance, two or three times at most. He eventually remarried and lived in Magazine Square.

Mam's health problems:

Mam was ill and in the Leicester Royal Infirmary. Her Colitis had returned with vengeance. It was a bitterly cold winter that year and with my brothers and sister away I was on my own. As a fifteen year old was not expected to cope on their own in an empty house, I'd been shipped out to stay with an Aunt and Uncle who lived on the other side of Leicester. (Annie and Wal)

As I worked near to where we lived a message was sent to my sister-in-law's home where she was living whilst Ted was in the Army.

'Could Elsie's mum give our Norman a hot meal midday otherwise he'd have nowhere warm to go to eat sandwiches?' The reply came back, 'Yes.'

Elsie, my sister-in-law, worked at the same place I did. She was in the office and I was the errand boy who rode the firm's carrier bike. That first day I waited for her and we walked home together to her house where I was to be fed. No sooner had we got into her house her mother made it very plain she considered I'd been dumped on her, her good nature taken advantage of, blah, blah, blah. I said nothing back but was close to tears. The next lunchtime, I didn't wait for my sister-in-law I just let myself into our cold and empty house. Even the toilet had frozen up and I was busting for a pee. I just sat. My Aunt hadn't packed me any sandwiches as she thought I'd be given dinner with my sister-in-law. Some ten minutes or so after letting myself in there came a knock at the front door. It was Elsie to ask why I wasn't at her mother's house for my dinner. I told her in a very nice way that I wasn't going to be a trouble to anyone, especially her mother. For all her faults Mam would never have been unwelcoming to someone who was hungry. I wanted the toilet but as ours was frozen (it was outside) I had to use a bucket and dispose of the contents in the garden, frozen though that was too.

When Mam's condition deteriorated Maisie was given compassionate leave from the WAAFs as it was touch and go whether Mam would survive. She was even put into a room on her own so other patients wouldn't be upset if she did die.

Maisie too had to survive in our frozen up house for the few days she was allowed home. So much for in-laws!

Eventually, thanks to a new wonder drug of the time (it was the same drug given to Churchill to cure his pneumonia) Mam's fever broke and she came home cured. I was there to welcome her home but was told off by Auntie for smashing up lumps of coal in the fender whilst getting a fire going.

Mam looked dreadful, she really did. They should never have let her out. That night I was so worried about her that I curled up on the rug in front of the fire in case she needed me during the night.

Mam was upstairs in the front bedroom and in the early hours of the morning I woke with a start. My name hadn't JUST been called; it was SHOUTED! 'NORMAN!'

I was bolt upright in an instant. 'Mam, did you call me?' No reply. I opened the stairs door wider. 'Mam, do you want me?' Again no reply. Timid and frightened, I went upstairs, through the open door and into the bedroom. Softer, 'Mam, did you call me?' Again, deadly silence.

The black-out curtains were shut so I switched on the light. She never stirred. I looked at her more closely; I swear her breathing had stopped. She lay so white and corpse like.

I turned away, my blood was like ice. 'She's dead, she's dead', kept going through my mind. What do I do? Who do I turn to? Slowly, I crept back down the stairs, and then,

'Norman, is that you, Norman?' SHE WAS ALIVE!

Not very long after this happened, I realised that the first voice that shouted my name wasn't Our Mam's, it was Mabel's! Years later, Mam told me that whilst in hospital she'd reached the crisis of her illness and was so far gone she was put into a room on her own. Although very ill, she was fully conscious and, as she was waiting for the end she saw a golden light was approaching the open door of her room. Then Mabel came into the room. Mam said she was as naked as the day she was born but her whole body was giving off a golden/ bronze glow. I quote Mam now,

"I strained myself up in the bed, holding my hands out to her, and she took them in hers and held them. Her flesh was as warm and alive as when a little girl and I cuddled her to me. Suddenly she smiled and gently shook her head from side to side, and began to pull her hands free from mine. I knew she was telling me she had to go, alone, for my time wasn't up yet. I wanted to go with her, I pleaded, please take me with you, but it was no use. I couldn't hold her. Her hands slipped through mine and she was gone. I knew then that I was finally going to get better."

Was it delirium, who can say? What I can say is that I too have seen that wonderful golden glow and it's just as wonderful as Mam described it!

Lodgers:

With so much room to spare, we now had lodgers; some Irish girls who worked in munitions. I was still helping with the housework and one of my jobs was to scrub the quarry tile kitchen floor. I undertook to do this because I hated to see Mam having to scrub a floor. Anyway, this Friday evening I'd just finished scrubbing when one of the Irish girls came out of the living room and walked across the still wet floor, leaving dirty marks. I looked into the living room and there they all were, smoking and laughing, talking and taking their ease. That did it. I stood up and slung the scrubbing brush and cloth into the dirty water and said, 'Finish! That's the last time I scrub a floor whilst the house is full of blasted women!' Mam burst out laughing, as she did whenever recalling the incident. I think our relationship changed for the better after that....but we still had a long way to go.

Around the time Our Ted was posted to Kenya, Mam took in a new lodger, the Irish girls having departed following a flaming row. We now had an old chap called Billy and, without being biased in anyway, all I can say about him is that he was a thoroughly detestable old sod. I was told he was an engineer and a very good one by all accounts. I'd put his age at mid sixty, though God knows he looked twenty years older than that. Billy was a small, wrinkled bloke with permanently screwed up eyes caused by the smoke from his fags getting into them. He was the first true chain smoker I'd ever seen. I couldn't guess what his consumption of cigarettes was but if I said over a hundred a day, I'm sure I'd be about right. From the time he got home in the evening he would just sit, smoking first one then another, lighting the fresh cigarette from the butt of the previous one. He always held his fags halfway down the first two fingers of his right hand, the fingers being stiffly extended. Then he would start to cough, and cough, and cough. I used to hold my breath for he was coughing so hard he couldn't draw air into his lungs. Then the saliva and spittle would run from his mouth in streams and he wouldn't be able to do a thing about it. Whilst coughing he was absolutely helpless. I used to think he was going to die. On top of everything else, what made me detest the man was his habit of trying to bully and cow me, simply by glaring at me. He only did this though when Mam was out. It went like this:

He always sat in a grandfather type chair at the side of the fireplace, puffing at a cigarette. I would come in at 10 o'clock from the Cinema or wherever and from then on until Mam got in from the Club he would just sit and glare at me through clouds of cigarette smoke; never saying a word. I feel sure now looking back, that had he been a younger man by ten years, that he would have 'tried it on' as the other dirty old men had 'tried it on before', after all, I was still basically an inexperienced boy and he was alone with me for long periods.

When Mam came home the 'creeping' would start. He called her 'Mother' and would fawn & flatter her, but as always happens in these cases he blotted his copy book eventually. You see, his coughing, which he couldn't control for 10 minutes or more at a stretch, not only woke me up but Mam as well, and she slept in the front bedroom. The spasms also caused him to be part incontinent so he wet his bed. Now, Mam was prepared to help the old gent, not knowing how his behaviour towards me was giving me the jitters, but then he messed his bed. He had to go, and he went both ways! In the bed, and out of our door! Goodbye Billy, you detestable so and so!

Our final lodgers were two young males. They were nice enough lads but only stayed a few months. One had particularly smelly feet and had to hang his socks out of the window to make the air in the bedroom they shared, bearable.

Ron on the farm/ Maisie in the WAAFS/ Ted:

Ronnie was now working on a farm miles from Leicester and had acquired a shot gun in order to bag rabbits and send them home to supplement our meagre meat ration. An adjoining field was prolific with rabbits so Ron approached the neighbouring farmer, who was known to be a miserable so and so, and asked very politely for permission to shoot some of the rabbits on his land. The farmer scrutinised Ron closely before giving a very surprised Ron, permission. With six rabbits in his arms, Ron prepared to leave the field when the farmer piped up, 'I'll have those, sonny!'

'But Sir,' began Ron, 'You gave me permission to shoot them!'

'So I did' said the miserable old bugger, 'but I never said you could keep what you shot!'

Norman left and Ron right

Maisie had joined the WAAFS (and very smart she looked in her uniform) and was based at a place called Bridgenorth, but where the heck was that? When asked, people didn't know, although they'd heard of North Bridge; everyone knew this was on the other side of Leicester City but Maisie wasn't based there.

When Maisie was on leave she told us a heart breaking story of how an old chap went into a pub near to where she was stationed putting up barrage balloons. He'd proudly shown off a medal awarded to his son posthumously. Congratulations and free drinks all round for the old chap but then tragedy; the medal so freely passed around had disappeared! Heartbroken, that old chap went home minus the medal. I always remembered this and it all came back to me after the war when a fellow was imprisoned for displaying a gallantry medal with the name of the hero almost completely filed off. I'm not sure but I think the old chap by then was dead.

When Maisie was on leave from the WAAFs she'd told us how there was a sex maniac on the loose in Birmingham where her Barrage Balloon Section were stationed. The WAAFs sleeping in a Nissan hut were too afraid to go outside to the toilets at night as it was a strict black-out and the section were right out of the way and isolated. But what to do when the toilet was needed? For the simpler of the two (a pee) a bowl was put on the table. Problem solved, and it was well used to over flowing. Late into the night one of the girls returned from leave and, not wishing to wake the sleepers did not put on the light whilst having a quick swill! The next morning when the penny dropped she said, or claimed to have said, 'I wondered why I couldn't work up a lather!!'

Maisie had also dropped a bombshell. We knew she'd been very friendly with a paratrooper from Glasgow whose father owned a bakery. Unfortunately, when doing a drop his parachute had candled, that is to say it didn't open properly before he landed, and he'd had to be discharged from the Army.

Maisie had also been writing to a young sailor, a Leicester chap, and although he rarely got any leave, they did correspond regularly. Les had been on HMS Worcester stoking the ship's boilers for long periods without a break whilst the troops were being evacuated from the beaches of Dunkirk. Les was interviewed when his ship next went to New York, during which time he commented that the American girls were very nice but he had a girl in England waiting for him. Her name was Maisie. (I have a photocopy of the newspaper article)

When Maisie announced she was going to wed Les, we had a big house party. It was an 'All Services Affair'; Maisie was in her WAAF uniform and Les (Thomas Leslie Foreman) was in his Navy number 1's with white trimming around his neck. Ted gave the bride away and the Maid of Honour/ Bridesmaid was another WAAF.

Maisie & Les's wedding day

Like all (or most) Matelots, Les liked a drink and didn't so much walk, as stagger up the aisle! What with her own nerves and emotions, Maisie, who saw all of this, began to laugh and, as she said later, Our Ted gave her such kick on the skins to shut her up! Once again, rations were pooled from both happy families and friends, and a good time was had by all. So much so that Maisie became pregnant virtually at once and became a mother 9 months and two weeks later. Of course, she applied for and was given her discharge. Perhaps as well really because she'd been told that some of the WAAFs were to be given special training to do with fixing contact bombs on the balloon cables for use against the Japanese.

With Maisie due to be discharged from the WAAF, the two young male lodgers who'd been with us for a few months, had to go.

Ted was now in the War Office where David Niven, the film star, was based. According to form, and I believe it to be true, my eldest brother was known to be the 'smartest soldier in the War Office!'

Ted was immaculate all his life.

His time in the 'Big House' coincided with the Blitz, and many times he came close to being killed. One night whilst asleep, the whole wall of his bedroom was blown out with him still in bed, perched precariously on the sagging floor. He decided to get out quickly and, grabbing his clothes, he scrambled into the street. Unfortunately, he couldn't find his trousers. Thinking they were still upstairs he was about to write them off as the building was sagging alarmingly, when a policeman came along with the missing trousers draped over one arm. They'd been blown into the next street.

Ted was sent overseas next and, having acquired his 'stripes' was moved up to Staff Sergeant. He was to see out the War working in the Nairobi General Hospital, Kenya, and finished as Regimental Sergeant Major.

I realise in reading back that I haven't painted Our Mam in a very good light, so let me try to make things clearer. I often wonder now if, with the others out of the way: Ron on the farm, and Ted and Maisie in the forces, she'd begun to see me in a different light. Certainly, as the only man about the house, she began to confide in me and, dare I say it, began to realise that if all else failed, I would never fail her or let her down. Years later an aunt, her sister, said in my presence to her,

'Mary, you had five children, but of all of them, your Norman, the youngest, had least of all, and yet he's the one who's stood by you all the way.'

I shall never forget the look on Mam's face. When she looked at me I think she finally had the truth of it all brought home to her.

Mam's parties:

With Mam's illness finally out of the way, she would look for any excuse to hold a party. I well remember she won a barrel of beer in a raffle at the Working Men's Club and Harold Ward, who kept the Outdoor Beer Licence on the corner, was brought in to tap it and help get that beer dispatched. My word, that beer was pasted!

All her pals and her sisters and their husbands would be invited and the war time food, rationed or otherwise, would be pooled. I can see it now; on one of those Beanos, Aunt Annie and her husband, Walter, turned up with Wal's

357

brother Jack. A 'sing song' started and Jack, who was a consumptive, was enjoying himself so much, and just for that night, he was a tenor extraordinaire, or so he thought! He stood in front of the fireplace, arms outstretched, singing as he'd never sung before! What a racket! He couldn't sing for toffee but we weren't going to tell him that, for we were too busy laughing! This was due to Walter, his brother, having reached down some ornamental brass bellows that hung at the side of the fire place and, standing behind him with the nozzle pushed gently against Jack's backside, he was pumping away like mad. Years later, Aunt Annie told me about the next piece of hilarity which followed the party. Somehow the three (Wal, Jack and Annie) had staggered home through the black-out. At least four and a half miles and no trams or buses! Too tired for supper they'd staggered to their respective rooms, and so to sleep. Around 3 o'clock in the morning, Auntie woke to find 'Old Toff' as she always called Walter, was not in bed beside her. Then she heard a hissing noise and, as she said, 'I thought that's funny, we haven't any gas in the bedroom.' Aunt Annie got out of bed and put the light on, and there was 'Old Toff' still sozzled, peeing into the open wardrobe!

Horace Allen:

Now Mam had a new gentleman friend, Horace. I reckon he was at least 15 years older than she was, and he was bearable, for whereas her previous 'gents' had liked to drink to excess which caused all sorts of problems, Horace would sit over a glass of beer, puffing away at his pipe and be quite affable.

Once Maisie was discharged from the WAAF it was just Mam, me and Maisie until, returning home from work one dinner time, Maisie greeted me with,

'You're to pay me your board now!'

'Why, where's Mam?'

Maisie then went on to inform me that Mam had married Horace that morning at the registry office. Well, that was the first I knew about it!

In retrospect it was obvious that the marriage was one of convenience; Horace wanted a cheap housekeeper cum cook, whilst Mam thought she was on easy street for the rest of her life as Horace had been a traveller with a secure job.

Horace retired soon after the nuptials but on several occasions Mam had to get a job to give herself some spending money so as to keep the brewery fluid flowing. Let me repeat though, I can never ever, hand on heart, remember seeing her the worse for drink; she just liked to be in company, the noisier the better, with a ham sandwich in one hand and a glass of beer or Guinness in the other.

Landlady Maisie:

As part of the deal for Mam getting the house for Maisie to rent after she'd moved out to live with Horace, Horace's daughter-in-law was to move in and share the house with Maisie and myself.

Hannah, for that was her name, had a little boy who'd been born some 5 years before; her husband, soon after, being called up into the Army.

I don't think the two young women got on that well and Hannah seemed to spend a lot of time in Oakham, at her mother's house. Eventually, she upped sticks altogether. Sometime after, I found at the back of the wooden mantelpiece, a letter from Hannah's husband which made it clear Hannah had written to him about the difficulties of a shared house.

Maisie gave birth in December 1943 and as Les, the father, was still away, I acted in many respects, as Michael's dad. He was a lovely baby and I could change his nappy and mix his feed with the best of them. If Maisie wanted to go out and visit relatives in the evening, then I would babysit even though I may have made arrangements to go out myself.

In the first few months of 1944, Les got some leave and was able to see his son for the first time. He was to see him one more time, and then never again, as we shall see.

Maisie

I decided I wanted to be in the war. I was only 16 years but I knew the Merchant Navy took youngsters for boy status, so I applied for and received an enrolment form. I took the form to my doctor and he gave me a medical. He said the Merchant Navy would probably accept me. Under my breath I said, 'only if they don't know about my childhood consumption, mate.' I was accepted, but then panic, as I'd gone into engineering, a reserved occupation.

I went to the local labour exchange to get permission to leave but was refused; my boss apparently felt I was too useful. I went mad. I argued that I was being used as nothing short of cheap labour; I felt I was learning nothing and the only engineering work I was doing was repetitive which could be done by a female. That's when I made my threat....I argued that unless I was allowed to leave engineering I would refuse to work, and that would be that!

Maisie had gone to the labour exchange with me and between us we shouted the man down to the point where he eventually said, 'Alright!' I'm only surprised he didn't add, 'NOW SOD OFF!'

I realise now that in leaving, things were made harder for Maisie, for she lost my board money and the loans I made her now and again, so she could write to Les.

Waiting to be sent for, I saw Les for the very last time. I can see him now, walking in a diagonal line from the Spinney Hill Park swing yard to get to his mother's house which was across the road from the St Saviours Church. He had just been made up to Stoker Petty Officer and wore a peaked cap and navy, square cut suit, which he hated after his 'tiddly' sailor outfit.

My travel documents and rail voucher arrived and, on a sunny Monday morning, I set off with Maisie on my mind. I knew she was worried to death as she hadn't had a letter from Les for a few weeks, and we knew he was now on a minesweeper which was the sort of job that ruled out any chance of getting life insurance cover. Just before going back after his last leave, Les had said,

'If we do hit anything Mais, I'll have no chance, being down in the engine room.'

We'd guessed that with the invasion (D Day), Les was in the thick of it. Maisie told me years later that going up the street, leaving for that last time, Les had cried. This was a man who'd been through Dunkirk, Greece and Crete. He'd been close when the battleship 'Barham' blew up and been on the battleship Queen Elizabeth when the Italian frogmen had blown her up. Did he have a premonition this time?

And so, as an old sea dog was to say to me later, 'having no friends, no money and being wanted by the police, you went to sea.' It was baloney of course but I think it did apply to some of the seamen I met later.

Ladies!:

One of my chums prior to going off to sea was a boy named Ray. He was several months younger than me and generally accepted by everyone because he was rarely, if ever, out of sorts and had a good sense of humour. Dear Ray; sadly he's now passed away but I can see him as if it were yesterday, with a big happy smile upon his face as he did what he was famous throughout the neighbourhood for..... FARTING! He'd do it with no effort or straining; farting to order!

Ray came from a very nice home. His dad was in the Home Guard in his spare time whilst his mum kept the house looking like a new pin. Ray also had a sister who was my age and I still laugh out loud to this day when I remember a time I was in their home waiting for my pal to get ready. Ray's sister was sitting quietly reading in the same room when our hero 'let off' a loud fart. With no discernible change of expression his sister, without even looking up, muttered ....PIG!

Another time Ray and I were on the Evington Golf Links when we spotted two likely looking girls; a butter blonde and a smaller dark haired girl who I'd mentally allocated to Ray. Of course, it was chat up time, and we lounged on the grass that lovely summer afternoon, doing famously as we sought to impress. Then, the stillness of the afternoon was broken by a muted 'fart.' Oh my God I thought, he's at it again! I managed to chat my way through the moment although I could see that my dream girl had heard it by the way her face went crimson and she tried not to laugh. Ray was looking angelic as usual and so I decided to ignore it and carry on charming. IT HAPPENED AGAIN.......so I kicked Ray's foot and glared at him only to be met with an offended glare in return and a mouthed, 'it wasn't me!' I mouthed back, 'Liar!' but only to see the butter blonde was now kicking her friend on the ankle. The penny finally dropped as I realised Ray WAS innocent; it was the butter blonde's friend who was doing the farting! That was IT then and what followed was a scenario no aspiring Romeo should ever have to endure for, not to be outdone in the farting stakes, Ray and the dark haired girl began farting alternately. So, that potential romance was ended although I did see the butter blonde again later on in life but only to say 'Hello', for by that time she'd married; a policeman I think!

19: Norman and the Merchant Navy

First to Birmingham then change to Gloucester, then Berkley Road and finally, along with 20 or so boys of my own age, I arrived at SHARPNESS and the training ship 'Vindicatrix.' There she lay on the Severn and Avon Canal, an old sailing ship dating back to the 19th century. As she lay on the canal she looked a picture; no sails, no engines and just a low dry stone wall some eight feet from her side. On the other side was the River Severn leading down to the sea.

We were greeted by a smiling Chief Steward who guessed that after our long journey we'd be hungry. Well, some of us anyway. A lot of the new intake were from Bristol etc and so hadn't come too far. Me, I was very hungry, having set off early from my home and, not realising how far I'd have to travel, had not thought to pack any food. Now it was mid-afternoon.

First we were detoured to a brand new, recently erected hut, where we left our suitcases. Actually, mine was a plywood box with a handle on it, painted matt black. My sailor brother-in-law had made it whilst at sea and then discarded it. Now it was to be mine for the duration.

After being allocated a bunk, we were taken across the lock gates to the other side of the canal, up a gang plank and onto the mess deck of T S Vindicatrix. We were invited to 'be seated gentlemen' at long, bare wooden tables, already set with cutlery and plates on which were a thick slice of gammon, a potato, and we were invited to 'get stuck in, and help yourselves to piccalilli.' To drink there were mugs of coffee. To tired hungry boys used to the basic of wartime food, this was Manna from Heaven.

'Righto my lads, you can have the rest of the day to let your mums and dads know you've arrived safely and had a lovely meal.'

Well, we fell for it hook, line and sinker! Duly primed, we all basically wrote the same thing: arrived safely, food marvellous!

Next morning it was turn to! Washing and getting dressed was done in double quick time because we had very few clothes and not many of us shaved, and we had visions of eggs and bacon!

Onto the mess deck it was porridge for starters. Honestly, I'm not exaggerating when I say the porridge was so thick and lumpy that if the servers (other boys) had not gently eased it onto the plate, they would have smashed it! Porridge needs sugar, right? Forget the sugar, there isn't any!

'Where do you think you are, on your daddy's bleeding yacht?'

Ah well, there's always the main course, and this was it! A piece of bacon as big as a matchbox and so white with salt it looked to be covered in frost! In addition there were two potatoes; I cut into the first and it was rotten all the way through, so I attacked the second. Only a third of this was untainted! To round off this repast was a mug of unsweetened coffee. That night every boy again wrote to their nearest and dearest,

'This is a hell ship; ignore the first letter; for God's sake send food!'

Those National dried milk tins that had contained baby Michael's dried milk were put to good use as famine containers and Mam sent me food as often as she could.

We were vaccinated and given a medical of sorts to see if anyone had fiddled their doctor's sheet. I sweated a bit as my doctor (Wooderson) had mistakenly put my chest measurement down wrong and Maisie and I had altered it to what it should have been.

I remember one boy who failed the medical broke down & cried when he was sent home. He had varicose veins on his legs like great blue drain pipes.

And so we settled in. I have no complaints about the sleeping accommodation, but all the time we were there the food never did improve. I maintain that someone who dealt with our food, even though it was rationed, was intercepting it and selling it before it even reached the galley store room.

One evening we were on the mess deck of the ship. It was Vindi soup on the menu; a truly dreadful concoction. Because of the time of year it was mainly peas, brought straight from the fields. It was probable the peas had been rejected by the market buyers for, as we were now finding out, they were full (and I mean FULL) of maggots. Any former Vindi boy will confirm that if you dipped in a spoon, a grey background behind the peas of well boiled maggots were fished out. We were so hungry though we ate them all.

Vindi soup was notorious for giving us boys the 'Vindis', another name for diarrhoea. I can clearly see one boy, a big fair headed chap, who had the runs so badly he was afraid to get off the bucket type lavatory. No doors for privacy either. Exhausted, he'd fallen fast asleep and was still there two hours later.

Other nights we had a round or two each of bread and dripping. Now, to spread the bread with either dripping or margarine, it was melted first then painted onto the bread with a 1 inch paint brush. The boys who were did this were fondly referred to as 'Rembrandt.'

Next we were lined up to be vaccinated. We were told that just down the road from Sharpness was the place where Jenner developed the vaccine for smallpox. On this night I knew my vaccination was on the blink. My arm was sore, swollen and tender. I could've put up with this but as I sat at the mess table the deck began to go around in circles. I staggered across to the Officer on Watch to explain how I felt and was ordered off to the sick bay.

The sick berth attendant, although wearing South Africa flashes on his uniform, was a Londoner,

'What the fucking hell do you want?' was how he greeted me.

Me: 'Please Sir, I think my vaccination's gone funny.

'Then why the fucking hell didn't you report sick at sick parade this morning, hey?' he sneered.

Me: 'Please Sir, I didn't feel sick this morning.'

'Right,' he said, 'you'll find a bucket over there, a scrubbing brush and 'soojee' clothes in here with the soft soap. There's plenty of hot water in the tap, so you can scrub the fucking sick bay out!'

An hour later I was finished, in two senses of the word but, I thought, now I'll be allowed to get into one of the beds. Some hope!

'Right, you can fuck off to your 'wanker' now', the BASTARD said.

Somehow, I made it back to my bunk and was delirious for the rest of the night. The next morning I reported sick at the Sick Parade. The Chief Steward and his wife were on duty. He pulled the plaster off my arm and whistled, then stuck a thermometer in my mouth. He took it out, looked at it and said,

'You'd better get into that bed quick, you need a doctor. Why didn't you report sick earlier?'

I couldn't be bothered to tell him. Eventually I returned to my group. That night one of the boys was delirious and raving. Everywhere was dark and the sick bay was closed. No sick berth attendant could be found. An hour later he turned up, pissed as a newt! He looked at the boy and diagnosed 'a slight chill, he'll be fine in the morning!' The next morning the boy was whipped into a local cottage hospital with double pneumonia.

Six weeks later, I was home and waiting for a ship. My arm still felt funny so I went to my local GP. He took off the plaster which had been put on 5 weeks previously and told me I needed a dry dressing on it; said it couldn't heal with a plaster that would keep it wet.

I think the £5 danger money paid to the boys under the age of 18, was paid with that drunken swine in mind.

In the classroom we had to set to, and learn the quarter points of the compass, then all the various sails of a lifeboat. Do you think they were trying to tell us something?!

We had to learn how to 'step a mast', how to 'tack' if in a lifeboat, how to lay officers' tables and which side to serve from, and finally, the dreaded Captain Angel would question you closely on the lifeboat and the points of its sails. I had to do a resit.

Whilst training I received a letter from my brother Ron. Maisie's husband, Les, was missing, presumed killed. Later, his death was confirmed. The minesweeper he was on, HMMS Pylades, was sunk by a German one man submarine off the beaches of France during part of the D Day invasion.

HMS Pylades

Les has no grave. Now I jump ahead in time: In 1990 and recovering from a triple bypass heart operation, I went to France with my wife, Joyce, and daughter & son-in-law. We went to see the famous Bayeux Tapestry and then to the D Day Museum close by. Just across the road was a huge War Cemetery which we entered. As you can imagine it was mainly soldiers. We were walking down on the left hand side and to my right was a huge expanse of grass with the Alter of Sacrifice in the middle, and then further over were more graves. Why, I do not know, but as though impelled, I left my family, walked across the expanse of grass and came to a stop in front of a gravestone. I looked to the left and right; everywhere were soldiers gravestones except for the headstone to which I'd been drawn that declared, 'A Sailor of the Royal Navy.' I can't remember exactly what was engraved on the headstone but it stated, 'three sailors known only to God, died July 1945.' This took me back over the years and I remembered how Maisie had told me that on the morning of Les' death, she had woken to find the misty outlines of three smiling young men in sailor's uniforms standing in the doorway of her bedroom. Baby Michael had whimpered which diverted her attention, and when she looked back the vision had gone. Not realising what had happened at this point, Maisie had gone to Les' Mam's house and told her of what she'd seen, adding that one of the sailors had looked like Les. Les' mother realised the significance at once, 'Oh no Maisie, don't say that!'

I still believe that some force took me and led me over to the graves that day. I wrote to the War Graves people but they said no records were kept when bodies were washed up by the sea.

Eventually, I completed my sea training and was word perfect with all things to do with a ship's lifeboat. But word perfect only, as I think in the six weeks on board Vindicatrix we only once went out on the canal in a small boat.

I joined the Dock Street, London Pool and for the rest of the war sailed deep sea on the North Atlantic convoys. I requested my discharge from the Merchant Navy in the middle of 1946.

Discharge from the Merchant Navy:

For a time after my return to peacetime living, I lived with Maisie who had remarried a Burma Veteran. I then moved into digs. It was from one of these digs that I was rushed to hospital with a burst appendix and peritonitis. Admitted to a ward I turned to speak to the chap in the next bed only to realise he'd died. Oh Gosh! I realised that I had to call Sister but before doing so I turned to inform the chap on the other side to me. Would you believe it, as I started to open with the words,

'Hey mate, this chap's dead'

I saw that this chap's eyes were rolling back, and he died as I watched him!! Discharged!!

Norman

My digs had been re-let so I had to go and stay with Mam and Horace, which pleased him not at all! I was terribly weak though and ignoring Horace's protests, Mam came up trumps. 'He's coming here until he's better and that's that!'

20: Closure

I will begin to bring mine and Our Mam's story to a close. Over the next few years my situation changed. I grew up! The Old Man disappeared off the scene and he married a war widow, Ethel. Ethel had two daughters from her previous marriage and one son, Roger, by the Old Man. From what I heard it would've been impossible to decide which of them disliked him the most.

The Old Man (right)

After the Old Man died, I visited Ethel. She was lovely. As near as I can remember, her exact words were,

"I had only been married to the swine for a fortnight when I realised I'd made a mistake."

Mam's second husband, Horace, died in 1962. We all knew theirs was a marriage that, had it not been for the fact they were resigned to putting up with each other, wouldn't have lasted. Each went their separate way in the home but I think he got the best of the deal. Mam looked after Horace, and fed him well, often using her own money to keep things going. His death caused her little grief, and if she'd gone first he would've felt the same.

Two items of the paranormal I will recount since I'm closing a chapter on him. In their house in the middle bedroom was a double bed. At different times, both my Aunt Sadie and Mam tried to sleep in that bed. The first was Aunt Sadie who stayed overnight:

In the night (this is Our Mam telling the story) I heard Sadie tossing around in that bed and muttering and talking. In the morning I said to her, 'What was the matter with you last night, Sal, you were restless?!' Sadie had replied, 'I was ever likely to be. I was just closing my eyes having put the light off, when I could feel the body of a woman in bed with me, and she'd got her knees in my back as she tried to push me out of the bed!'

Two years later, Mam went for a sleep in the afternoon on that bed and the same thing happened to her. The two of them made a joke of it and nicknamed the apparition 'Sheila'. Not long after there was a horse in a big race called 'Sheila's Cottage,' and for a laugh the pair of them bet on it. IT WON!

Sometimes when on leave from my Merchant Navy trips, I would stay overnight at Mam's and I can swear no ghostly woman tried to kick me out of bed but, as God is my judge, as soon as I got in that bed and put the light off, a feeling of calm peace would descend upon me and strange bed or no, I had a wonderful feeling of being watched over. Who was the woman? Well, Horace was a widower, and he did have a son by his first marriage who was well loved. Draw your own conclusions.

Mam was now living on her own although occasionally she would take in a lodger or two. The house had been bought by Horace and, quite rightly, he'd left it in his Will for her to live in during her lifetime. However, Mam was hankering for a council place because she was responsible for the upkeep of the house and its repair and, only being on the basic pension, she found major repairs difficult to finance. Ever one to keep her thoughts to herself, she now had a plan. The first I knew of this was when she came to my house one night and said she'd got some startling news. What this boiled down to was she'd found what was supposed to be a ground floor flat; in reality it was just one ground floor room in a house. I put on my coat and told her I wanted to see this place. When I did I could have wept; It was a dump and I told her in no uncertain terms that I would not let her live there. To this she told me she'd already posted a letter to young Horace, telling him she'd be relinquishing his father's house. 'Then I'll have to un-tell him!' I told her! With that, I raced home to get my trusty bike which I pedalled four miles just to push a note through young Horace's door. 'Forget it, and ignore my Mam's note. She's staying.'

As a result of this I then visited each of my brothers and sister to tell them I could understand Mam worrying about the deterioration in the house and suggested we all got stuck in and decorated it to make it more presentable. Although I was the youngest sibling, and had the youngest children in the family, the onus always shifted to me when matters to do with Mam were decided. Eventually, understanding her financial situation, the council relented and allocated her a top floor flat in Goodwin House on the St Matthews Estate. The view was marvellous but the height!! Phew! After the flat, Mam did a swap and moved to a ground floor flat in Gleneagles Avenue.

From the time of Horace's death I had taken it upon myself to visit Mam twice, and sometimes three times a week, usually with some home grown vegetables from my allotment, and I can honestly say that never once did she plead poverty or ask me for money or a loan, and she was still coming up with a modified version of, there's plenty worse off than me! Indeed, she kept herself remarkably smart and well dressed. She always looked, as did her sisters, like 'the Quality.' She always had gentleman friends, the last being 'Fred.' He was a real pal to her and lived not far away.

During a holiday with Fred to Skegness, Mam had a fall and broke her arm quite badly, but she didn't let a small thing like that spoil things and came home heavily plastered. It wasn't far off the time the plaster needed to be removed when I visited to check she was ok. She was obviously in great pain and complained the plaster was cutting in and hurting. I decided to take her to the Leicester Royal Infirmary and told the nurse who saw her that she was in pain from the plaster even though this shouldn't have been the case. The nurse gave mum's arm a cursory glance before declaring, 'Nonsense, the plaster is quite alright!'

I looked at my Mam's drawn face and said, 'If my Mam says she's in pain, then she's in BAD PAIN!'

A passing Sister heard and offered,' let me have a look!' Sister then told the nurse that the plaster should be removed at once as it was digging into Mam's arm.

A much stronger bond was now evident between Mam and me.

By now, Mam was 85 years and I'd noticed that her 'Mentals' were going downhill. She was repeating herself far too much but still coping. I was visiting more regularly and as long as she wasn't struggling, I decided to let her carry on.

Mam's eldest son, Ted, very rarely appeared, Ron was an infrequent visitor due to his health problems and Maisie visited when she could.

Old Fred rang me. 'Your Mam's ill, Norm, can you come? I went! First I asked her whether the doctor had been. 'Yes' was the answer. Have you been given any medicine was my next question, 'No' came the reply. That night, it was a Saturday and I slept, or tried to sleep, on her settee. I left late morning, shattered, after getting her some breakfast which she didn't want.

I rang Maisie, and she said she was able to go in later that day. That evening, about teatime, Maisie rang.

'Norm, Mam's vomiting faeces!'

We agreed the emergency doctor should be called, but he didn't want to come out; Maisie insisted! When the doctor arrived and Maisie told him what Mam had been bringing up, his response was, 'I don't think so!' To her credit, Maisie was ready for him and played her 'trump card'. Shoving an enamel bowl under his nib's nose and whipping off the cover, Maisie asked, 'Really, then perhaps you would be good enough to tell me what this is?'

Very embarrassed, the doctor said he would send for an ambulance as it was clear Mam had a complete stoppage in the bowel. By this time, Ron had turned up. I don't know where Ted was but he always did have a knack of being missing when a crisis arose.

At the Infirmary the doctor confirmed the diagnosis, adding 'of course you know your mother has breast cancer!' Breast cancer! We nearly died! Typical of Mam! She'd known for months but it was in remission so she said nothing to us!

Mam was admitted to hospital so we went home to await developments. Two days on and I got a telephone call from Maisie.

'Norm, the Infirmary have just rung. They have to operate but Mam won't sign!' Would you believe it, just 10 minutes before I got that call the local composting plant had dumped off a load of manure and it was completely blocking the pavement outside my house.

'Maisie, you'll have to get Ted out of work and I'll come down as soon as I can!' One hour later Maisie rang me again.

'It's bad news Norm. Mam did sign for the operation but the surgeon showed us an X ray and told us a mass in Mam's stomach is cancer. They're going to operate but we've been told there's little chance Mam will pull through and will you go and kiss her 'goodbye' for the last time!'

I was shattered to say the least! Well, they operated and found the mass wasn't cancer; it was Diverticulitis. I raced to the Infirmary that evening; Mam was still out. I remember leaning over her and repeating again and again, 'It wasn't cancer, it wasn't cancer!' After an hour I finally got through. She roused a little and said, 'Thank God!'

Well, she made a speedy recovery, or did she, for, whether something went wrong in the operation or the anaesthetic, she was hopeless in her 'Mentals' and what made things far worse was she was urine obsessed.

For example, taking her back to my house for her Sunday dinner one day, as we went into my house she said she needed to go for 'a wee.' On her return she sat down, but immediately stood up again saying she needed 'a wee!' When I pointed out she'd only just been, she said 'she couldn't help it' and off she went again. This went on for the duration of her stay with us, but when I encouraged her to stay for tea as well she said she had to get home 'because I might need the doctor!'

I contacted Social Services for I realised that some form of Residential Care would be needed before too long as she would not stay for any length of time with me. In the meantime her old friend, Fred, would ring one or the other of us nearly every night saying, 'can you come quick; your Mam is gravely ill!?' She wasn't ill in the sense Fred meant but she was confused and miserable over the feeling she was filling up with water. She wasn't though, as her very fed up local GP could testify.

Then we started 'the rounds' and by that I meant Mam and me. The others kept right out of it. I took her to The Towers Hospital to be assessed but they couldn't help. I got her into the local Blind Home on day only care as she was nearly blind in one eye but after checking by driving past the place and finding her wandering the street, I gave that up. Mam's social worker arranged for her to go into a residential home on a two week trial. When this period was up I saw the Matron who informed me, 'your poor mother needs full time care,' but would the social worker agree to this? No way! 'She'll be far better off in her own home' was the argument, but she wasn't! As she was still feeling the need to wee, Mam would go round to ask her sister (who lived in a flat above Mam) if she would ring the doctor for her as there was something wrong with her 'water works'.

Other residential homes were tried for two week respite periods and every Matron of every Home in Leicester must have been tried; every one said the same thing,

'Mr Hastings, your mother needs full time care!'

My answer to them was always, 'tell that to the bloody social worker, for I can't get through!'

What made it worse was that on fetching her home when her two weeks were up, she'd accuse me of dumping' her! Often, and I'm not ashamed to admit it, I would cry as she shouted at me!

This state of affairs went on and on. Fortunately, I was working on the district where she lived and going in several times a day to check she wasn't wandering the street.

On Friday evenings, I would check her pantry then go and buy her bread, butter, ham or pork pie, eggs, bacon and whatever else was needed to get her through the weekend. On Saturday I would leave home early and, after dropping my wife off in town, would drive to her flat to change her bed linen, taking the soiled bedding home for my wife to wash. Mam may have been water obsessed but she never wet or soiled her bed clothes. I would then clean her flat from top to bottom, at times even cleaning her windows. Her friend and prop, Fred, would arrive from just down the road and I would say, 'now, what are you having for dinner?' The reply was always, 'could you fetch us some fish & chips, me duck?' I would of course oblige and then go for my own meal. Mam had Meals on Wheels during the week but on Sunday I would return home from the allotment at 12 noon to pick up a Sunday dinner with all the trimmings and a sweet, and jelly and cakes for Mam's tea. The food would be put into hot casserole dishes, wrapped in newspaper, then placed on hot water bottles on the floor of my car, and I would race to her flat and watch her eat it all up, finishing with me rolling her a cigarette. She went to her grave saying how lovely her Sunday Meals on Wheels were!

After settling her down for her rest, I would next check her larder. Nearly empty!

'Mam, where's all that food I brought you round? It should have lasted you until Monday night!'

'Oh well, me duck, Fred's been round for some meals and Old Fred's got a good appetite!'

Honestly, I didn't mind; having Fred close by took a lot of the worry off my mind.

And so it went on. Thank goodness, Mam's 'Mentals' seemed to stabilise. She wasn't getting appreciably worse but I daren't let one day go by without checking she was alright. One incident I remember very clearly though was going in to see her and Old Fred met me with,

'She had to go to the doctors. There was blood in her urine!'

'Are you sure? I said, to which Fred replied, 'Oh yes, her water was all red when she showed it to me!'

'Mam, what did the doctor say?' I asked.

'Nothing' was her reply! 'He just looked at the sample and emptied it down the sink!'

Fred saying 'red' gave me the clue........

'Did you enjoy the beetroot I brought you?' I asked.

'Oh yes' came her reply, 'me and Fred cleared it all up in one go!'

'I don't suppose you checked your urine, did you Fred?'

It took a moment or two for the penny to drop!!!!

After having another go at the social worker, she agreed Mam could go into Curzon House for a fortnight to give me a break. It was marvellous to be able to relax. Two weeks later the social worker rang me.

'We're having a case conference on your mother this morning and I'll be recommending she's to be returned home.'

I exploded! 'Ok, but I give you warning now. If you send my mother back to her flat and anything happens to her, then I'll hold you accountable and see you get maximum publicity.'

I then rang Maisie and told her what the woman had said. Maisie went up in the air!

'Does Mam's doctor know about this woman's recommendation?' she said.

'Mam's doctor is as fed up as we are! Mam practically lives at the surgery!'

Maisie rang the surgery and spoke to the doctor, recounting what the woman had said. In return, the doctor confided that he knew about the case conference and that the social worker knew how he felt about Mam being rejected for care time and time again! He admitted he hadn't intended going to the case conference but, in view of what Maisie had just told him, he would be attending and, 'we'll see if she tries to overrule me!'

Lunch time came and the telephone rang. It was her!

'I've decided your mother may stay at Curzon House!'

'Really?' I couldn't resist saying, 'you decided that did you? Well, now I know she'll no longer be under your supervision, such as it was, my advice to you is DON'T LET ME SEE YOU ANYWHERE NEAR HER AGAIN!'

Mam settled down at once, and I can say without fear of contradiction that the two ladies in charge enjoyed having her there. She was no trouble at all, in fact when she was asked whether she was happy and liked being there, Mam's answer was, 'it's lovely; just like being in a top class Hotel!'

Now and again, Mam would ask me if her house was alright. After a month we were still checking her flat because she'd yet to sign to agree to stay at Curzon House. I reported this to Shirley, the lovely lady in charge.

'Do you know, Norman, I'd quite forgotten!' she said, and opening her desk drawer she took out a form. 'Come on, we'll do it now.'

Mam was sitting in the lounge.

'Mary, do you like being with us?'

'Oh yes', said Mam.

'Well, I need you to sign this then,' and with that Shirley pushed the form under Mam's nose.

Mam was still rabbiting on about 'better than a first class Hotel' but paused to ask, 'what's this?'

'When you've signed this, Mary, you'll have a permanent room here with me.'

'Oh me duck,' said Mam, 'that would be lovely!'

I danced all the way home!!

I should say here that whilst all this was going on, it was just me and Maisie who were taking the burden. Ted had emigrated to Australia but if he'd still been here it would've made no difference, for he didn't visit her right up to him going.

Poor Ron was fighting Reynaud Disease and was in really bad health. The expert on the complaint would take visiting and training doctors to see him, saying it was doubtful they would ever see a worse case of Reynaud than this. Over the next few years, Ron lost most of his fingers which had turned to gangrene, and then they took his hand off. Finally, it went to his feet and legs. Death was a merciful release. God Bless you Ron. As children we went through so much together. It created a special bond and though we had our arguments, we never, ever fell out. You were the best!

Every week, I would go and see Mam. Mam being Mam, she soon had one of the old chaps following her around like a little puppy dog. Several times she needed to be seen at the Leicester Royal Infirmary for her water works trouble, which I say to this day, was all in her mind, for she never ever wet herself. Still, it gave her a run out. (And three guesses who usually took her!?)

Some three years passed, then Mam became ill. I was at the Home every day and followed the ambulance in my car when she was sent to the Groby Road Hospital Geriatric Ward. I visited the first day after admittance and remember being surprised at how few nurses were available with whom I could discuss Mam's condition. In fact it seemed to me that the old folk were rather neglected, and this was borne out when, on the third day Mam seemed to be having problems with her throat. When I asked her to open her mouth so I could take a look, I was horrified to see her mouth full of what appeared to be desiccated coconut. Obviously, mouth hygiene was low on the list of priorities. I called a nurse over and asked if she'd seen the state of Mam's mouth.

'What's the matter with her mouth?' she asked, and when she saw, this angel of mercy just said, 'oh, she just needs some mouth hygiene!'

Two hours later and I was still waiting for the hygiene to begin..........

The next day Mam's mouth was clean. I say this in all fairness.

On the fourth day I went into the Ward, Mam was sitting out of bed in a chair, slumped over and unconscious. I lifted her head and one look at her eyes said it all. I just shouted.......'For God's sake, SOMEBODY!! My mother's dying!!!'

There was no nurse in sight, but as luck would have it, two young doctors were passing the foot of her bed. They rushed over, took one look at Mam's face, said, 'Oh Christ', and one each side, they grabbed hold of her and threw her onto the bed. I was pushed out of the way and the curtains were pulled to; they, and Mam, were out of my sight. Ten minutes later and one of them emerged to say Mam had 'no chance'. Her kidneys had packed up and it was just a matter of time....not long in fact.

The next afternoon, Mam was in a room of her own and deeply unconscious when I arrived. A few minutes later my niece walked in, not knowing how close to death her Nan was. Pat had brought in some yogurt and, after being brought up to date said, 'let's see if we can get some of this into her.' We persevered, feeding her like a baby, and most of it, by reflex, was swallowed.

'I think Nan's bowels have moved' observed Pat. (I'd already noticed the smell) Pat set off to find a nurse which wasn't all that difficult as we could hear screams and filthy language coming from a store of some sort situated just across from the room. A very disgruntled female in a nurse's uniform followed Pat into the room.

'I think my Nan's soiled herself' said Pat.

'I'll go and get some pads' said our Angel of Mercy.

One hour later she'd still not returned to us, although the screams from the store cupboard HAD started up again!

Pat set off again to find her, and I heard her say, 'if you're too bloody proud to change my Nan's soiled pad then give me the buggers here and I'll change her!!'

That brought results, but maybe it was Pat breathing fire that did the trick!

The next day I couldn't believe it! Mam was sitting up back on the Ward! She wasn't with it though. Her mind had nearly gone.

The following day she was back in isolation, slipping in and out of a coma. Her mouth was dry and parched and so I lifted her head after filling a glass of water from a jug at the side of her bed. I saw at once that she hadn't been given a drink since the day before. I hated to do it but, just to check, I marked the jug and the level of the water in it. The next day I checked. It was the same jug only with more dust floating on the surface. The water was now very stale and still as I'd left it the day before.

Maisie was going to the hospital as often as she could and between us we were giving her a drink, but we never saw any sign of consumed food on Mam's locker.

One day, although still not with us, I saw as I opened her mouth to give her a drink, that there was a large blister on the end of Mam's tongue. I'd just noticed it when Maisie came into the room.

Mams got a damn great blister on her tongue' I said.

'Yes, and I know how she got it!' said Maisie.

Maisie went onto explain that whilst she was sitting with Mam the day before, a nurse had come in with a beaker of scalding tea. When Maisie had said not to give it to her because it was too hot, the nurse had left. A moment later another nurse had come in with the beaker and, before Maisie could do anything about it, had pushed the spout into Mam's mouth, scalding her in the process. As unconscious as she was, Mam had let out a scream and that silly bloody woman had run out.

Things were now at such a pass, I was going into the Ward every day to wash Mam's face and hands, and to make sure she got a drink of water.

The attention she, and the other poor souls in the main ward each side of her room got, can only be described this way. Both Maisie and I got used to hearing a thud or crash as some poor soul went down due to there being no nurse in the room to supervise them. Meantime, the screams and the filthy language was still coming from the store room where the young male cleaner held sway.

Every day I found myself picking up medication from the floor, tablets that Mam should've been having. Then I found out why. A very bossy, officious, senior nurse came into the room. I was at the sink swilling out Mam's water glass and she didn't see me. In her hand this Angel of Mercy held several tablets which, having pulled Mam's head up she promptly crammed the tablets in her cupped hand into Mam's mouth. Remember now that Mam was nearly unconscious! No water was offered and so feeling something foreign in her mouth, Mam promptly began to push them with her tongue.

'Oh, so that's your game is it, Madam!' said our Ministering Angel and, without attempting to pick the tablets up off the bed, she turned to leave the room. Then she saw me and saw I was not best pleased!

'How do you expect an old lady of 89, who is more often than not unconscious, to take tablets that are just forced into her mouth without a drink of water?'

I received no answer.

By now, Mam's urine bag was more often than not, full of blood and it was clear time was running out. During the last week, I was bending over her cleaning her mouth, when one of the more caring nurses saw me and said,

'Be careful, she'll go for you!'

'No way' I said, 'if she's gone for anyone of you it will be because you've hurt her in some way.'

Of course, this was denied, but I'd seen and heard too much of it with my own eyes and ears.

At no time did I or Maisie see Mam turned every hour or so, as to prevent bed sores, and when I did see the state of her elbows and buttocks with bed sores, I could've cried.

That last week: I had just finished washing her hands and feet to freshen her up. She was well under and hadn't stirred. I leaned over and looked down at her tired old face, remembering the lovely, vital young woman she'd been, heard that tune she'd hummed to me so many years ago as she nursed me on her lap before both our worlds fell apart; when I'd been crying with ear ache, nursing me, loving me. The years in between were gone, and I felt my tears welling close to the surface as I said those words to her, that to the best of my knowledge I had never said before, 'MAMMA, I LOVE YOU.'

Those words must have gone in deep, stirring some chord in her subconscious, for she dragged herself to the surface from that deep, deep sleep of near death she was so close to and, for the first and last time she said those words I'd waited a lifetime to hear,

'I love you too my baby!'

And so, she went to her adored and adoring Mabel.

I took over arranging her funeral and collected the death certificate.

'Carcinoma of the breast' was the main cause given.

Burial or cremation: Ted was out of the country; Ron opted for burial; Maisie said cremation. What to do? Who to satisfy? Solution! Cremate then bury her ashes in the family grave with her brother, Jack, and beloved Mabel. Was that it then? No, not quite. I'd told the hospital that when Mam's time was near, day or night, they were to ring me and I would come at once as I didn't want her to die alone, however, if she did slip away before I could get there I asked to be phoned first and I would tell the others in the family. I didn't want Maisie to be unduly upset. So, what happened......at 7o'clock on the Saturday morning, Maisie rang me.

'Norm, the hospital just rang. Mam died at 4am.'

21: Peace

More years ago than I care to remember, I was in the Belgrave Cemetery in Leicester visiting the family grave, when a gentleman stopped me to ask if I'd seen a grave marker inscribed with 'such a such' name. I had to confess the answer was in the negative, and seeing he was so upset at my answer, I remarked,

'Are you sure they're in this cemetery?'

He admitted he did not, and I remember I said,

'Does it matter? After all, they're safe now and all that remains here are the empty shells. Their spirits are all around us; they haven't changed.'

He commented that I seemed very sure, and how could I be so sure? This is what I told him,

'As a young man, I was in lodgings with a lady who had two boys. Peter, about 12 years, and Philip (Pip) 3 years younger. The landlady had a lovely sense of humour, and myself and the other lodger loved being in her home. I remember it was Pip's birthday and I went out and bought him a toy canon which shot matchsticks. It wasn't cheap and I wasn't earning big wages, but the pleasure on his face was reward enough. If Peter played his mum up, I was at hand to sort him out. We were all the best of friends. Mrs S slept in the big front bedroom with Pip, Peter slept in the small front box room, the other lodger slept in the front room downstairs and I slept in a single room in the back bedroom. I remember so clearly that I was fast asleep upon this night and dreaming. Suddenly, a curtain came down upon that dream and I was standing at the bottom of the stairs, looking up at the bathroom door which was closed. Slowly, the door began to open and a most beautiful golden bronze light streamed out, in

389

the centre of which I could see a shape which I thought was a monk because of the long robe. As I stood transfixed, not at all frightened, the name 'Jim' came into my mind and, as it did so, the door began to close and that wonderful light faded. I was at once in my bed where I'd been all the time, still fast asleep and, as the curtains had come down upon my dream, so now it lifted, and the dream recommenced exactly as it had been when the curtain came down. The next morning at breakfast, I told Mrs S I'd had ever such a funny dream that night; it was about someone called 'Jim'. Mrs S told me not to say anything more about it now but to wait until that night when the boys were playing in the garden. That evening, Mrs S asked me to tell her about my dream so I recounted it all, as it had happened. Then I got to the name 'Jim.' At once she began to weep and rushed upstairs. I was bothered and wondered why she was crying. A moment or two later she returned. She explained she'd been married twice and that Peter and Pip were half-brothers. Jim had been Pip's father and he'd died of cancer. She asked about the robe the figure was wearing and, holding up a dressing gown, asked whether it was this? Then she put it on. Mrs S was a very tall woman and it came nearly to her ankles. Mrs S told me that during Jim's illness he used to wear the dressing gown and as he wasn't as tall as she was, it used to cover his feet. Here Mrs S paused.

'You've been so good to the boys, Norman, and my little Pip loves you, calling you Uncle Norman! My Jim knows this and is trying to warn you something is going to happen. It's a warning, of that I'm sure, that's why my Jim came to you. Be careful!'

A week to ten days later I was rushed into hospital. My appendix had burst and I had peritonitis followed by abscesses on the site internally where the appendix had been removed. It was nearly four months before I was halfway fit again. I didn't go back to Mrs S. As a widow she needed the board money and had re-Let my room. I went back to see her twice, and each time she said the same thing,

'You see Norman, I was right. My Jim was trying to give you a warning. It was your health.'

Time passed, and now I was a young married man with a baby son. My first little house cost me £250 cash; 26 Gordon Street, Leicester. It's since been demolished. Right from the outset the baby, whose cot was in the back bedroom alongside the frame of a single bed, seemed unable to settle at bedtime. As soon as he was put down, even though fast asleep, he would wake and begin to cry. One night in particular, on hearing him crying, I went up to him. The nights were dark and as I pushed open the bedroom door my hand went to the light switch. As the light came on my eyes swept across the room and passed over the single bed to the baby's cot. I registered he was standing up before my eyes focussed on the single bed. What I'd seen but not registered for a split second, was a little elderly lady, fully dressed, sitting on the edge of the bed frame. The bed had no mattress. I knew just what to do. I clicked the light off and then spoke thus.......

'I know who you are. You're Mrs Davie. (The previous owner who'd been dead some six months) I know this used to be your home but it's our home now. Please Mrs Davie, go in peace for the baby can sense you in the room and is frightened even though I know you intend him no harm. Go then, and may God Bless you,'

I put on the light and, apart from the baby and myself the room was empty. In those few moments my son had lay down and was fast asleep. From that day until we sold the house we had no more broken evenings.

In our new home a neighbour called me to her garden where a sparrow was crouched upon the grass with its beak shot away. It was in agony with no chance of survival. I had a spade in my hand and I raised it up to put the bird out of its misery. As I brought the spade down I was looking at the poor little thing. Just before its life was ended I swear its tiny eye transformed to a human eye. I ignored that, for at that moment, as the spade ended its life, a voice thundered in my head 'thank you!' Sitting as I had for so many times, listening to those Sunday sermons whilst in the choir at St Barnabas Church, I remember that what I found hard to come to terms with were those words from the Bible that went something like..... 'Even a sparrow cannot fall from the heavens without the Lord your God knows of it.'

For many years and to interest our children we kept budgerigars in a cage in our living room. On this particular day I was coming down the stairs when my wife said she didn't think a bird was very well as he was lying on the cage floor. I went into the room and yes, he just lay there. Now, the room had a chimney breast for a coal fire with a recess each side of it. The cage stood on top of an old Gestetner Duplicator cabinet in the left hand recess. I opened the cage door and lifted the bird out, my fingers gently wrapped around its body lest it tried to fly away. I remember saying 'I think the bird's dead' when suddenly, it began to struggle. I had never realised just how strong that seemingly frail body could be. I felt my fingers being forced open one at a time and couldn't hold it; it was so strong. Now it was free. The only way past me was close to my head, and I felt the displacement of the air and the dry rustle of feathers close to my face. Then a wing tip caught the side of my face on the cheek so sharply that instinctively I put my left hand up to see if there was any blood. It felt so sharp.

I glanced down to my right hand, but my fingers were still closed around the budgie and it lay just as it had when I lifted it out of the cage. Had I felt the soul of that little bird leave its body? To this day I say 'Yes, Yes, Yes!'

My wife, Joyce, and I were on the Isle of Wight and had marked down a church we wanted to visit; old churches had always fascinated us. We set off walking along a lane with fields each side and deserted except for two ladies sitting at the side of a hedge on an old rustic bench who we bid 'Good Day' to as we passed. I remember my wife and I were in deep conversation and when looking up I saw a lady walking towards us. Who she was, what was she wearing, what she looked like just didn't register but, ever the gentleman, I stepped off the causeway into the road to let her pass between us, which she did. As she passed I caught her perfume and commented, once I thought she was out of hearing, how 'out of this world' her perfume was!

'What lady?' Joyce said.

'Why, that lady who just passed us!'

My wife looked at me as though I'd gone mad.

'Nobody passed us,' was her reply.

As I insisted there was, I turned around to point the lady out, but apart from the two ladies seated in the lane, the lane was empty! Had I dreamed her?

'I wondered why you stepped off the pavement into the road!'

One thing I'm sure of, well, two things really. First was the smell of her perfume as it was still in the air and second, if it could have been duplicated and bottled I could have made a fortune.

And so, this is what I recounted to the man in the Belgrave cemetery. To me there was nothing super natural about any of this. No ghostly wailings; no hair standing up on the back of my neck with fright. What I saw was perfectly normal in all respects and I believe that is how we will all be eventually. What did he say? He told me his mother was a psychic and instrumental in setting up a spiritualist church but, he would give his right arm to see or experience what I had. So, am I a confirmed believer in Spiritualism? The short answer is 'No'.

The last so called medium I saw at De Montfort Hall was so patently phoney that after sitting through the first half of what he was trying to con the audience off with, I just got up and walked out!

And so my story and Mam's story, comes to a close. What I have learned is that love is a miraculous abstraction, and that all the love I gave Our Mam in her last few years, came back to me a thousand fold.....AND I AM NOT BITTER ANYMORE!

NORMAN HASTINGS

Norman would often say 'children grow up in spite of their parents.' This is true, but because of his own deprived childhood Norman remained a children's champion throughout his adult life and coined the phrase 'every child matters' before it became a 21st century social care slogan.

Norman passed away 27 August 2011 aged 84 years following a short battle with cancer. Whilst he never lived to see his book published the drive to tell his and his mother's story remained strong to the end. I am proud to now be doing this on Mary Wileman's and Norman's behalf.

If you liked reading this book, Norman will return in his second book: Norman: Through My Eyes Too, where Norman recounts his life as an Education Welfare Officer in Leicester.

1999: Norman (right) with Roger Wileman, an American cousin

Printed in Great Britain
by Amazon

51006812R00241